The
Post-War History
of
The London Stock Market

The
Post-War History
of
The London Stock Market

George G Blakey

2000

First published in 1993
New paperback edition published in November 1994 by
Management Books 2000 Ltd
125A The Broadway, Didcot, Oxfordshire OX11 8AW
Tel. 01235-815544

Set in New Brunswick by Management Books 2000 Ltd
Printed and bound in Great Britain by The Alden Press,
Oxford.

British Library Cataloguing in Publication Data is available

ISBN 1-85251-137-0 (hardcover)
ISBN 1-85252-139-2 (paperback)

FOREWORD

I am pleased to be able to introduce this book because I think it fills an important gap in the history of the last fifty years.

The period has been one of dynamic change in the stock market, and George Blakey, who has been in the City for much of it as a working stockbroker, has captured the spirit of the times.

In this account he places stock market events, which have quickened the pulses of traders and investors, in the context of the economic and political movements which have affected the whole nation.

This makes it a good work of reference for historians of the period and, for interested observers of the London Stock Exchange, a warmly entertaining story with a genuine feel for the equities market.

I was specially intrigued by his story of the flowerings, and in some cases the subsequent witherings, of the corporate impresarios of the period.

There are serious messages here for those who are still engaged in bringing regulation to bear on issuers and traders of securities. We must protect vulnerable private investors from reckless promoters but we should be careful not to 'protect' professional fund managers from corporate innovators.

It is perhaps significant that the story starts with the nationalisation of the coal mines and the imminent disappearance from the Official List of the sector called Home Rails. Today we are looking forward to the privatisation of British Coal and British Rail. When that happens we will indeed have come full circle.

At the same time we at the Stock Exchange will continue our relentless march to support the markets effectively and to maintain their integrity and reputation.

Sir Andrew Hugh Smith
August 1993

PREFACE

The inspiration for *The Post-War History of the London Stock Market* was the work of the same name covering the period 1945-1980 written by the late Alec Ellinger and Harvey Stewart of Investment Research, Cambridge. It was much more compact and written from a chartist's point of view, but it still provided practically the only background to the stock market for a newcomer to the investment business. That this has remained the case despite the huge expansion of market size and activity was always a matter of surprise to me and I planned in due time to write a more comprehensive and detailed version of their book. However, an unexpected turn of events leading to the premature interruption of my career in the City, has given me the opportunity to do so rather earlier than intended.

My aim has been to do no more than present the facts together with the comment of the day, and to this end I have used the *Financial Times* – the acknowledged authority in financial reporting – as my principal source material. Wherever possible I have still checked the corporate histories with the companies concerned, and with one notable exception have received their broad approval. However, where certain controversial issues are involved, if comment might be interpreted more as criticism, this is likely to be in cases where the objective reporting of the *Financial Times* has been supplemented by personal experience which may have given rise to a measure of prejudice on my part.

The sheer volume of information revealed by a study of over fifty years of stock market history has led inevitably to a considerable degree of editing, and although many more companies and personalities merited inclusion, it was not possible to feature more than a representative selection within the confines of a single volume.

ACKNOWLEDGEMENTS

I am indebted to my agent Jacintha Alexander for her diligence in seeking out a publisher, and to Robert Postema of Mercury Books for recognising that there could be a place on a business book list for a work about the stock market which was neither academic and full of mathematical formulae, nor 'popular' in the sense that it was a parody of City life portraying all the market professionals as knaves and the investing public as fools.

My thanks too to Martin Hall, John Aarons and Brian Bartholomew at the Stock Exchange, and to Chris Davis, Chairman of the Institute of Investment Management and Research, for their support, and to Bill Jamieson of the *Sunday Telegraph,* John Percival of *Currency Bulletin*, David Sawyer and Raymond Salami, for their invaluable help and advice.

I am grateful also to the *Financial Times* for providing me with the raw material to work on, and to Datastream International and BZW Research for supplying the charts, as well as to the Universal Press & Picture Agency, the Press Association, the Central Office of Information, the National Museum of Labour History, The Treasury, The Bank of England and many individual businessmen and politicians, for providing the photographs.

Last but by no means least, I wish to express my appreciation for the help and encouragement provided by my wife, Kristin, during the two years it took to research and write this book.

INTRODUCTION

The history of the UK stock market since 1945 has reflected not only the struggle between the competing economic philosophies of the two main political parties, but also the relative success of the economy in spite of it. The fact that the economy and the stock market have managed to grow and prosper against such a background is a tribute more to the skill and adaptability of British businessmen than to the actions of a succession of Chancellors of the Exchequer, well intentioned but still governed by political timetables, or often simply overwhelmed by events.

Steady and sustainable economic growth accompanied by an improvement in the standard of living, all without too much inflation and unemployment, are admirable goals, but the means employed in trying to achieve them have been so diverse and haphazard that the occasional brief successes have occurred more by luck than judgement. Nationalisation, denationalisation, and renationalisation followed by privatisation of the commanding heights of the economy with all the uncertainty thrust upon key industries, cannot be interpreted as the reasoned implementation of long-term economic policy in the national interest.

To go back to 1945, it is difficult not to admire the idealism of the first post-War Labour government that gave rise to the conviction that it must 'arm itself with anti-slump powers so that never again as in past years shall prices and productivity and employment all fall away through the failure of private enterprise'. Idealism, however, was not enough. After an initial burst of enthusiasm, the market soon relapsed when that vision faded thanks to a plethora of bureaucratic controls and the failure of organised labour to respond to the exhortations of its political representatives.

At the same time, the creative destruction of the War years had killed off the militaristic traditions in Germany and Japan and led to the the emergence of a new professional business class in both countries which was soon to make them formidable competitors in Britain's traditional markets. Indeed the first sterling devaluation in 1949 coincided with the introduction of the German currency reform, which involved a massive revaluation and laid the foundation of that country's economic miracle. For Britain devaluation did little more than mark the first of a series of soft options.

In such a climate it was not surprising that the FT30 remained locked in the 100-150 range for nearly a decade. It broke out only in 1954 after the first post-War Conservative administration had been in office for three years and its moves towards decontrol had at last begun to work through. Unfortunately the transition from a regime of strict control to one of relative freedom was not the key to economic success. The trade unions had never accepted controls under 'their' government in the first place, while the corporate sector, which had done so to a great degree, was now eager to make up lost ground.

It was doubly unfortunate that these first steps towards a market economy coincided with the outbreak of the Korean War in June 1950. Coming so soon after the 1949 devaluation, it provided a major inflationary boost as commodity prices rose worldwide. The cost of imports shot up 50% over the next two years, affecting final output prices directly and also indirectly through wage bargains revised in line with the cost of living. By the end of 1952 prices were up nearly 25%, and by 1958 the cost of living had risen 50% on immediate pre-devaluation levels. Inflation was here to stay. The stock market responded, practically doubling to 338 by the end of the decade, reversing the yield gap in the process in August 1959 as the urge to get out of fixed interest stocks and into equities gathered pace. No longer would equities have to yield more than gilts in order to compensate for a supposedly higher risk. They had proved themselves to be much more exciting and profitable. Capital gain as well as dividend growth was now factored into the income calculation and 'total return' had become the name of the game.

The first half of the 'sixties saw little progress for the stock market at the tail-end of a tired Conservative administration, but the break through the 400 level of the FT 30 in October 1967 owed less to hopes for the success of Labour's National Plan than to expectations of its certain failure. Devaluation three weeks later, accompanied by undertakings to a supranational body, the International Monetary Fund, were an acknowledgement by the Labour government of its inability to manage the country's affairs, sabotaged as it was at every turn by its natural supporters, the trade unions. Their attitude to negotiations remained dominated by the folk memories of Tolpuddle and Tonypandy, and without their cooperation all attempts at planning the economy were doomed as surely as those of the Attlee administration in 1945-1951.

By the end of the 'sixties, the motor industry had provided the classic illustration of what was going wrong with much of British industry. In the late 'fifties, Japanese car manufacturers stopped making the Austin Cambridge under licence and began to produce their own models for both home and export markets. In 1958 they produced 50,000 cars. In 1961 the figure had risen to 250,000, and in 1970 to 3 million, making Japan the second largest manufacturer in the world outside the US. Similarly, even as early as 1956, the once war-devastated German motor industry had toppled the UK from first place in Europe, and by 1968 at the time of British Motor Corporation's £400 million merger with Leyland, Volkswagen had become the biggest carmarker in the world outside the US. Production in the UK reached a peak of 1.9 million in 1972 and since then it has been downhill all the way, a performance symbolized by the fate of British Leyland, once the country's biggest exporter. Plagued by bad management, shifts in government policy and constant industrial disputes, and in spite of being propped up with over £3 billion of taxpayers' money, twenty years later British Aerospace was paid, quite literally, to take away what was left of the group.

But during this same period, fortunately for the economy, another side of British industry began to emerge. Entrepreneurs like Arnold Weinstock at GEC (1961), Raymond Brown and Ernest Harrison at Racal (1961), James Hanson and Gordon White at Hanson Trust (1964), James Goldsmith at Cavenham Foods (1965) and Owen Green at BTR (1969), laid the foundations of industrial empires and had no difficulty in raising through the stock market, the capital they needed to expand.

There was no reason for the next Conservative government to congratulate itself. Not only did it have to contend with the same obstructive trade unions but also with its own undisciplined supporters, the banks and the other lending institutions, as Chancellor Barber embarked upon his 'dash for growth'. To complicate matters further, the good years of economic management in the US were coming to an end. Vietnam War spending had taken its toll of the economy, the mighty dollar crumbled and in 1971 the system of parities established at Bretton Woods in 1944 finally broke down. America's failure now became the world's failure. The absence of a level playing field in economic management has to be taken for granted, but the fact that neither party of government could rely upon the cooperation and self-discipline of its own supporters left no alternative for Britain but to elevate the policy of 'muddling through' to the appearance of a virtue in a climate of national and international free-for-all.

The late 'sixties and most of the 'seventies witnessed an extraordinary boom in real assets, helping to form attitudes and set trends that persist to this day. During this long period of broadly rising inflation, interest rates lagged and it rapidly became obvious that it paid to borrow in order to invest in assets, whether in the form of a private house or an office block. In 1970, for example, when borrowing costs were around 8%, the yields on residential and office properties were of the order of 14% and 9% respectively. As property prices rose in acknowledgment of what was perceived as an anomalous situation, this yield gap also went into reverse, and the new order of things managed to survive the 1973/74 shakeout that followed over speculation fuelled by excessive lending. The shakeout was inevitable as the Barber Boom peaked, but the oil crisis in the autumn of 1973, which saw the price of oil quadrupled in a matter of weeks, made it a worldwide one and intensified the impact on the UK economy. In one sense, OPEC did the industrialised world a favour by pointing out the folly of relying upon the cheap and plentiful supply of a commodity, the production of which it no longer controlled, to subsidise its prodigality in other areas. It was another milestone along the road towards living in a competitive market economy.

The trade unions were not prepared to cooperate with the Heath administration's brand of interventionism designed to face up to this new reality and inflation took off. Ironically, it was left to a Labour government to try to deal with the aftermath of the Barber Boom, and to preside over the collapse of financial confidence in 1973/74 that saw the

FT30 back to below 150 amid talk of industrial breakdown and even rumours of a coup d'etat. The coincidence of an explosion in public spending with a new oil price rise accompanied by the failure of Chancellor Healey to produce a workable pay policy or avoid a record level of strikes, created the feeling that inflation had almost become a way of life. Reaction against this attitude paved the way for the return of the Conservatives under Mrs Thatcher in 1979 and the first practical efforts to get a grip on an economy that had given up the competitive struggle and was close to descending into anarchy. The event coincided with a very similar hardline approach by the US authorities, and real interest rates soared in response to a restrictive monetary policy designed to squeeze inflation out of the system.

British industry was hard hit, especially the manufacturing side, but a growing flow of North Sea oil took the strain on the current and capital accounts. Helped by Chancellor Howe's 'Medium Term Financial Strategy', with its emphasis on reducing public expenditure allied with personal and corporate tax cuts and tax reforms, the FT30 responded by breaking above 600 for the first time. On Wall Street, the Dow topped 1000 and then moved decisively into new high ground as investors became convinced that the inflationary momentum of the 'sixties and 'seventies had been broken. That view quickly became current in practically every capitalist economy and equities and bonds moved strongly and consistently upward.

The continuation of that boom owed much to the collapse of the oil price as well as that of many other basic commodities, as the laws of supply and demand reasserted themselves during three recession-hit years; to the benefits of enforced reorganisation and rationalisation showing up in a dramatic increase in corporate profits; and to giveaway prices for privatisation issues. All these factors served to boost the appeal of financial assets.

The final seal of approval to the Thatcher government's 'There is no alternative' policies was conferred by the crushing defeat of the politically inspired miners' strike of 1984/85 and then of the print workers' rebellion at Wapping. Coupled with the introduction of legal curbs on trade union freedoms, these events not only effectively ended half a century of industrial strife but they also put the unions out of the regulatory business. No longer were they 'combinations in restraint of trade'. Once again the financial establishment still had lessons to learn. A new wave of disruption and loss was soon to follow from the irresponsible lending in the new climate of deregulation, by banks and financial institutions, ever eager to fuel the consumer booms and corporate hyperactivity upon which they battened.

The process was aggravated by the continuing obsession with asset appreciation, this time driven not by inflation, but by competition and the apparently unlimited willingness of the banks to fund property development and investment. The October 1987 Crash provided no more than a brief interruption to such excesses which were not to burn themselves out for another two years. But while these areas had acquired a 'haven' status for institutional funds to the detriment of what was seen as dull and unreliable manufacturing industry, the market still managed to provide the backing for a second generation of entrepreneurs like Nigel Rudd and Brian McGowan at Williams Holdings (1981) and Greg Hutchings at Tomkins (1983), enabling them to launch their ambitious plans for transforming key sections of manufacturing industry.

The recovery of the broad market since the dramatic but short-lived collapse of 1987 owes much to a degree of international cooperation over policies designed to avert what was perceived as a threat to the world's financial system. But the problems of GATT and the ERM experience show that such unity is precarious. The present market level is less likely to be a 'permanently high plateau', than a tentative one waiting for the real economy to catch up. Furthermore, the belief that while inflation might abate it can never be conquered, remains prevalent. It bears a heavy responsibility for the sluggish state of the property-based UK economy and for the idea that it is only a revival of the property market which will spark an economic recovery.

Although the aim of this book is to do no more than set the movements of the stock market in the context of changes of government and government policy and world events, by simply recording the facts together with the comment of the day, this study of the good, the bad and the positively ugly in both the political and business spheres over the course of nearly half a century inevitably begs certain questions.

For example, if the manufacturing sector has declined so significantly as a proportion of the national economy, what would have happened to it without the efforts of Lords

Hanson and White, Lord Weinstock at GEC, Sir Owen Green at BTR, Sir Ernest Harrison at Racal, Nigel Rudd and Brian McGowan at Williams and Greg Hutchings at Tomkins? All these companies are involved almost exclusively in manufacturing. All have been extraordinarily successful to the benefit of employees, shareholders and national economy alike. Furthermore, they have taken over and made equally successful many of the best known companies in the country, which without their intervention would in many cases have gone the way of such once great names as Alfred Herbert, Davy Ashmore and Stone Platt. In this context mention must also be made of Glaxo, which under the leadership of Sir Harry Jephcott, Sir Alan Wilson and Sir Austin Bide, during the post-War years graduated from being principally a maker of baby foods and veterinary medicines to a world leader in pharmaceuticals.

If continuity of sound, debt-averse management is largely responsible for the consistency of the success of the great companies already mentioned, perhaps nowhere is the lesson more evident than among the retailers. They have had their share of shooting stars as opportunistic new managers caught the upwave of the spasmodic consumer booms of the post-War years, but those that continue to shine like Marks & Spencer, Great Universal Stores and Sainsbury, all have strong family traditions to provide that continuity through boom and recession alike.

Interestingly, the financial services industry with its much-vaunted contribution to the country's invisible earnings, has thrown up few heroes. World-renowned Lloyds of London will take years to recover its reputation. The general run of insurance companies which, like the banks, regularly succumb to the seductive lure of bricks and mortar can no longer lay claim to the status of successful investment trusts hampered only by being tied to the 'boom and bust' underwriting cycle. Many of the banks and merchant banks, some bearing the most hallowed names in the City, have blotted their copybooks in one way or another, and perhaps only the Warburg Group, a relative newcomer and the creation of another outstanding personality, deserves to rank among the great post-War success stories. By contrast the leisure and media industries have seen the emergence of a number of entrepreneurs like Sir Maxwell Joseph of Grand Metropolitan Hotels, Lord Forte, Cyril Stein of Ladbrokes, and Rupert Murdoch of News

International, all of whom have turned small domestic operations into major international corporations, in spite of a
tendency towards overgearing at times.

In short, it is difficult for the objective observer to draw
any conclusion other than that economic progress since
1945 has been achieved solely due to the actions of 'a few
good men' just as at other critical periods in our history.

We are still a long way from Adam Smith's (and many
other people's) ideal world in which a national government's
sphere of influence is restricted to defence, law and order,
and foreign affairs, with economic policy left to businessmen, but at least by using the exceptional business
talent available to give a measure of continuity to economic
planning, governments could defuse a great deal of the criticism directed against them. There are some encouraging
signs in that today's voters no longer face the stark choice
between State Planning and Free Enterprise – only the
most reactionary of Labour politicians would now seriously
advocate the reimposition of exchange controls and the
repatriation of overseas investments – and it is abundantly
clear to everyone now that the direction of economic,
monetary and industrial policy is too vital to be left to the
mercy of the politicians with their rival ideologies.

This is not the end of history for the market but the
beginning of a new and critical chapter. The Pandora's Box
opened by deregulation and globalisation can never again
be closed, and this record of examples of the wisdom and
folly of the past may help to put the present in perspective
and provide some pointers to the future. On past experience
it is a future not without hope. The transition from a
protected command economy to an unprotected competitive
market economy was bound to be difficult and painful, as
the former Soviet Union and its Eastern European satellites
are now discovering. No longer can anyone doubt that the
'moving finger' is firmly attached to the Invisible Hand.
Fortunately for the London stock market, 300 years of
evolution may have ensured that it will continue to strike
the delicate balance between liberty and licence which in
the last half century has allowed its many successes to
outweigh its occasional failures. One Hanson makes up for a
dozen Polly Pecks.

George G. Blakey
October 1994

PRELUDE 1939-45

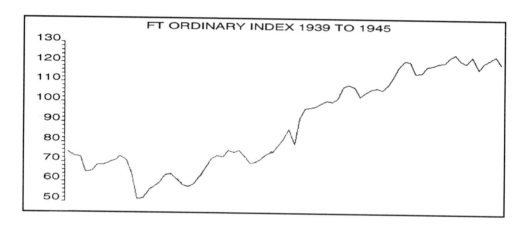

FT ORDINARY INDEX 1939 TO 1945

A review of the war years

"Buy when blood is running in the streets" is the most reliable, if the most difficult to follow, of time honoured market maxims. It was true, quite literally, in June 1940, a month which witnessed the evacuation from Dunkirk, the entry of Italy into the War, and the fall of France. German forces appeared poised to cross the Channel and the *Financial Times* Ordinary index plunged to a low of 49.4.

Fears of the coming war in Europe had depressed both gilts and equities in the two years leading up to the outbreak of war and the actual event came as not so much of a shock as it had in 1914. The Stock Exchange bowed to the dislocations of war and closed from 1st to 6th September 1939. When it reopened gilts and equities were only fractionally lower with their indices at around the 100 and 80 marks, respectively.

Strict control of the capital markets was the cornerstone of the government's war financing policy. Bank Rate was cut from 4% to 2%, minimum prices were set for gilts, and interest rates were simply not permitted to rise as the war went on. In addition, a whole package of emergency financial measures was introduced. It included large increases in taxation, both personal and corporate, higher duties on tobacco, beer and spirits, and the levying of purchase tax on a wide range of consumer goods, the prices of which were in most cases strictly regulated. At the same time, in order to avoid a sharp rise in the cost of living and its unsettling effects on the working population, the prices of essential foodstuffs were heavily subsidised. In combination all these measures gave a degree of artificial stability to markets.

At this stage, the principal beneficiary from war prospects was Home Rails, and in anticipation of greatly increased activity their index, which had begun 1939 at close to 40, reached 47.4 by the beginning of 1940. There was, however, no rush for gold or gold shares. Gold was a fixed-price commodity in 1939 and had been since 1934. The price was raised marginally to 168/- an ounce, but government restrictions on the distribution of profits and the prospect of disruption of production, meant that gold shares failed to benefit.

The military disasters of June 1940 proved a major test

Wall Street at War

Wall Street's performance during the War years paralleled very closely that of London. The Dow Jones Industrial Average had reached a post-1929/32 recovery high of 194.4 in 1937 but declined sharply in the wake of the recurrent clashes between the Administration and business. Political factors continued to block any sustained recovery as did anxieties over the course of the War in Europe. The attack by the Japanese on Pearl Harbour and their initial successes in the Far East pushed the Dow to a low point of 92.92 in early 1942, but thereafter it was recovery all the way. The 1937 peak was matched by VJ Day under the influence of post-War prospects judged to be very promising in the light of the huge increase in productivity in the war era, the large rise in national income, and the political commitment to full employment. All these factors were expected to sustain both income and profits at levels well above pre-War peaks, and by the close of 1945 the Dow had crossed the 200 mark.

of the stability of financial markets. Gilts, sustained by the official cheap money policy and encouraged by the Churchill leadership, maintained their levels even in the country's "darkest hour". Industrials and Home Rails, on the other hand, both slumped dramatically but from that point on, recovery was practically continuous. There were minor reactions on the news of the German invasion of Russia in June 1941 and when the Japanese attacked Pearl Harbour in December, but the industrial index still managed to end the year at 85. Anxieties over the fall of Singapore and then Rommel's push into Egypt caused industrials to slip below 80 in February and again in June 1942 but the recovery was swift and subsequently aided by the Allied landings in North Africa in November, leaving the index at 93 at the year end. The turn of the tide in 1943, marked by Russian successes on the Eastern Front and then confirmed by the German and Italian surrenders in Tunisia in May, led to all-round gains and by the end of the year the gilts index stood at 112.8, the FT 30 at 100.6 and Home Rails at 67.6.

"Awaiting the sunrise"

Markets could now begin to set their sights on post-War prospects and the advance gathered pace after the Normandy landings in June 1944. A combination of low returns in investment quality stocks and high taxation prompted a search for more remunerative, if more speculative, holdings. Investors remained cautious, however, balancing the potential trials and tribulations of the post-War economy with consideration of the new and exciting commercial opportunities created by changes in habits and taste acquired during the War years coupled with the benefits of accelerated research.

The worries were well-founded. Britain was now heavily in debt to the rest of the world. Invisible earnings, always a big component in British calculations, had halved and the country's ability to rebuild its export trade had greatly diminished thanks to a 30% reduction in its merchant fleet and the dislocation, destruction and rundown of so much productive capacity at home. At the same time, government expenditure abroad, mainly for maintenance of the armed

Prosperity in Store

Stores edged up slowly during the later War years. Their dividend yields were modest but it was widely forecast that they would benefit in peace time from a renewed wave of consumer spending after five years of enforced restraint. At the same time, investor enthusiasm was tempered by consideration of the difficulties stores would have in obtaining stock, increasing floor space and finding enough counter staff. The investment statistics of three principal stores in March 1945 were as follows:

Company	Shares in issue	Price	Earned %	Paid %	Dividend Yield %
Woolworth	5/- Ord. 30.0	78/6	68	45	3.0
Marks & Spencer	5/- Ord.& A 8.45	73/6	70	35	2.0
Debenhams	1/- Ord. 10.0	12/-	100	25	2.0

forces, was five times as great as it had been pre-War. A contemporary US survey estimated that Britain would have to double its exports to regain pre-War living standards.

Neither was it going to be a simple matter to devote physical resources to building up the export trade. The civilian population and returning service personnel had endured great hardship and deprivation during the War and their needs, especially in terms of housing and clothing, had to be met. There was no alternative but for the government to make a virtue of necessity and create a strong domestic market upon which to build the export trade. Certainly the demand existed and, fortunately, so did the ability to pay. As a whole the population was much better off. The cost of living in 1944 was 50% higher than in 1939 but weekly earnings were 81.5% higher and spread among an employed population that had grown by 3 million during the War years.

Moreover, the War had stimulated technological break-throughs which had created new industries. This was in sharp contrast to the period after the end of the 1914-18 War when the emphasis had been more on reviving the old staple industries of the nineteenth century. Now there were

The Coming Motoring Revival

Motoring was obviously going to resume and increase its popularity in peacetime and from early 1945 investors intensified their search for bargains in the industry. During the War private motoring had virtually come to a standstill. Many cars had been requisitioned and all available production went on military and official use. Furthermore, there was no petrol. Garage prices suffered greatly and their share prices all languished well below pre-War levels. **Lex Garages**, with its many depots in and around London, began to attract buyers and rose from 3/- in January 1945 to 5/3 in May. Midlands-based **Kennings** also became a target and over the same period advanced from 20/- to 26/6, with prospects further enhanced by its involvement in hire purchase, property development and agricultural and commercial vehicle distribution. Interestingly, even at the higher prices, Lex was capitalised at just £145,000 and Kennings at £1.58 million. Among motor manufacturers, **Jaguar Cars** also found buyers. Originally SS Cars – the name had been changed at the outbreak of war for obvious reasons – the marque had always had an enthusiastic following, but at 16/6 in 1945 the price was still a long way from its pre-War peak of 25/6. Jaguar's equity market capitalisation in October 1945 was just £400,000.

new developing industries like electricals and electronics, radio and television, synthetic textiles, chemicals, pharmaceuticals and plastics, automobiles and jet engines, all of which would come into their own in peace time. Industrially, Britain had taken the decisive leap into the twentieth century. The whole country was looking forward and no longer back.

"War Babies"

"War Babies" was a term used affectionately by investors to describe companies whose development had been greatly aided by wartime orders and where the potential for further growth post-1945 was reflected in their share prices. Two leading high fliers in this category were **Decca** and **De La Rue**. Neither had been very successful pre-War but electronic expertise transformed the prospects of the former, and plastic technology those of the latter during the War. Decca invented a navigational system which was widely employed by the Allied forces and is still in operational use today, and then developed a revolutionary gramophone and record system ready for the peacetime market. De La Rue, although best known as a security printer, set up a plastics subsidiary in 1941. It developed Formica, a brand name which became practically a generic term for plastic, and with no timber being imported at all, demand for plastic substitutes soared. By the end of 1945, Decca's share price had risen from 16/6 to almost 70/-, and De La Rue's from 25/- to over £11.

1945-50

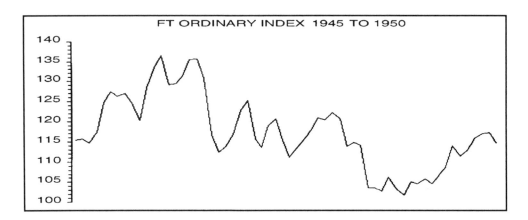

FT ORDINARY INDEX 1945 TO 1950

Labour takes charge

It was this spirit of change which led to one of the most dramatic political upsets of all time. Against the most pessimistic computation in House circles of a majority of as low as 30 seats for Churchill and the Conservatives, the Labour Party under Clement Attlee swept into power on 26th July 1945 with a 146-seat lead. The FT Industrial index, which had risen to 118 on the eve of the declaration of the poll, confident of the maintenance of the political status quo, slumped to 115 the next day. The selling continued and at the beginning of August the index touched a post-election low of 105.9. Gilts largely held their prices on the prospect of a continuing cheap money policy under Hugh Dalton, the new Chancellor, while gold shares and dollar securities moved up on hedge buying. A measure of the shock to the City can be gauged from the *Financial Times* editorial on 7th August. It referred to Labour's victory as "the most serious reverse since the dark days of 1940", adding that the market's reaction was "a commentary on the hopes and fears engendered throughout the world of investment by the advent of a Socialist government whose clearest intentions seem to be embodied in the one word 'nationalisation'." And the King's Speech, announcing the proposed nationalisation of the coal industry and the Bank of England, did nothing to allay these fears. Even Wall Street juddered on the view that "if it can happen there, it can happen here".

Properties out of favour

Property companies remained the Cinderellas of the stock market after the War, right up to the early 'fifties. Their investment standing was impaired by a combination of factors, namely: (1) war damage, particularly for those companies with large holdings in the City of London; (2) the difficulty of getting licences to repair or rebuild; (3) rent restrictions; and (4) the unsympathetic attitude of the Labour government which was in power from July 1945 until October 1951. **City of London Real Property** (CLRP), with nine acres of freehold properties in the City and seven acres of leasehold, did not begin to pick up until the Conservative election victory of 1951, when controls began to be relaxed. Priced at 19/- in 1939, six years later the shares were 14/6 to provide a market capitalisation of around £6 million against a 1944 asset value of £12.1 million. **London & County Freehold & Leasehold**, the proprietor of Key Flats, was the largest operator in the private rented sector. Its properties were in the balance sheet at their 1928 valuation of £10.25 million and, in 1945, at 23/-, the company was capitalised at £5.7 million.

But just as Dunkirk presented the investor with a buying opportunity, so did the Labour victory. Less than three months later, on the eve of Chancellor Dalton's first budget, the industrial index had managed to recover practically all the ground lost since the election. The budget itself was hailed by the *Financial Times* as a "tonic for both industry and labour". Income tax was cut by 1/- to 9/- in the pound, Excess Profits Tax (EPT) was slashed from 100% to 60%, personal allowances were increased, and many consumer items were freed from purchase tax. The stock market responded by having its most active week on record and industrials moved into new high ground at 119.6, just topping the previous peak of 118.5 achieved on 30th April.

£sd

The pre-decimalisation currency in everyday use until 1971 was complicated in the extreme and a mystery to all foreigners. There were 240 pence or 20 shillings to the pound. Decimalisation retained the pound by consolidating every 2.4 pence into one new penny. Thus a shilling made up of 12 old pence become one containing 5 new pence.

Old	New
£1 (20/-)	£1 (100p)
15/-	75p
10/-	50p
5/-	25p
2/6	12.5p
2/-	10p

Terms relatively commonly used until 1971 were 'guinea' for 21/-, 'crown' for 5/-, 'half a crown' for 2/6 and 'florin' for 2/-.

Clearly markets, too, were becoming imbued with the spirit of change and were prepared to give untried Socialist policies the benefit of the doubt. Even nationalisation had lost its terrors. Investors now welcomed the prospect of receiving compensation for old and rather dull holdings and the ability to reinvest the proceeds in new and more exciting ventures. Consequently, when on 21st December the government announced its plans for the nationalisation of the 850 undertakings that made up the coal industry, colliery shares rose and other equities rose with them.

The Dalton "cheap money" era

Even the Investment Control Bill, introduced in January 1946, was greeted as a bull point for equities in that by restricting the supply of new issues, it would prolong the bull market by leaving investors' demand for stock unsatisfied. There is little doubt that a year earlier such legislation would have been regarded by the City as part of the socialist apparatus for the control and direction of industry to its certain detriment.

Industrials had moved broadly sideways since the ending of the War in May 1945, albeit staying at the upper end of the range, and it was only after Chancellor Dalton's first full budget on 9th April 1946 that investor enthusiasm really began to take hold. Chief among the measures was the scrapping of Excess Profits Tax by the end of the year, and there was no mention of limitation or onerous taxation of dividends. Investors were both surprised and relieved and the industrial index topped 120 by the end of the month on record turnover. The market clearly had warmed to a Chancellor who believed it was the aim of the government "to cheapen money and to lower rates of interest to the greatest extent that economic and financial conditions permit". Of course, the cheap money policy had not been a creation of the new Labour government. It was one which had been determinedly pursued by successive administrations since 1932, the year 5% War Loan had been converted to a 3.5%

Hugh Dalton was the first post-War Labour Chancellor. His aim was to "cheapen money and to lower interest rates to the greatest extent that economic and financial conditions permit".

coupon. Low interest rates had been designed as a key feature of the full employment policy between the wars, then became a cornerstone of financing during the Second World War, and post-1945 they were regarded as an absolute necessity to see the economy through the vital period of reconstruction and rehabilitation.

Sentiment was further aided in July when US Congress voted its approval for a $3.75 billion loan to help the UK "over the hump" in restoring its economy and covering its adverse balance of payments. This was a great relief to the market. Approval had by no means been a fait accompli. Initial negotiations had been undertaken with the Churchill administration and there were real doubts that Congress would vote through a loan to a socialist government.

Chinese or Japanese Bonds?

Immediately after the ending of the War in the Pacific, there was no doubt among investment commentators that Chinese bonds were the ones to buy, not Japanese. Their reasoning was that the US would pour millions of dollars into China to help rebuild its war-devastated economy and that the Chiang Kai-Shek government would thus inevitably triumph over its Communist opponents. Japan, on the other hand, was considered likely to be crippled by reparation payments for the foreseeable future, quite apart from the widespread conviction that it was morally repugnant to invest in that country. As a result, in 1946 Chinese bonds were selling at around £70-80 as against £17-25 for the principal Japanese loans. However, it soon became clear that investors preferred the "speculative" attractions of Japanese bonds to the "investment" merits of the Chinese, an approach which was soon seen to be fully justified when the Communists seized power in 1949 and the Chiang Kai-Shek administration decamped to Taiwan. By now Chinese bonds were back to £12-16 while those of Japan had crept up into the £35-55 range. The Korean War put the finishing touches to this role reversal as the US turned its attention to bolstering Japan's position in South-East Asia as a bulwark against the spread of Communism. By mid-1951 Chinese bonds were practically a nominal market at £8-12, while Japanese loans were actively trading in the £50-80 range.

Inflationary pressures build up

However, it was at about this time that some commentators began to point to inflationary dangers ahead. All the signs were there, they argued. Crowding in shops, queues, waiting lists and a flourishing black market, all indicated a physical inability of current production to satisfy the pent-up demand for goods and services by a public that had gone without for five years. Prices began to rise and the inflation hedge argument for buying equities made its appearance. As an *FT* editorial pointed out at the beginning of May, industrial equities were practically the only example of pre-War prices remaining in a world where real values had appreciated by 50% or more. As if to confirm this view, a 16.66% rise in rail charges at the end of May was greeted with a surge of buying of leading equities under conditions of acute stock shortage, taking the index to 126.2.

The Chancellor's cheap money policy now began to come in for criticism. While the provision of cheap capital to government and industry at a time when high expenditure was required to rebuild the country's infrastructure was clearly desirable, it was not without its dangers. After all, critics pointed out, the whole policy rested upon interference with the normal functioning of supply and demand in the capital markets. The increasing unimportance of the debt

---

The Financial Times
Industrial Ordinary 30 Share Index (FT 30)

On January 1st 1947, the *Financial Times* decided to discontinue using its broader Industrial index, and to establish its index of 30 leading industrial ordinary shares as the new market barometer. The FT 30 had been compiled first in 1935 with a base value of 100.

The 30 constituents on 1st January were:

Guest Keen	Watney Coombe Reid
Vickers	Imperial Tobacco
United Steel	Tate & Lyle
Murex	London Brick
EMI	Associated Portland Cement
General Electric	Pinchin Johnson
Rolls Royce	Imperial Chemical
Hawker Siddeley	Dunlop
Courtaulds	Turner & Newall
J&P Coats	William Cory
Lancashire Cotton	Swan Hunter
Patons & Baldwins	Morris Motors
Harrods	Leyland Motors
Woolworths	P & O
Distillers	Spillers

In this text, for the sake of ease of comparison year by year, we have quoted the FT 30 throughout to record the movement of equities even though they may be referred to as "industrials" and "ordinaries". Following its introduction in 1962, the FT Actuaries series is also quoted, and from 1984, the new FT-SE 100 share index tends to become the principal yardstick.

---

burden could encourage wasteful spending by government and industry, and also act as a disincentive to reduce debt. On the other side of the coin, cheap money could discourage saving to a point where the holders of capital might prefer to spend it on consumer goods and services rather than invest it for the benefit of industry. Such considerations did not appear to worry the Chancellor or investors. Later in the year he issued an irredeemable stock with a 2.5% coupon at par, and it was snapped up.

There were two developments in the autumn of 1946 which could have had serious repercussions on London equities. In the event, they caused nothing more than a relatively minor and short-lived reaction in the indices. One was a severe shake-out on Wall Street, pulling the Dow back from over 200 in mid-July to 163 in mid-October. The other was the prospect of an acute coal shortage threatening industry with shutdown. But at the time investors were far more concerned with seeking a better return on their capital than that available on government stocks, and in pursuit of this aim they competed for a limited supply of good quality industrial debentures and preferences and for leading equities. In July a £6 million offering of a 3.5% Debenture from Dunlop was seven times oversubscribed, and a general shortage of prospectuses for new issues led to a Stock Exchange ruling that investors could make their applications on ordinary notepaper. The attraction of equities was further enhanced during the second half of the year by a great number of high percentage dividend increases and even though the FT 30 had risen from 112 to 134 since the beginning of the year, the average dividend yield was still 3.54% whereas that on Consols had fallen from 2.74% to 2.54%.

Equities were given yet another boost in November when compensation terms for the nationalisation of the railways were announced. Stockholders who had been enjoying yields of about 4.5% were to be bought out at market value with government stock carrying the rate of interest found to be ruling on 2nd January 1948, a figure widely assumed to be 2.5%. These terms were condemned as confiscatory, and started a scramble for good class industrial equities which were yielding a full point more on average. Not surprisingly the year ended in fine form with both the gilt and equity indices at new peaks.

The Fuel Crisis

As is so often the case in the markets, a strong move up in the face of what appear to be serious and obvious problems, does not necessarily mean that these problems have been adequately discounted. On 2nd January 1947, ironically the vesting date for the nationalisation of the coal industry and in the middle of one of the severest winters of the century, Electrical & Musical Industries (E.M.I.) announced that it was on the verge of a total shutdown as a result of the lack of fuel supplies. The next day the FT 30 hit a new peak. It continued to rise until 18th January when it touched 140.6, but reality reasserted itself in February and the index crashed to 126 as industry after industry was forced to curtail production. By March industry was practically at a standstill.

The government's honeymoon period with the markets was nearing its end. The curbing of private enterprise was coming to be seen not only as a political act offering no compensating advantages, but also as one which had created an economic void nationalisation was incapable of filling. There were plenty of departmental plans and targets but a lack of planning and control to cover the whole economy. Hence the coal crisis and the acute shortage of practically every essential commodity accompanied by swingeing price rises.

Much of the blame for this state of affairs now began to be laid at the door of organised labour. While politicians on both sides of the House stressed the need for greater productivity to overcome the shortfalls in production, the TUC was demanding a 40-hour week and "closed shop" agreements, and absenteeism in the coal mines was recognised as a major cause of the fuel crisis. Because of its historic links, the Labour government was able neither to control the demands of the TUC nor to disassociate itself from them.

More austerity measures

A better than expected budget in April followed by a bumper crop of dividend announcements prompted a strong rally in mid-May which almost reached the January peak, but that was the market's swansong. Gilts also failed to regain their best levels of November. The first post-War bull market had run its course. The three props of cheap money, scarcity of investments and weight of funds looking for a home, had been around for so long that they had lulled markets into a false sense of security. It was soon to be dispelled as the economic background deteriorated. In July the Chancellor introduced the first of a new series of austerity plans, cutting dollar imports of tobacco, petrol, newsprint and films. Investors sensed that the government was losing control. Heavy selling hit gilts, pushing yields up to 2.75% and undermining the relationship with equities, which also fell away sharply.

There was one bright spot on the horizon. It was the Marshall Aid proposal to help reconstruct the European economies by channelling in £6 billion a year for the next three to four years. Unfortunately the complexities of the deal meant that the negotiations were unduly prolonged, and news that they had been adjourned until the following January led to an all-round fall in markets. The last week of July saw 4.5 points knocked off gilts and nearly 10 points off the FT 30, taking it to 120. An appeal to the nation from

---

A Star is born

1947 saw the public launch of **Glaxo** when the subsidiary of that name took over the parent, Joseph Nathan & Co., in a share exchange deal. Originally a New Zealand-based produce merchant founded by East London emigré Joseph Nathan in 1873, the company pioneered the development of dried-milk babyfood in the early 1900s, and graduated to pharmaceutical production in the inter-War years. Glaxo Laboratories was formed in 1932 and rapidly grew in importance to the group. It became a major provider of medical products during the Second World War, including the newly-discovered substance, penicillin, for which it developed mass-production methods. At the time of the reconstruction, all the former operations of Joseph Nathan were disposed of and 100,000 Ordinary 10/- shares in Glaxo were issued to the original shareholders. The move attracted buyers, and with the share price at £29 the new group was capitalised at just under £3 million as compared with today's figure of close to £20 billion.

Sir Stafford Cripps, a leading left-wing socialist and wartime Minister of Aircraft Production, warning that the country's economic survival was at stake, did not help matters and there were calls from all quarters for the government to come up with a plan of action to deal with the crisis.

The "plan" when it came on 6th August did nothing to reassure markets. The measures comprised further powers to cut imports and direct exports, and with the agreement of the TUC the government also acquired control over labour with the power to direct it for the benefit of the country's basic industries. Later in the month additional measures were enacted, including a ban on pleasure travel outside the sterling area, the scrapping of the basic petrol ration, and a reduction in the meat ration. Only essential motor cars were to be manufactured for domestic consumption and all others were to be for export. And sterling, which had become convertible in mid-July in accordance with the terms of the Anglo-American Loan agreement, was promptly made inconvertible again.

The government's actions were widely criticised as panic measures that would do little to solve the underlying problem of the economy, which was lack of production. Much was made of the fact that, despite the huge shortfall in coal production, earlier in the year the miners had been permitted to move from a six-day working week to one of five days, and had then refused to honour agreements to change their working practices to boost productivity. The country was 'hanging by a thread' said Minister of Fuel and Power, Emmanuel Shinwell, and the miners should "play the game by the nation", but such exhortations fell on deaf ears and indeed were counterproductive – quite literally – in that they resulted in a wave of pit strikes. By the end of the first week in September, gilt yields were well in excess of 3% and the FT 30 had fallen to 104.2.

The remainder of the year saw a slow but steady recovery in equities. They had taken heart from a speeding up of the Marshall Aid plans for Europe and from what was seen as a more realistic approach to the country's economic problems by Sir Stafford Cripps, who had become Minister for Economic Affairs at the end of September. His drastic measures to reduce the dollar outflow by more import cuts and by a reduction in domestic capital spending in order to leave more materials available for export, were viewed as unpleasant but necessary, and did not hinder the market's recovery.

Chancellor Dalton resigns

There was some nervousness about what action Chancellor Dalton might take in an autumn budget, and it was widely feared that a large increase in distributed profits tax was likely in order to strike a political balance against a further reduction in the huge bill for subsidies. In the event equities remained firm ahead of the budget and even the doubling of profits tax and further increases in purchase tax failed to stem the advance. Gilts, on the other hand, took a sharp knock the day after the budget, when Mr Dalton resigned after admitting to having inadvertently disclosed details of the budget to a journalist minutes before his speech, and was replaced by Sir Stafford Cripps. While the former's commitment to an ultra-cheap monetary policy was never in doubt it was thought the new Chancellor might adopt a more flexible approach and be tougher on inflation.

Vesting date for the nationalisation of the railways was rapidly approaching and the prospect of the pending rein-vestment of the compensation proceeds was a major factor behind the burst of strength in equities towards the end of December which left the FT 30 at 128.3, up 23% from the September low. Gilts, meanwhile, had settled around a 3% yield basis on the assumption that the Transport stock to be issued to former Home Rail stockholders would be given a realistic 3% coupon on 1st January 1948 and not an untenable 2.5% one.

Marshall Plan to the rescue

Speculation towards the end of 1947 that the summer collapse had perhaps constituted the shortest bear market on record did not last long into 1948. Despite an improving domestic situation characterised by rising production and sharply higher coal stocks, February saw a deterioration in

Sir Stafford Cripps took over as Chancellor after Hugh Dalton's resignation in 1947, becoming the personification of the austerity programme.

the external situation. The US loan was down to the last $100 million and more gold sales had to be made to counter the drain on the country's dollar reserves. There were fears, too, that the post-War US boom was collapsing and already the Dow was testing its 1946 low point. The scene was set for another round of austerity measures from the new Chancellor. His wages and prices policy was seen as a threat to equities in that as well as turning the screw on inflation, limitation on profits and dividends had to be a political quid pro quo for the restriction on incomes. The FT 30 slipped back to 111.3 in March on rumours of a dividend freeze, but when it became a reality in the budget a month later, the index, which was already back to 118.1 ahead of the news, went better again.

The passing of the Marshall Plan by Congress helped sentiment further. The austerity measures had met with a degree of success and now US aid was giving the country a breathing space to put its house in order. This period of relative calm was abruptly shattered in July when the Russians sealed off Berlin. The index touched its low point of the year at 109.2 but then began a slow recovery as the airlift proved a resounding success and the situation stabilised. President of the Board of Trade, Harold Wilson, gave the upward movement a further boost with his "bonfire of controls" on 5th November.

In December, the Chancellor detailed his Four-Year Plan for the UK, to be ready for the ending of Marshall Aid in mid-1952. As might have been expected, it called for a greater proportion of imports to be raw materials and essential foodstuffs and for the export drive to continue unabated. With industrial production recovering to a new post-War peak and the gold and dollar drain stemmed following the coming into operation of the Marshall Plan, equities were not unduly depressed by the restraint on profits and dividends, and closed the year at 121, a fall of 6%. Gilts held steady throughout the year and the Government Securities Index, which had been 112.88 at the end of December 1947, stood at 113.66 precisely a year later. Golds were the year's worst performer as ever rising production costs set against a fixed selling price, inevitably took their toll of profits, and the index closed the year down 22.7% at 94.67, its lowest since 1932. All in all, 1948 was a year in limbo for the stock market with the low level of investor interest resulting in the smallest turnover to date in any post-War year.

The first devaluation

If 1948 was the year in which the government faced up to the realities of the economic situation and began to take steps to deal with it with some apparent success, 1949 demonstrated that problems of such magnitude were not easily solved. Exports were rising, the balance of payments was moving towards equilibrium with the large dollar deficit offset by US aid, thus taking the pressure off the country's gold and dollar reserves, but the recovery was still fragile and susceptible to external shocks. The shock, when it came, was from the US in the shape of a business recession causing a substantial reduction in purchases of UK goods in the context of an export market where the criterion had changed from one of availability to one of price. There was a renewed decline in the country's gold and dollar reserves and its cost structure was exposed as excessively inflated. Drastic measures were called for and on 18th September the pound was devalued against the dollar from $4.03 to $2.80.

The event meant that the Government had been forced to acknowledge that it was trying to do too much with the resources available. Attempts to modernise and expand UK industry and to increase exports, at the same time as extending the social security system, were simply unrealistic and overambitious. As a result, growing inflationary pressures undermined the international status of sterling, and demonstrated the fragility of the foundations of an economy based on a policy of full employment and a welfare state.

The size of the devaluation – or the "change in the rate of exchange" as Sir Stafford Cripps preferred to call it – was greater than had been expected. Equities, nevertheless, responded positively to the news and the FT 30 gained 1.9 to 110.1 but losses in gilts ranged up to £2. The real beneficiaries were gold shares. They had been edging up since the summer when rumours of a coming devaluation were rife, and on the now certain prospect of at least doubled mine profits, their index jumped 20% to 129.63. However, the absence of any significant supplementary action by the government suggested that perhaps too much reliance was being placed on devaluation as a cure for all the country's economic ills. In particular, doubts were expressed that the reduced dollar yield on exports could be outweighed by a proportionately greater increase in volume, and equities failed to hold their initial gains. In mid-November, the index slipped to a new post-War low of 99.8, recovering to 106.4 at year end for an overall loss on the year of 12.25%. Over the same period the Government Securities Index recorded a loss of 7%.

The Korean War and rearmament

The failures of 1949 made 1950 a critical year. The coming election in February meant that the government had to tread warily, and after winning with only a 17-seat margin, the prospect of any economic crisis rapidly turning into a political one dictated that the more controversial contents of the manifesto had to take a back seat. As one of the Opposition members put it, there could be no more "frog-marching of doctrinaire legislation through the House". Fortunately for the government, a boom in the US, a better flow of raw materials and the coming on stream of much of the capital investment undertaken since the end of the War, were good for production and for exports and equities began to respond. The FT 30, which had fallen 2.4 to 105.6 on news of the election result, was already up to 110 ahead of a tax-cutting budget and the announcement at the end of May that petrol rationing was to end.

The outbreak of war in Korea towards the end of June was a shock, but recovery was rapid as the demand for sterling area commodities increased and the balance of payments strengthened. Rearmament to meet what was perceived as a worldwide Communist threat, now became an industrial priority but inevitably inflationary pressures began to increase as this new burden was imposed upon an already overstretched economy. This meant trouble ahead,

---

The way we were...
Sterling Exchange Rates
Currency Units per £
31 December 1950

France (Franc) 9.80
Germany (DMark) 11.76
Italy (Lira) 1750.00
Japan (Yen) 1012.00
USA (Dollar) 2.80

---

but fired by the prospect of steel nationalisation funds looking for a new home following vesting date early in 1951, equities ended the year on a strong note at 115.7, up 8%, with a momentum which carried on well into the New Year. Wall Street also provided an encouraging background. The long bull phase that began in the spring of 1949 had passed the Dow's May 1946 peak of 212 in April 1950 and was not set to run out of steam until September 1951.

1951-55

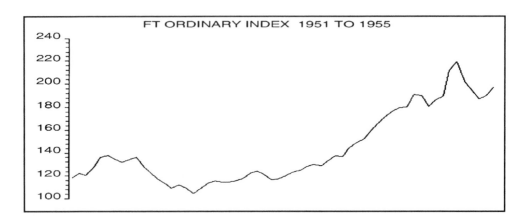

Conservatives back in power

The first half of 1951 witnessed a gradually gathering economic crisis. The devaluation of September 1949 had bought time for the Labour government but policies based on the assumption that public expenditure could not and indeed should not be reduced, that wage and dividend restraints could continue indefinitely, and that exhortation and patriotism would look after the export drive, could lead only to disaster. By the middle of the year imports were rising sharply, and exports lagging as a recession in the prices of dollar-earning commodities from the sterling area, combined with higher dollar purchases, reopened the dollar gap. The balance of payments was weakening again and a deficit of £500 million in the first half threatened to grow to £1.2 billion by the end of the year. The new Chancellor, Hugh Gaitskell, felt compelled to reverse the tax cuts of the previous year.

In order to back up its calls for wage restraint, the government, noting that even a 50% distributed profits tax was not keeping dividends in check, imposed statutory dividend limitation in late July. This was hardly effective in dealing with what was rapidly becoming a major crisis, and feeling that his administration needed a new mandate, Mr Attlee called a general election for 27th October. The Conservatives, led by Mr Churchill, won with only an 18-seat majority, and Mr R.A. Butler became Chancellor. The FT 30, which had risen 3.3 to 138.6 a month earlier when the date of the election was announced, began to fall away as soon as the Chancellor revealed his emergency measures, reaching 121.9 by the end of December.

Chancellor Butler's measures

His actions were conventional enough in that they included a £350 million cut in imports together with sharp restrictions on domestic capital spending, but the monetary measures marked an important change of principle in the way the new government would exercise control of the economy. Bank Rate was raised from 2% to 2.5%, the foreign exchange market was reopened, and a number of commodities were decontrolled and left to the workings of the price mechanism. Markets continued to take a cautious view, and at year end the FT 30 was back to 122, with the Government Securities Index depressed at 96.03 on higher interest rate fears. Few doubted that these drastic measures were necessary to deal with a

'Rab' Butler, first post-War Tory Chancellor embarked upon the first major moves towards de-control.

crisis situation but investors preferred to wait until the first Conservative budget before celebrating. Perhaps they had become cynical after seeing the early promise of the Labour government dissolve in crisis after crisis, and were simply not prepared to take the new Conservative administration on trust.

The budget, when it came in March, was shaped by two overriding factors. One was the defence requirement and the other was the need to improve the balance of payments. Chancellor Butler called it an "incentive budget", but while it did bring longer-term benefits to industry, the raising of the Bank Rate to 4%, the introduction of the Excess Profits Levy, and further restrictions on capital investment, were not well received by the markets. Funds fell by up to 3.5 points, pulling the Government Securities Index back to 92.73, and the immediate reaction of the FT 30 was a 3.9 fall to 109.3. Confidence did not return until the beginning of the second half of the year when it became clear that the gold and dollar drain had been stemmed and that the balance of payments was moving back into surplus. At the end of the year, the FT 30 had recovered to 115.8 to show a loss of 8%, while Government Securities at 94.41 was down just 2%.

The bull market gets under way

The improving trend of the economy carried on into 1953, and the confidence that it engendered in investors was now, slowly but surely, beginning to be reflected in the stock market. The first major post-War "popular" bull market was getting under way. It was popular in the sense that investors were making money, not out of shares in exotic companies from "far away places with strange-sounding names" like Mexican Eagle or Wiluna Gold, but from shares in stores, breweries and motor car manufacturers they came into contact with every day. Everybody knew Marks & Spencers in the High Street and it was comforting to know that by buying their shares as well as their merchandise, a capital gain and an ever increasing dividend were assured. In fact, 1953 could almost be pin-pointed as foundation year for the cult of the equity and the share-owning democracy. Stores were very much the darling of the developing boom, and every new set of results from Marks & Spencer, Great Universal Stores (widely known as Gussies) or Woolworth, was eagerly awaited to see, not only how many new bonus shares were to be issued, but also whether the dividend was going to be maintained on the last increase of capital.

Investors were rarely disappointed more than momentarily in the wake of the liquidation after a pre-results surge of speculative buying.

Considerable additional excitement was brought to the party by bid activity. In the early 'fifties few companies had bothered to embark upon a revaluation of assets – even ICI had been taken to task by the *Financial Times* for complaining that to do so would be too costly and time-

---

Savoy under Siege

The opening shots in the long-running battle for control of the Savoy Hotel came in the autumn of 1953. Charles Clore and Harold Samuel of Land Securities were both interested in what they saw as the underdeveloped property potential of the group, and both had quietly accumulated shares. In order to foil a suspected takeover attempt, the Savoy board, led by Hugh Wontner, formed a special subsidiary company to hold the group's properties and keep them separate from the hotel operating side. Charles Clore then sold his stake to Harold Samuel, who promptly tried to use his resulting 37% holding to block this defensive move through the courts. However, after talks Harold Samuel agreed to sell his stake to the Savoy board and "friends" at 62/6 a share, a price which gave him a £1.3 million profit on the deal. This is probably the first reported case of "greenmail".

---

consuming – and most had their land and buildings in the balance sheet at often absurdly low pre-War cost prices. Furthermore, conservative boardroom practice, reinforced by Labour's dividend restraint policy, meant that dividends were often covered four and more times by earnings. The British industrial scene thus represented a happy hunting ground for entrepreneurs like Hugh Fraser, Charles Forte and Charles Clore, all of whom were to lay the foundations of their business empires during this era.

The budget in April was welcomed by the *Financial Times* as "good for the public, good for industry and good for the market". Its principal provisions were 6d off income tax, a 25% cut in purchase tax, and the ending of the Excess Profits Levy on 1st January next. After some initial hesitation, equities resumed their steady rise aided by a stream of good economic news in the shape of a post-War peak in new car registrations, record aircraft exports and a sharp recovery in textiles output. It was now clear that the trend in profits was changing quite dramatically. Reported profits had been disappointing earlier in the year, but they were reflecting conditions in 1952. It was now possible to look at the production figures and the obvious signs of prosperity all around and anticipate a sharp improvement later in 1953 carrying on well into 1954.

This sort of intelligent speculation was good for the equity market; confidence was further boosted in September by a cut in Bank Rate to 3.5% and the following month by the announcement of the terms for the offer to the public of denationalised **United Steel**. Even Wall Street, which had been depressed all year, now weighed in with a sharp recovery, casting doubts on the validity of earlier fears of a recession. As a result, 1953 ended on a strong note with the FT 30 up 14.9% to 130.7, Government Securities up 5.8% at 100.21 and only Golds disappointed, down 5.17%. Since industrial profits had fallen by 8% during the year, the auguries for 1954 were good.

Into new high ground

At the beginning of 1954 there was much talk of, not whether, but when the index would surpass its January 1947 peak of 140.6. The big event took place on 3rd April, just ahead of the budget which was well received, confirming the breakthrough. It was widely noted that the peak prices of April 1954 looked far more sustainable than those of January 1947, in that industrial dividend yields were now geared to a more realistic level of interest rates than that ruling in the Dalton cheap money era. A period of rising dividends also meant that with equities yielding around 5% on average, the yield gap was much wider than in 1947, providing them with what could be regarded as a greater margin of safety. It should be remembered that this was the time of the "yield gap", long before the advent of the "reverse yield gap", when equities yielded more than gilts in order to compensate for the higher risk attached to them.

There was no stopping the market in 1954. Company profits and dividends appeared set on a permanently rising trend and every key announcement sparked a new round of buying. The stores continued to reveal brilliant results as did the motor car manufacturers, with Ford reporting doubled profits in April. In May Bank Rate was again reduced, this time to 3%, a move interpreted as a sign of the government's confidence in continuing industrial recovery and its belief that production and exports could continue to rise without risk of inflationary pressures building up again. Furthermore, the underlying balance between the dollar and sterling areas was moving strongly in favour of the UK, and trade with the OECD countries was yielding a substantial monthly surplus. And also powering the upward drive in stock prices was the simple fact of too much money chasing too little stock. The performance of equities vis-à-vis gilts was not lost on the institutions and the composition of their portfolios was undergoing a sea change in favour of ordinary shares.

There had to be a spectre at such a feast and it turned out to be the familiar one that had haunted the last days of the Labour administration in 1951. A combination of acute labour shortages, big wage claims and awards, rising personal consumption, heavy capital investment by industry and increasing government expenditure, served to put an intolerable strain on productive capacity which in turn led to lengthening delivery dates and a deterioration in the balance of payments as imports rose and exports fell. The shape of things to come was evident in the fact that German car output had risen by 38% in 1954 to 675,000 vehicles of which 300,000 were exported. None of this seemed to worry investors very much during the last days of 1954 and equities entered the New Year on a rising trend. Gilts, however, had a better nose for dearer money and failed to share their enthusiasm, ending the year with just a 3% gain against one of 53% for equities.

The brakes go on

The opening days of 1955 saw increasing activity in equities and the latest of the denationalised steels, **Colvilles**, received applications totalling £169 million for the £13 million of stock on offer. Then at the end of January, Bank

Rate was raised by 0.5% to 3.5%, not, it was stressed, to remedy a critical situation but to ensure that one did not arise. It did not work. Gilts continued to fall and the Government Securities Index, which was 103.94 on 1st January, had slipped below the 100 mark by the end of the month. Sterling also failed to respond and the drain on the gold and dollar reserves persisted. It was now time for the government to show that it really meant business in its anti-inflationary drive. Accordingly, at the end of February, Bank Rate was raised a full point to 4.5%, and hire purchase restrictions were introduced for a wide range of consumer goods, cars included, specifying a minimum 15% deposit and a maximum two-year repayment period. Gilts promptly fell by up to four points, the FT 30 lost seven points to 177, and sterling steadied.

The markets quickly recovered their poise, for the consensus was that the country was flourishing and that some degree of inflation was inevitable in a full employment economy where unfilled vacancies actually exceeded the number of unemployed. Thus the Chancellor's measures were regarded as necessary to nip inflation in the bud, to protect the balance of payments and to remove uncertainty in markets as to the government's intentions. In the budget in mid-April, the Chancellor seemed to confirm this sanguine view of the state of the economy by cutting the standard rate of income tax from 9/- to 8/6, and halving purchase tax on some consumer goods. By May there were some signs that the original credit squeeze was working. Furniture sales were down by over 30% in March compared with a year earlier. This sort of restraint on domestic consumption was precisely what was intended and, coupled with evidence of an improvement in the gold and dollar reserves and in the balance of payments, the market lost its nervousness ahead of the election, reaching 196 on the eve of the poll.

The Conservatives win again

A Conservative victory with a majority of 60 seats against the 17 of 1951 was exactly what investors wanted and the result was greeted with a surge of buying which carried the

FT 30 through the 200 level for the first time. US buyers now came in for such international stocks as Unilever, Bowater, ICI, Ford and BP (formerly Anglo-Iranian Oil). Gilts, on the other hand, paid more attention to the domestic background, where large pay claims were often accompanied by the threat of strikes, and the strikes, when they occurred, were followed by large pay awards, and then in rapid succession by large price rises. Equities, nevertheless, pressed on regardless, touching a high of 223.9 in late July, despite the announcement of a sharply widening trade gap in June which indicated that the credit squeeze was failing to reduce the excessive demand for imports. A few days later the Chancellor countered with a tightening of hire purchase controls by increasing the minimum deposit from 15% to 33.33% and by requesting the banks to reduce advances to private customers.

The June trade figures, showing imports up by 14% on those for the first half of 1954, seemed to confirm the need for this new wave of restrictive measures. After all, as an *FT* editorial argued, the benefits of the last devaluation had been exhausted, and if the value of the pound was to be maintained, the reserves strengthened and provision made for investment, then credit had to be restrained. Despite consideration of the probability that the credit squeeze would lead to caution on the dividend front, equities took the restrictions very much in their stride. Forced selling in a thin market in the wake of the banks cutting back on overdrafts, pushed the FT 30 into the 180/190 range in August but even further increases in purchase tax (including that on motor cars from 50% to 60%) failed to do any more harm and the index ended the year back at the 200 level. Meanwhile gilts were in broad retreat, victims of what was now realised to be a worldwide trend towards dearer money on the emergence of inflationary pressures everywhere. Increasingly, the Dalton era of cheap money was seen as nothing more than a brief and temporary interruption of this trend, to which markets were having to make a belated adjustment. The Government Securities index was down by 12.8% over the year to 90.

1956-60

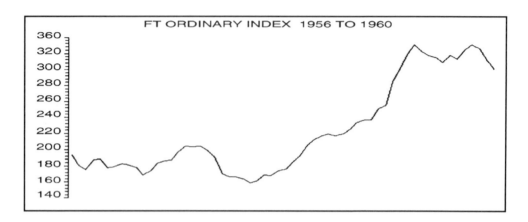

The squeeze begins to hurt

In the first few days of 1956, it was clear that the new Chancellor, Harold Macmillan, was not going to be able to preside over any relaxation of the restraints imposed by his predecessor. There was a sharp decline in the gold and dollar reserves in December, leaving them at their lowest level for three years, and the December balance of payments figures showed imports up by 15%. There were already signs that the impact of the credit squeeze was being felt in the motor industry, where some factories had already begun short-time working. Nevertheless, Mr Macmillan was not convinced that enough had been done to damp down home demand and in mid-February he raised Bank Rate to 5.5% and brought in a new package of restrictive measures. The motor industry once again was singled out for particularly harsh treatment and hire purchase deposits were lifted from 33.33% to 50%. In addition, the investment allowances introduced in the April 1954 budget were suspended, the capital spending programmes of the nationalised industries were to be cut in 1956/57, and the Capital Issues Committee was directed to take a more "critical" look at prospective new issues.

The ordinary share and Government Securities indices were already trending downwards from the beginning of the year and these latest moves depressed them further in early March to 170 and 85 respectively. Such falls appeared more than justified by a rapid succession of announcements from industry detailing the drastic effect the squeeze was having. Huge stocks of new cars were building up and more and more companies were forced to lay off production workers. The same situation applied to the domestic appliance manufacturers, and the radio and television makers were reporting production cuts of up to 40%. The fact that both equities and gilts rallied strongly to 196 and 88 by the end of April suggests that markets sensed a degree of overkill in the Chancellor's measures, pointing to a rapid reversal of policy in the not too distant future. Support for this view was drawn from a progressively narrowing trade gap in February and March, accompanied by a sharp recovery in the gold and dollar reserves. With the crisis in the motor industry aggravated by import restrictions operating in two of its largest overseas markets, Australia and New Zealand, this theory had a lot to recommend it on the reasoning that the abrupt change from expansion to contraction would cause alarm in government circles.

Nasser seizes the Suez Canal

Then in July, Colonel Nasser seized control of the Suez Canal and created a more serious crisis which was to dominate the economic and political scene for the rest of the year. The initial reaction to the news was a relatively minor fall in the ordinary share index to 183.2, with the largest declines being registered by shares in oil and shipping companies on the prospect of having to pay higher dues to the new owners of the Canal. However, the lack of any real progress towards achieving a settlement and the growing shortage of oil supplies soon began to erode investor confidence and the index was back to 175 when the shooting war started at the end of October. The political embarrassment caused by the withdrawal of the Anglo-French forces under pressure from America and the United Nations was matched by the economic damage resulting from the closure of the Canal. The UK was now faced with the double problem, first of all, of getting enough oil to keep industry going, and then of paying for it without deci-mating the gold and dollar reserves. By the end of November, the FT 30 had reached its low point of the year at 161.5 with the

Harold Macmillan, as Chancellor of the Exchequer in 1956, had to deal with the problems raised by the Suez Crisis.

Government Securities index similarly depressed at 82.38. The introduction of petrol rationing in December was a further blow to the motor industry, where one fifth of the workforce was already on short-time, and it prompted the first selective reflationary move, which was a reduction in the minimum hire purchase deposit from 50% to 20%. December witnessed a modest recovery in the markets despite news of the Russian crushing of the Hungarian uprising, and the FT 30 closed the year at 178.8.

Bank Rate to 7%

The political legacy of Suez was shaken off in January 1957 with the resignation of Anthony Eden and his replacement by Harold Macmillan, with Peter Thorneycroft taking over at the Treasury. The economic legacy, however, persisted with restricted oil supplies which were much more costly and thus a severe drain on the country's gold and dollar reserves. Although alarmed by their decline, less than a month after taking office the new Chancellor lowered Bank Rate by half a point to 5%. Such anxieties failed to dent the rally in equities which had begun in the previous December, and by the end of April the index had breached the 200 level once more. Mr Thorneycroft's first budget had been anything but restrictive, and a number of wage disputes had been settled on generous terms, both of which factors served to encourage further pay claims, many of which led to serious strikes. All this provided an ideal background for the wave of currency speculation against the pound in the second half of the year in the wake of the devaluation of the French franc. The cost of defending the pound led to another sharp fall in the gold and dollar reserves, and the Chancellor decided to act.

Chancellor of the Exchequer Peter Thorneycroft resigned in January 1958 over government spending plans.

The two-point rise in Bank Rate in September to 7% stunned the City. The move was accompanied by a brake on investment spending by government departments, local authorities and nationalised industries, and by instructions to banks to limit loans to the private sector. The immediate reaction in the markets was an 8.7 point fall in the FT 30 to 183.5 and one of 3.99 in Government Securities to 77.52. The decline continued and by the end of November the ordinary index was down to 162, and while gilts had steadied, their prospect of recovery was not helped by a report from the Church Commissioners that they had just trimmed their gilts portfolio by £11 million to £35.8 million. The feeling of apprehension among investors was heightened when the government announced its intention to take a firm stand against exorbitant wage claims regardless of strike threats, and confirmed its resolve by vetoing a 3% pay award to Health Service workers. However, Chancellor Thorneycroft felt that the Prime Minister's firmness was more apparent than real, and believing that the will to curb actual government spending was lacking, he resigned in January.

The recovery begins

The year had ended on a quiet but more hopeful note after a sharp improvement in the November trade gap and a marked revival in the motor and steel industries. There was now a widespread feeling among investors that markets had discounted a great deal and that in 1958 things could only get better. They were right. The disinflationary measures of 1957 were to prove more successful than the government had hoped, and served to provide a period of rest and recuperation for the economy in 1958 which paved the way for the boom year of 1959. January saw a sharp improvement in the gold and dollar reserves, and a significant reduction in the December trade gap to the lowest monthly level for seven years. This set the pattern for the rest of the year and encouraged the new Chancellor, Mr Heathcote Amory, to embark upon a series of Bank Rate reductions beginning with a 1% cut in March. The figure of 154 touched by the FT 30 in February proved to be the low point of the year, and from then on the advance was practically continuous, boosted by a mildly reflationary budget in April, and by each successive cut in Bank Rate. The last one, which brought the rate down to 4% in November, saw the index within just a few points of the 1955 high of 223.9, and on the last day of the year it broke through. Investors had good reason to believe that they "had never had it so good".

Equities had gained 36% and gilts had topped 6.7%, providing a fair reflection of the recovery in the economy during 1958. That recovery had been greatly assisted by two factors. One was a much milder recession in the US than had been expected, which meant that the UK was able to take full advantage of the opportunity offered by a favourable change in the terms of trade. Of course, Wall Street's performance was no drawback either with the Dow Jones adding nearly 150 points to reach a new record high of 583.65. The other was the government's drive towards financial liberalisation with the elimination of a great many of the controls that had hampered the free working of the economy ever since the war years. Industry was confident that it was entering the New Year in good shape, and secure in the knowledge that it had a large enough margin of spare capacity to meet home and export demand without running into production bottlenecks and stirring up new inflationary pressures.

The Great Aluminium War

One of the major corporate events of 1958 was the battle for control of **British Aluminium**, which was a milestone on the road towards the formulation of the City Takeover Code. BA supplied about one third of aluminium demand in the UK and appeared an attractive target to two American aluminium producers, both looking for a stepping-stone into the fast-growing European markets. One was **Reynolds Aluminium** and the other was **Alcoa**, the Aluminium Company of America. In order to make its planned takeover of such a key industrial company more acceptable to Britain, in September 1958 Reynolds went into partnership with Tube Investments, and both began buying BA shares in the market using nominees. In November, Reynolds and Tubes, advised by Warburgs, a relative newcomer on the merchant banking scene, met with the BA board, advised by Lazards and Hambros, to try to reach agreement on the terms of a bid. The meeting broke up with BA flatly rejecting the approach.

In December BA announced that it had agreed a deal with Alcoa, justifying it on the grounds that only a one-third stake would pass into American hands whereas in the case of the Reynolds-TI bid, all the BA stock would be held by a joint company with a dominant American partner. By the end of the year, neither offer had received sufficient acceptances, a stalemate which sparked an independent offer by a consortium of institutions. This new offer, supposedly, was not on behalf of BA but since the

Sir Siegmund Warburg, founder of the Warburg Group (from a painting by Rayment Skipp).

accompanying letter to BA shareholders was signed by the chairmen of Lazards and Hambros and called for the Reynolds-TI offer to be rejected "in the national interest", there was little doubt whose side they were on.

This manoeuvre turned out to be ill-judged, and on two counts. One was that it gave the impression that the City establishment was trying to slam the door in the face of newcomers, especially those who did not instantly accede to its wishes. The financial press was not happy with this and neither were many of the other financial institutions, some of which were holders of BA stock. The other was that Reynolds and TI were goaded into instant action and Warburgs promptly began buying BA stock in the market, much of it from those same disgruntled institutions. Within ten days, it was all over. The Reynolds-TI camp had amassed 80% of the issued capital of BA and some of the oldest and most revered institutions in the City had suffered an embarrassing defeat.

The yield gap goes into reverse

The year 1959 was an "annus mirabilis" for the equity investor. If the bull market of 1952/55 had laid the foundations of the cult of the equity, then the first real construction work on those foundations was done in 1959. It was also the year the yield gap finally went into reverse, just twelve months after the move had been pioneered in the US. There were still many household names among the top performing shares of 1959 just as in 1955, and Steels and Motors were up by 160% and 100% respectively, but the stars were two of the new acquisitive industrial holding companies, and two of the many new issues that had flocked to the market during the year. Two headline making bids had also served to prove to the enthusiastic investor and speculator that no company, however exalted, was safe from the attentions of the new breed of entrepreneurs.

The year opened in a mood of cautious optimism but sentiment soon became adversely affected by the start in January of another strike in the motor industry involving both British Motor and Standard. The suspension of the Capital Issues Committee in February prompted a revival of interest in that it was seen as another important step along the road to financial decontrol, giving companies freedom to raise capital for the first time since the outbreak of war in 1939. It was the budget in April that finally convinced investors that the government, if not exactly throwing caution to the winds, at last believed that it was safe to put the economy back on an unashamedly expansionist path. There was a cut in the standard rate of income tax, further reductions in purchase tax, 2d off a pint of beer (supposedly a great psychological boost for the working man), and investment allowances were restored following their suspension two years earlier. The next day, the FT 30 finally recovered all the ground it had lost since the beginning of the year and edged to a new high of 226.1, with Government Securities reaching 86.3, up nearly two points over the same period.

Car exports boom

From that point on, it was good news all the way. Production rose rapidly, and the recovery spread from consumer goods to capital goods. Productivity gained dramatically too, with the increase in employment lagging well behind the rise in production. Exports soared, particularly of cars. These were the days when British sports cars were conquering America, and over 50% of UK car exports in 1959 went to North America, which had taken over from Australia, New Zealand and South Africa as the most important market for British cars. In May, BMC announced that it was planning to step up production in the face of "overwhelming demand", and after unveiling the new Mini (priced at £497 including purchase tax) in August, it reported that its home market order book stood at three times the level of the year before. British aircraft, too, were very popular with overseas buyers, and the Vickers Viscount became the staple of airlines in many parts of the world. And all this was against a background where the new upsurge in profits was seen as certain to bring a delayed benefit to shares, the current rating of which in terms of earnings and dividends still reflected the near-stagnation of the years 1957/58. Not surprisingly, on 28th August, the yield gap at last went into reverse with the FT 30 at 256 yielding 4.76%, or 0.01% less than Government Securities at 85.09. The equity revolution was now complete. Fixed interest stocks no longer figured in the calculations of the average private investor constructing a portfolio. Equities were much more exciting and profitable.

The bids for Harrods and Watney Mann

The two bids that aroused the most interest during the year and made a significant contribution to the cult of the equity, were the one for **Harrods**, London's best known department store with its internationally famous flagship building in Knightsbridge, and that for **Watney Mann,** one of the biggest brewing groups in the UK. After a hard fought, three-cornered battle, Harrods eventually fell to the fast-growing Glasgow-based stores group, **House of Fraser,** for £37 million, but Charles Clore's £20 million bid for the property-rich brewer was withdrawn after a vigorous defence by Watney and the bidder's unwillingness to raise his offer. Unsuccessful though it was, the bid for Watney served to highlight the hidden property potential in all sorts of companies well beyond the circle of the breweries. There were also a number of mergers in the insurance world, and towards the end of the year the big aircraft manufacturers embarked upon the amalgamations necessary to make sure they had the clout to compete successfully in world markets.

As for the two best performing shares of the year, these were **Harper Engineering & Electronics**, up 450%, and **Arusha Industries**, up 400%. Both had been "shell" companies, in the sense that they had disposed of their original businesses and used the proceeds to go on the acquisition trail aided by the provision of further funds from shareholders. They were thus the forerunners of the fast-growing industrial holding companies that were such a feature in 1986/87 leading up to the October crash.

Among the many new issues floated during the year, **Berry's Magicoal,** with its electric imitation log and coal fires, was an instant success and recorded a 355% gain. **Shannon**, which made innovative business systems, also caught the imagination of the investing public and rose 360% over the year. Other newcomers to be welcomed by the stags were **Showerings**, the makers of Babycham, **Daintifyt Brassieres, Roy King Properties**, and, one of the few companies still independent today, **Frank G. Gates**, the car dealers, which raised £140,000 by a public offering of 27% of its equity. The year also witnessed the original flotation by Raymond and Sybil Zelker of **Polly Peck**, who offered 250,000 of the one million 2/- ordinary shares at 6/- each.

The Conservatives re-elected

If there was one element lacking in this booming market, it was confirmation of the political stability of the Conservative government. It was duly supplied by the October election when the Macmillan administration was returned with a majority of a hundred seats. The market had been rising strongly ahead of the poll and on news of the Conservative victory, the FT 30 leapt an unprecedented 16.1 points to 284.7 and kept going day after day to reach 338.4 by year end. There were few doubters during the boom, and optimism was reinforced by the fact that the bull market was a worldwide phenomenon and that dividend yields in the US and in Germany, for example, at 3% and 3.3% on average, were much lower than those ruling in the UK. Towards the end of the year, an editorial in the *Financial Times*, wisely if cynically observed that "the surest sign of future trouble is present prosperity", and pointed prophetically to rising world interest rates, fast-growing imports, and a pick-up in extravagant wage demands, as all signs of possible trouble ahead. Another indication of a peaking market was a fine arts boom culminating in the record price of £275,000 paid for Rubens' Adoration of the Magi, although it should be noted that it was bought by a college and not by a tycoon.

The Trustee boomlet

The performance of the equity index in 1960 demonstrated very clearly the truth of the market adage that it is better to travel hopefully than to arrive. The rise in profits, earnings and dividends so firmly established in 1959, accelerated dramatically in 1960, but it had been well discounted. After a rise of no less than 50% in the FT 30, most of it in the last three months of the year, investors had turned cautious. Past experience had taught them that it was time for a touch of the brakes. A wave of New Year enthusiasm carried the index to a new record high of 342.9 in the first week of January, but there was no follow-through. By the end of the month, it had lost more than twenty points in the wake of a BBC Panorama programme warning of the unstable nature of stock exchange booms and dearer money fears, which were soon realised by a 1% hike in Bank Rate to 5%. This was the first increase since November 1958, but it was well received, being regarded as a "stitch in time" necessary to trim the marginal excesses from the boom and keep it healthy. After touching 321.5 on the Bank Rate news, equities rebounded smartly on institutional buying. At least part of this buying was in anticipation of the implementation a year hence of the government's proposal to widen the investment powers of trustees to permit them to hold up to 50% of their funds in equities. The LCC (London County Council) had already obtained powers to invest up to 25% of its superannuation and provident funds in equities and announced that it had been "active" in the equity market. Unit trusts were increasing in popularity and in numbers, and their policy was to invest on setbacks.

Curbing the boom

However, it soon became clear that the rise in production was being constrained by difficulties in the supply of labour and other resources rather than deficiencies of demand, especially on the home front. In consequence, imports began to rise faster than exports. Wage claims and strike threats became very much a daily routine, and the April budget was appropriately restrictive in an effort to strengthen sterling and bring the expansion back within bounds without reviving dangers of inflation and balance of payment problems. One of the provisions was a requirement for the banks to deposit with the Bank of England 1% of their reserves of liquid assets, thereby reducing their ability to expand advances. The FT 30 reacted by slipping below 300 in early May to 295.8, close to its lowest point of the year, but by the end of the month it had recovered to 320. The rally was dented only briefly in June when the Chancellor tightened the screw once more by lifting Bank Rate another point to 6% and by upping the banks' Special Deposits from 1% to 2% in order to restrict their lending powers even more. By September, the rally was a spent force and after peaking at 340, the broad index declined to reach the year's low point of 293.4 in early December before staging a recovery to 305.5 at year end after a second half-point cut in Bank Rate had brought it down to 5% again.

Still, this apparently lacklustre performance by equities, as evidenced by an FT 30 down almost 10% on the year, masked a great deal of activity as institutions switched from sector to sector, causing a new pattern to emerge rather than a new level. The Financials, Properties, Stores, Plastics and Foods all moved up, while Consumer Durables, especially Motors, Household Appliances and Radio and TV, took a back seat as it became clear that their profit margins were being squeezed by a combination of flat demand, rising wages and constant final prices. Attractive new issues were often substantially oversubscribed, and in January the House of Fraser-related offering of 3.6 million shares in **SUITs** (Scottish Universal Investment Trust) for £2 million, received applications for £50 million. Indeed, but for the fact that the FT 30 was predominantly an industrial index with no Financials represented at all, it is more than likely that a decline from the January 1960 peak would not have registered at all. This was also a year of consolidation for Wall Street after a near hundred point rise in 1959 to 680. By the middle of March, the Dow had slipped below 600 again, and had great difficulty in holding the line until a year end rally carried it up to 614 as investors began to share in the popular enthusiasm for the charismatic new Kennedy administration.

If equities had an uneventful year, Gilts and Golds had a rotten one. The Government Securities index fell almost six full points from 85.09 to 79.12 in response to a double blow. One was from institutions rejigging their portfolios in anticipation of the changes in the Trustee Act, and the other from the banks which were heavy sellers of gilts to fund a rising level of advances following the ending of the credit squeeze in mid-1958. The effect of all this was to push up the gilts yield to 5.68% from 5.04% at the end of 1959, but thanks to dividend rises the reverse yield gap actually narrowed, with equities yielding 4.82% against 3.74% a year earlier. Golds fared even worse. Reports of the Sharpeville shootings in March, followed by the declaration of a State of Emergency, prompted panic selling of Kaffirs which knocked the index back to 70.2 at its lowest point against a figure of 88.8 at the start of the year.

1961-65

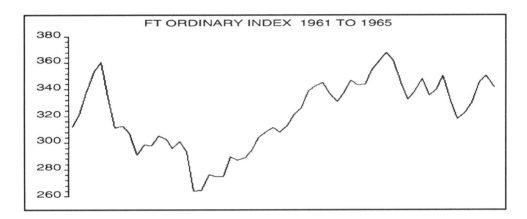

FT ORDINARY INDEX 1961 TO 1965

Bids and mergers dominate

The New Year opened strongly, continuing the recovery from 1960's low point of 293.4 touched in early December. There was a good two-way business in the market with sentiment helped by a rash of bids and mergers featuring many well known names. **Thompson Newspapers** announced in January that it was planning a merger with **Odhams** to form the UK's largest press group, and was then promptly outbid by the **Daily Mirror Group**. January also saw the merger of Charles Clore's property flagship, **City & Central** with Jack Cotton's **City Centre**, and in February they launched a joint bid – ultimately unsuccessful – for the capital's top property company, **City of London Real Property**. And in March, **Ind Coope** merged with **Tetley and Ansells** to form the biggest brewery group in the country. Another bid in March, the significance of which was not widely appreciated at the time, was **GEC**'s agreed offer for **Radio & Allied Industries**, the makers of MacMichael and Sobell radios. The managing director of

Radio & Allied was Arnold Weinstock and he retained this position in relation to the new combined undertaking. Without doubt the bid of the year was that of **ICI** for **Courtaulds**, which at £200 million was the largest ever mounted in the UK. It was a hard fought battle with Courtaulds pulling out all the stops to escape ICI's clutches, and when the offer closed ICI had failed narrowly after receiving acceptances from holders of 38.5% of Courtaulds' stock. There was also a new issue boom, with many of the new flotations

Arnold Weinstock became Managing Director of GEC in 1961 when the ailing company acquired Radio and Allied Industries.

instantly establishing huge premiums thanks to enthusiastic public participation.

A new all-time peak of 365.7 was attained in May, but those early months of the year had witnessed a dangerously large and growing excess of imports over exports, together with a new surge of wage claims in the wake of a sharp fall in unemployment. Mr Selwyn Lloyd, the new Chancellor, was keen to put his stamp on the economy by ensuring that the expansion would not be pursued in such a way as to endanger the position of sterling, the balance of payments or the stability of prices. It was not going to be an easy task. International competition was increasing apace and traditional export markets were no longer the exclusive preserve of UK industry. Neither was the domestic market safe, following the abolition of import controls. Two straws in the wind, with very significant longer-term implications for the UK motor industry, were the fact that Nissan had stopped making the Austin Cambridge under licence and had begun producing its own models both for the Japanese domestic market and for export, and that Renault was beginning to export its Dauphine model to Britain in considerable numbers. Clearly, continuing economic success was going to depend on a very real effort to be competitive in international terms, and in this context there was much discussion of the merits of joining the EEC. General de Gaulle remained opposed to Britain's entry but negotiations continued with the stock market broadly in favour, seeing membership as providing a wider target for UK exports, greater stability for the economy and better management, as well as providing increased US interest and investment in the UK as an operating base within the EEC.

Bank Rate to 7% again

In anticipation of a new round of restrictive measures, the ordinary share index had retreated from its May peak well before the Chancellor unveiled his formidable July package. Bank Rate was hoisted to 7%, indirect taxes were subjected to a 10% surcharge, there were to be cuts in government and local authority spending including a 'pay pause' to put a brake on public sector wages, and restraints on building. Special Deposits were raised to 3%, and worst of all, for market operators, was the announcement of the long feared and long awaited plan to tax capital profits. The initial reaction of equities was a fall to 305, but a strong rally developed in August as the new Trustee Act came into operation.

However, the rally soon petered out and the index relapsed to 285 before recovering to end the year practically unchanged at 304.8 after two half-point falls had reduced Bank Rate to 6%. Gilts did not fare so well and the effect of sales by trustees switching to equities pushed the Government Securities index to 72.01 in the first week of August, its lowest level since the compilation of the index forty years earlier.

Just as in 1960, fairly narrow fluctuations in the index concealed a good deal of switching between sectors as investors became more sophisticated. Capital Goods shares were out of favour as it became clear that increased foreign competition had eroded profit margins, causing large and unsettling swings in profits and dividends. Steel plant suppliers like **Davy United** and **Wellman Smith**, whose share prices had risen more than fourfold between 1955 and 1960 as orders and profits boomed, now began to fall back, as investors turned their attention to companies benefiting from more reliable consumer expenditure and rental income. Low-yielding shares were also greatly sought after on the assumption that they offered superior growth potential, and buyers were rarely disappointed in 1961 by their investments in Stores, Insurances, Merchant Banks, Properties and Electronics.

The year also witnessed the fall from grace of **Harper Engineering & Electronics**, the industrial holding company that had topped the best performing share table in 1959. Just like its successors in 1986/87, it had expanded too fast and neither wisely nor well. In July, the interim dividend was passed and lower profits were forecast for the year just ended, the chairman citing the familiar litany of provisions for losses and overvaluation of stocks and work in progress among its recently acquired subsidiaries, all resulting in a severe strain on the group's financial resources and necessitating an operational and financial reorganisation. Its fellow star performer in 1959, **Arusha Industries**, followed much the same pattern and had declined by some 80% by early 1961. Among new issues, the most notable without doubt was **Racal.** Described by the FT as "one of the most interesting newcomers in recent months despite its short history", the placing of 25% of the shares at 20/3 capitalised the whole group at £1.3 million. Despite caveats about heavy dependency on government orders, the shares topped the most active stocks list on the first day of dealing, establishing a premium of 64% on the issue price.

Trading places

Equities continued to drift for the first six months of 1962 despite three half-point reductions in Bank Rate, taking it down to 4.5% by April, and a broadly neutral budget, apart from the introduction of short-term Capital Gains Tax. To use a phrase of the 'eighties, the economy seemed to be "dead in the water". Earlier assumptions of a rise in consumer spending fuelled by a rise in personal incomes, appeared to be wide of the mark regardless of the Bank Rate cuts, the easing of restrictions on bank lending and the lowering of minimum HP deposits. Industry, too, seemed to

---

FT Actuaries Indices

Introduced in June 1962, the FT Actuaries Indices (so-called because they were devised by the *Financial Times* in cooperation with the Institute of Actuaries), provided a much more representative and thus more accurate picture of what was happening in the UK stock market. The broad indices like the All Share and the 500 Industrials break down into main groups of Capital Goods, Consumer Durables etc., and then into individual sectors, i.e. Electricals, Stores, Properties. It was now possible to look at the performance of a single share in relation to its sector as well as to the market as a whole. The indices are based on an arithmetical mean and weighted for market capitalisation to reflect the growing – or declining – importance of companies and sectors.

---

have pulled in its horns. Stocks were being run down and capital expenditure reduced as company profits fell back and confidence waned.

In May, this mood of depression deepened when Wall Street took fright at what it saw as President Kennedy's anti-business stance after he had forced the US steel industry to withdraw its price rises. The Dow Jones index was already well down from its January peak of 726, but on 29th May a shock 35-point drop to 563.4 panicked London into an 18-point slump to 261.3, its largest one-day fall since Hitler's ultimatum to Czechoslovakia in September 1938. Although the lows in both centres were not touched until the following month (535 and 252.8), the violence of the falls served to clear the air and a base was established for a new primary rise. The advice of Lord Ritchie, Chairman of the Stock Exchange, given at the height of the May panic, that "small investors should put their heads down and let the wind blow over them", was particularly appropriate at the time.

Selwyn Lloyd resigns

Political factors now began to assert themselves. A run of disappointing by-election results had persuaded the Prime

Minister that his Chancellor was not presenting the right "image" to the electorate, and in July Selwyn Lloyd was invited to resign. His successor was Reginald Maudling, at 45 one of the younger members of the Tory hierarchy, described by the *Financial Times* as "a gregarious man, with experience of economic matters, an acquaintance with businessmen and a mind of his own". With retail sales stuck on a plateau, unemployment rising, and an encouraging surge in exports leaving

Chancellor of the Exchequer Selwyn Lloyd was "invited" to resign in July 1962.

room for expansion at home, the new Chancellor might have been expected to provide some new stimulus for the economy. In the event, he stood pat on the measures of his predecessor, influenced by evidence that expansionary forces were already well underway.

At 275 in October, the equity index had staged a modest recovery from its June low, but there was little to encourage further progress. Gilt-edged stocks, on the other hand, were enjoying a revival as anxiety over the prospects for industrial equities, coupled with the reductions in Bank Rate, brought in new buyers. Already well up from the August 1961 low point, the Government Securities index was back to 85 again in October. Both gilts and equities, however, had a surprise in store when the Cuban missile crisis blew up at the end of that month. Although the world teetered on the brink of nuclear war, markets reacted with relative calm. In the wake of the Dow losing 10.5 to 558, the FT 30 dropped 7.8 to 264.4 and just over two points were knocked off Government Securities. The rapid resolution of the crisis prompted an instant rebound and, by the end of December, equities at 281.6 had recorded a loss of just 7.5% while gilts were up by no less than 14%. The revival in equities had been helped in November by a package from the new Chancellor designed to restore business confidence and provide a moderate stimulus for the economy. The measures were targeted at the weak spots in the economy, namely the motor industry and industrial investment generally. They included a reduction in purchase tax on private cars from 45% to 25% (which brought down the price of a new Mini from £509 to £448), more generous investment allowances and a quicker write-off for outlay on heavy capital goods.

Rebirth of Rolls Razor

One event in May 1962 was to occupy the attention of investors and the financial press for the next couple of years. This was the return to the market of **Rolls Razor**, a "shell" company whose shares had been suspended in January 1960 pending details of the reorganisation following "an agreement for the manufacture and distribution of Electromatic washing machines". Approximately 10% of the capital was made available to the

John Bloom (28), Managing Director of Rolls Razor, tried to challenge the domination of the domestic appliance market by the big manufacturers.

public by way of a tender offer at 23/- a share. The issue was only modestly oversubscribed but before long Rolls Razor was regularly featured on the list of active stocks. Its managing director was John Bloom, 28, son of an East End tailor, determined to challenge the domination of the domestic appliance market by the big manufacturers. His chosen method was direct selling using newspaper advertising backed up by a highly motivated sales team. The shares rose rapidly following a production deal with Pressed Steel, and then a £10 million HP financing arrangement with Sir Isaac Wolfson's Drages, but after touching 36/3 in September, they fell back to 27/6 in October when John Bloom was served with a writ for enticement by a husband who had already been charged with the murder of his wife, the subject of the enticement. In November, there was also a spate of adverse rumours about the company, concerning its methods of trading, the quality of its products, and its general solvency. A vigorous denial, authorised by its eminent trading partners, settled any doubts investors may have had and the shares ended the year at 36/9.

De Gaulle says "Non"!

Shares entered the New Year on a high note, continuing the post-Cuban crisis recovery and helped on their way by a cut in Bank Rate to 4% in the first week of January. Thereafter progress was slow, particularly during the first half of the year, when a number of political shocks had to be absorbed. The first came later in January when General de Gaulle, at a press conference, effectively vetoed Britain's entry into the Common Market and ensured the failure of the Brussels talks two weeks later. The market dropped from 292 to just under 280 on the press conference statement, but rallied strongly on the final decision not to enter, relieved that a period of uncertainty had come to an end.

The FT 30 was soon above 300 again and, following an "expansion without inflation" budget giving widespread tax reliefs and encouraging share buyers by halving Stamp Duty to 1%, looked set to continue its advance. Then in June, the Profumo scandal broke, casting doubts over the future of the government and of Mr Macmillan in particular. Despite pressure from many in the Conservative party to hand over the reins, Mr Macmillan stayed on until October when he was replaced by Sir Alec Douglas Hume. The index had just managed to hold above 300 at the height of the Profumo revelations in June and July, and had recovered to the 330/340 range by October in anticipation of a change of leadership putting an end to the whole dreary episode. The week of Sir Alec's appointment duly saw a 5.8 rise to 344.1. By November it was clear that the economy was responding to the expansionary measures of late 1962 and of the budget. The Chancellor had no wish to apply the brakes after such a long period of stagnation, and given that a useful margin of spare capacity remained, his wish appeared justified on more than simply grounds of political expediency.

President Kennedy assassinated

The final shock of the year was the assassination of President Kennedy on 23rd November. The Dow had been falling in the four days ahead of the event – it would be interesting to know if the Warren Commission looked at the short interest opened during that week – and on news of the shooting the Dow fell 20 points to 711.59 before trading was suspended at 2.20 pm. The news broke on a Friday after the London close, leaving a whole weekend for the implications of the event to be absorbed. On Monday the FT 30 opened 6.7 lower but closed only 3.9 down at 334.8 as Wall Street came in with a strong rally, eventually closing up 32.03.

The FT 30 ended December at 348.3 in "very active" trade to record a gain of 23% on the year and one of 37% on the June 1962 low point of 252.8. Gilts had a relatively uneventful year and the Government Securities index ended down 1.4% at 84.78. It seemed that the market had shown itself to be much more resilient to major political upsets and changes than might have been expected, and that the state of the business recovery had been the overriding factor to influence investors. And on these grounds, the prospects in 1964 were encouraging. There was no doubt that the economy was expanding. Car production had reached new peak levels, machine tool orders were picking up, and bank advances were increasing. A high level of pay settlements, however, showed that the Chancellor's efforts to continue his predecessor's plans for an incomes policy were not having much success. This failure, inevitable though it may have been, was to haunt him in the latter part of 1964.

On the corporate side, 1963 was an active year. John Bloom's **Rolls Razor** went from strength to strength in share price terms after announcing a succession of new ventures, including the sale of his own holding to **English & Overseas Investments. Shell** and **BP** made a £290 million bid for **Burmah** and **English Sewing Cotton** tried to buy **Tootal** for £5.6 million. Both bids failed.

Harold Wilson becomes Labour leader

For many market commentators the apparently excellent prospects for 1964 were marred by the likelihood of a change of government. This anxiety had been heightened by the elevation of Harold Wilson to the leadership of the Labour party following the death of Hugh Gaitskell. Others were less worried. Despite his pro-left reputation, they saw Mr Wilson, variously described as "enigmatic", "pragmatic" and "empirical", as perhaps not such a damaging alternative to a Conservative administration that was looking tired after thirteen years in power that had culminated in the Profumo affair and then led to an unseemly leadership tussle. Mr Wilson's plans for a harsher capital gains tax and for the introduction of corporation tax in place of income tax and profits tax had been well aired, and it may have been the prospect of their implementation that kept market activity at a low level throughout the year. Nevertheless, 1964 was not without its moments. Belief that Mr Maudling would be forced to take a more restrictive line early in the year, evidenced by a 1% rise in Bank Rate to 5% and a record January trade gap, depressed the share index to 322 in February, but when it became clear that he was committed to his 4% growth target, shares began to rise again. A rise in imports, it was argued, was inevitable as manufacturers adjusted their stocks to the higher levels of output, and exports would rise in due course. In the meantime, any deficit could be accommodated by drawing on the IMF. The budget was not at all restrictive in any broad sense, save for increased duties on tobacco, beer and spirits, and the FT 30 rose by 6.5 to 352.5 on relief at its unexpected mildness. The advance of the index continued, despite an obviously deteriorating trade balance, and in early October a new record high of 377.8 was reached against a background of public opinion polls indicating a Conservative victory in the election scheduled for the middle of the month.

Labour inherits a bed of nails

Two factors then contributed to a sharp reaction. One was a sudden change in the message from the polls, which now indicated a strong swing to Labour. The other was increasing evidence that the deterioration in the balance of payments was not going to be a temporary affair. It was now clear that exports were actually falling, and that imports had begun to include a large element of finished capital and consumer goods, both manifestations of the deficiencies of production at home. The September trade gap at £111 million was the third largest on record, and in the same week that it was announced Labour won the election, albeit with only a five-seat majority. The index dropped another 5.4 points to 359.4 and then paused to see what the new Chancellor, James Callaghan, would do to combat a trade deficit for the year that looked like approaching £800 million.

His task was not made any easier by an almost imme-diate post-election run on the pound, sending it to a seven-year low against the dollar. Furthermore, foreign confidence was not helped by Chancellor Callaghan's failure to consult with his trading partners before imposing a 15% import surcharge in his first emergency package at the end of October. The autumn budget two weeks later, in which he raised petrol duty by 6d a gallon and gave early warning that income tax would go up by 6d the following April when the new capital gains tax and a 40% rate of corporation tax would become effective, was also seen as unnecessarily anti-capitalist in a crisis situation. The pound continued to slide amid talk of another devaluation and even a shock 2% rise in Bank Rate to 7% failed to stop it. What did turn the tide was the announcement two days later that the Bank of England had arranged with the Bank of International Settlements (BIS) and other central banks a $3 billion support operation for sterling. The situation remained fragile, however, since it was clear that Labour's 4% growth target for 1965 was no longer viable and that priority would have to be given to the defence of the pound and the boosting of exports, aims which must necessarily involve a major check to home consumption and cuts in public spending. The "hundred days" of action promised by Mr Wilson had begun so badly that the inevitable comparisons were being made with Napoleon's road to Waterloo.

Ordinary shares had not taken too kindly to this succes-sion of post-election impositions nor to the sterling crisis, but after dipping below 330 on the rise in Bank Rate, they rallied to 335 by year end on expectations that the worst was over. Gilts were less resilient with Bank Rate at 7% and the Government Securities index showed a loss of 6.7% on the year at 79.07.

Hanson makes his debut

The corporate news in 1964 was a striking mixture of the good, the bad and the positively ugly. In the first category, March saw the launch of **Wiles Group**, a Yorkshire-based fertiliser manufacturer and sack hirer, with the offer for sale of 41% of the equity or 350,000 shares at 11/- each, valuing the whole company at £370,000. Three months later, Wiles made a double bid for Oswald Tillotson, motor engineers, and for Commercial Motors (Hull). On completion of the deal, a director of Tillotson, named J.E. Hanson, joined the board of Wiles Group. Thereafter, the new board began to carry out the aim laid down in the March prospectus "to consider the acquisition of further businesses, to be run in addition to present activities". The shares gained 4/6 on news of the bid to close at 18/-.

Among the flood of new issues in 1963 and 1964 notable newcomers were fresh produce distributor **Albert Fisher**, valued at £350,000; Robert Maxwell's **Pergamon Press**, in a £962,500 offer of 29% of the equity; and two companies whose lives were much shorter and less spectacular namely the 177 times oversubscribed **Headquarters & General Supplies**, and **Vehicle & General Insurance**.

Beginning of the end for Rolls Razor

The corporate scandal of the year was provided by **Rolls Razor**. The shares had peaked at 47/9 in November 1963 but were still 39/6 at the beginning of 1964, boosted by a flurry of new ventures including the acquisition of businesses overseas and the launch of a gift stamp scheme with 12,000 outlets, 35 redemption shops and a fleet of 20 mobile showrooms. Then in March the first clear danger sign appeared when Pressed Steel announced the closure of its Swansea plant and its intention to terminate the production agreement with Rolls Razor because of "overcapacity in the refrigerator market". The shares fell to 33/- on the news. They continued to fall, dropping to 23/6 on the results in May despite a doubled dividend providing an 8.8% yield. Talks with rival Duomatic failed to stem the slide and by the time of the Annual Report in June forecasting "considerably lower" profits in the current year, the shares were down to 14/-. There had also been reference to an improvement in the second half following "vigorous action" and the coming on stream of "new ventures", but by the time of the AGM in the first week of July, the price was down to 10/3. The meeting opened with the announcement of the resignation of five directors, including the Chairman, Mr Reader Harris, MP, and shareholders were told that trading was not very satisfactory and that there would have to be a rights issue to improve liquidity. Despite the well attended meeting, there were no questions.

Two weeks later, while John Bloom was in Bulgaria arranging a travel deal for the tourist arm of English & Overseas, the rest of the board of Rolls Razor petitioned for the company to be voluntarily wound up. There were "wild scenes" on the floor of the Stock Exchange as the price crashed to 1/-. The next few days were taken up with frantic talks to implement a last-minute rescue but no one was prepared to come up with the money and on 31st August, the quotation was cancelled, the final price having been ¾d. The failure of any rescue operation was understandable in the light of the liquidators' report that "in the latter stages of the company's business, documents were not properly kept, minutes not followed up, and a state of complete confusion existed".

Given that the decision to liquidate had been taken just two months after the publication of the annual results, the Stock Exchange almost immediately issued an ordinance requiring quoted companies to announce interim reports to show "early warning" of profits trends.

Chancellor Callaghan gets tough

The year 1965 opened with the announcement that "a strict review" of all government expenditure was to take place. In the first stages, defence spending was the principal casualty, but when duty increases in the April budget and curbs on bank lending and hire purchase in May failed to boost overseas confidence as reflected in sterling, in July the Chancellor brought in a new package of spending cuts. This time, capital projects by government and local authorities were to be cut back and building licences were reintroduced into the private sector. On the plus side, the import surcharge had been reduced to 10% in April, and Bank Rate to 6% in June, but sterling obstinately failed to respond.

The stock market reacted by going to ground, and activity fell by 25% to its lowest level since 1958, but despite the general air of uncertainty the market was buoyed to some extent by consideration of the supposedly much more professional approach that the Labour administration of Harold Wilson was taking to the country's problems. The new Department of Economic Affairs (DEA) under George

George Brown was the first (and last) supremo of the Department of Economic Affairs, created by the Wilson Administration in 1965 with the aim of producing a national economic plan and formulating an incomes policy.

Brown with its National Economic Development Councils (Neddies) and its National Plan, was an attempt to remedy the deficiencies of overall planning that had bedeviled the first post-War Labour government, and although the aim of a 25% growth in output in the period 1964-70 was doomed to failure by the restrictive policies that the Chancellor was forced to pursue, large sections of business responded positively by continuing to invest, to hoard labour and hold down prices. The idea that the DEA would prevent the Treasury from thwarting a Labour government's plans for a new socialist Britain seemed to have quietly faded away. Sentiment was also aided by the government's apparent eschewing of doctrinaire socialism in favour of a more "pragmatic" attitude towards the economy, although the cynical pointed out that with such a tiny majority – it was down to just two in the summer – this was more a matter of necessity than of choice. Certainly there was no chance of steel being renationalised during the life of this Parliament, and mention of it was omitted from the Queen's Speech. Meanwhile on the other side of the political fence, Sir Alec Douglas Hume had resigned the leadership of the Conservative party in July, and was succeeded by Mr Edward Heath after a democratic election.

The ordinary share index ended the year up just 4.7 points at 339.7 after reaching a high of 359.1 in May and a low of 313.8 in July. Gilts were practically unchanged at 78.74.

Cavenham comes to market

Among the more significant corporate events of 1965, although its importance was not realised at the time, was the flotation of **Cavenham Foods**. During the two preceding years, James Goldsmith, then 30, described as "a French businessman", had acquired controlling interests in Procea, the specialist bread manufacturer, Carson's, a maker of chocolate and cocoa products, and Carr & Holland, a confectionery company, all through the medium of Lanord, his

James Goldsmith, after acquiring controlling interests in ailing UK food companies, floated Cavenham Foods in the summer of 1965

private French food company. In the summer of 1965 all these holdings were put into a new group called Cavenham Foods, which now had a turnover of £27.5 million and negligible profits. There were 5 million Cavenham 5/- ordinary shares in issue, but there were another 5.6 million in Deferred shares, all owned by Cavenham Trust controlled by James Goldsmith and his French associate, Baron de Gunsberg. It was announced that a quotation would be sought and in July the ordinary shares were floated at 6/- on the basis of a profits forecast of "not less than" £215,000 in 1964/65 and one of "substantially more" the year after, a level which was judged by the *FT* to be "looking some way ahead for a group with a lot of problems to be put right". On the first day of trading, the shares opened at a small discount.

1966

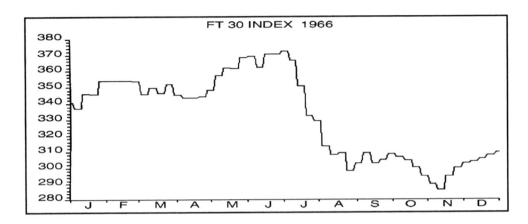

FT 30 INDEX 1966

Labour increases its majority

At the beginning of 1966 the Prime Minister had forecast that it would be a "make or break" year. In the event, it was neither but simply a continuation of 1965 with government policy still dictated by concerns over sterling and the balance of payments. At least the second Wilson administration could feel that it had a freer hand in dealing with the economy. By-election results in January showing a 4% swing to Labour, had prompted Mr Wilson to go for a snap election in March, and as a result a majority of three was increased to one of 97. Steel renationalisation was back on the agenda. The equity market took the event calmly enough. With the polls giving Labour an 11% lead at the end of March, a Labour victory had been well discounted. So too had the likelihood of further consumer restraints in the wake of the February trade figures revealing that imports were continuing to rise, and already down from a mid-February high of 358.6, the FT 30 was practically unmoved at 345 on the election result.

Mr Wilson had asked for a clear mandate from the country to "get on with the job". Having got it, the onus then fell on his two chief economic ministers, James Callaghan at the Treasury and George Brown at the Department of Economic Affairs, to tackle the problems embodied in the disparity between wage rises running at 9%, price increases at 5%, and productivity gains at 1%, a situation dubbed by one commentator, "Fahrenheit 951", representing the temperature at which economies burst into flames! Certainly numbers like this were not conducive to achieving any sort of growth target, and in an attempt to find an answer to the problem by keeping wages in step with production, a voluntary early warning system for the notification of proposed price increases and wage claims was introduced.

The IRC is born

Another of the methods chosen to achieve the country's necessary economic transformation was by the creation of the Industrial Reorganisation Corporation (IRC) with a pool of £150 million of public money to be used to devise and promote mergers aimed at improving the UK's competitive position in world markets. Mergers would provide the size vital to meet the challenge to industry on an international scale and rationalisation would produce the necessary degree of efficiency. The application of the 'white heat' of the technological revolution would do the rest. That such a body was the creation of a Labour government may seem strange today, but to a very large extent the IRC was an agent of government directing the fate of large sections of industry which otherwise would have been left to the interplay of market forces. The ICI bid for Courtaulds and the joint Shell and BP bid for Burmah had caused great consternation in the ranks of the opposition and they made it very clear that in their view, contests involving such key industrial groupings had to be subject to the test of national interest. The creation of the IRC was therefore an inevitable consequence of the next Labour government.

Selective Employment Tax introduced

The budget in April saw the introduction of the controversial Selective Employment Tax (SET), designed to give teeth to the socialist conviction that it is more virtuous to make things than to provide services. This tax on employment in the service industries had an immediate deflationary impact by adding something like a 3 to 4% imposition on services, with the benefit of premium repayments to manufacturers not scheduled to begin until February of the following year. Taken in conjunction with Corporation Tax at 40% and one side of a prices and incomes policy, the implications for company profits and dividends were not favourable, but once again the market was prepared to give the government the benefit of the doubt, and by mid-June the FT 30 had reached 374.2, just three points short of its all-time peak of October 1964. This enthusiastic response turned out to be premature, however, when hopes and expectations of renewed stability for sterling and further progress towards eliminating the balance of payments deficit had to be deferred as a result of a lengthy seamen's strike and the Rhodesia crisis. Chancellor Callaghan saw no alternative but to introduce a new deflationary package in July. First of all he raised Bank Rate to the familiar crisis level of 7% and a week later brought in a twofold series of measures to reduce the balance of payments deficit, one by direct action on government expenditure abroad, and the other by indirect action aimed at deflating home demand. The latter was especially onerous and included measures tightening hire purchase terms and building controls, the postponement of many public expenditure projects, further restrictions on bank lending, a 10% increase on all direct taxes, a 10% surcharge on surtax payers, and a six-month standstill on all wages, salaries, prices and dividends. Already weakening ahead of the Chancellor's moves, by mid-August, the index had fallen 20% from its June peak.

The market slumps

September saw a brief rally to just above the 300 level, but it failed to hold and by early November the index was back to 284.2, closing the yield gap and touching its lowest point since 1962. To a great extent the market slump was a reflection of a serious loss of business confidence. The deflationary impact of the Chancellor's measures on home demand had been very great, resulting in a four-point fall in the industrial production index for October. This was the largest decline in a single month since that of January 1963 when snow and ice had brought the construction industry to a virtual standstill.

However, by the end of the year, hopes were rising that the balance of payments would now begin to improve. It was also perceived that if the cost of this improvement had been a long period of stagnation and a relatively high level of unemployment, then the pressure on the government – especially a Labour government – to reflate demand was bound to grow. There had already been some mild reflationary moves in the autumn in the form of a temporary increase in investment grants, and an easing of the credit squeeze on house-builders. Confidence had also been boosted by a series of currency swap agreements with the US and other central banks coupled with the Chancellor's vigorous assertion that another devaluation was neither necessary nor desirable. Buyers began to reappear and by the end of December, the FT 30 had recovered by 9% from the November low to 310.3, but still showed a loss on the year as a whole of 8.6%. Gilts were practically unchanged, despite a 7% Bank Rate, at 78.20 against 78.74 at the beginning of January. It is also worth noting that Wall Street failed to set a bullish example in 1966. The Dow had begun the year by hitting a new record high of 970.82, but with fears of a recession becoming a reality during the subsequent months, it was down below 800 again by the end of December.

Australian nickel boom gets underway

Almost unnoticed behind the meanderings of the London equity market in 1966, were the first stirrings of one of the most remarkable speculative booms of all time. This was the Australian Nickel Boom in which fortunes were made and lost, and mostly the latter as far as the small speculator was concerned. The first hint of excitement came with an announcement in early April of a strike by **Western Mining** at Kambalda to the south of Kalgoorlie, the principal mining town in Western Australia, revealing a "high grade nickel sulphide orebody". The shares of Western Mining rose 2/9 to 26/9, a new high, on the news, and tiny **Hampton Gold Mining Areas**, with land adjoining the location of the find, doubled to 6d. At this stage there was no popular appreciation of the significance of the discovery and it remained the province of the mining columns. Nevertheless, Western Mining ended the year at 55/3, while Hampton Gold soared to 4/- for a 1500% gain on the year. There was more excitement to come in 1967.

1967

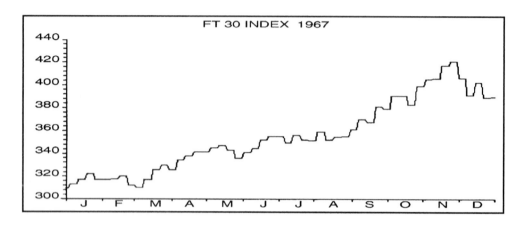

FT 30 INDEX 1967

Another Arab-Israeli War

Speculation about an imminent cut in Bank Rate provided equities and gilts with a firm start to 1967, and sentiment was helped by a sixty-point gain in the Dow Jones to 850 during January. The expected cut to 6.5% duly came, but the index marked time in the 300/320 range until mid-March when it suddenly came to life on news of three by-election results showing a strong swing to the Conservatives. The breakout was encouraged by a further reduction in Bank Rate to 6% and by early April the index had moved above 330. The budget was broadly neutral given that the economic recovery was expected to gain momentum as the year progressed, and also because the delicate state of the balance of payments appeared to rule out any early expansionist moves. Nevertheless Bank Rate was taken down another half point to 5.5% at the beginning of May. Equities also drew some encouragement from the government's formal application to join the EEC, and investment interest began to focus on those companies likely to benefit from access to a wider market.

The outbreak of the Arab-Israeli War and the closure of the Suez Canal in early June led to a 7.5 point fall in the FT 30 to 332.1 on fears that a potential oil shortage could adversely affect the trade balance and restrict even further the Chancellor's room for manoeuvre. In the event the early resolution of the conflict, coupled with a mild reflationary move in the shape of a relaxation of the severe hire purchase controls introduced in the previous July, prompted a rapid rebound and by the end of the month the index stood at a new peak for the year of 356.8, thereby demonstrating at least some confidence in the achievement in due course of the Chancellor's projected 3% growth rate.

July provided a very clear illustration of the government's dilemma. The unemployment figures had topped half a million in June to reach the highest monthly total for twenty-seven years, the trade gap for that month had deteriorated sharply, and profits and dividends were at their lowest point for twenty years. Yet while any new expansionary measures looked bound to lead to another sterling crisis, Mr Callaghan denied categorically that he had any intention of resorting to devaluation. Later in the month, the government managed to defeat a 'no confidence' motion, and subsequently announced plans to more than halve the rate of growth of state spending to 3% over the next three years. The Chancellor's policies were not popular with the trade unions or with his own back benchers, and it seemed politically inevitable that further reflationary measures had to be undertaken almost regardless of the risk. In a "hands on" gesture designed to bolster confidence, the Prime Minister took over at the Department of Economic Affairs, sharing responsibility with the Chancellor for the conduct of the economy, and at the end of August hire purchase controls were further relaxed with special concessions to the hard-pressed motor industry for the second time that year. The FT 30 responded by adding 4.6 on the news to 361.2.

New peak for the FT 30

The sharp contrast between the buoyancy of the stock market and the parlous state of the economy was not lost on the editorial writers. In mid-September the index rose above 380 to surpass its June 1966 peak of 374.2 and its all-time high of 377.8 achieved in October 1964. In the same month, the country's gold and dollar reserves fell to their lowest level for two years, the Bank of England warned of a setback in world trade delaying the UK's return to an external surplus, and company profits and dividends were still trending downwards. The explanation for this apparent contradiction was that long-term institutional buyers were convinced that the worst of the recession had been seen and were prepared to wait for a recovery in profits and dividends in the wake of the inevitable reflationary measures. Furthermore, while the personal sector was still a net seller of equities, rising savings meant that more funds were going into pensions, life policies and unit trusts and thus back into the market. There was also a stock shortage factor at work in that the advent of corporation tax had tended to dry up the supply of new shares, capital gains tax had inhibited selling to some extent, and continuing merger activity was taking equity out of the market. And in the wings was the prospect of steel renationalisation creating substantial reinvestment demand just as it had under the first Labour administration's programme for public ownership.

Countdown to devaluation

The autumn of 1967 was marked by a further widening of the trade gap, growing industrial unrest, persistent weakness of sterling – and new highs for ordinary shares. Even the lifting of Bank Rate to 6% in response to rising US interest rates failed to hinder the advance and in the last week of October the FT 30 crossed the 400 barrier for the first time in its thirty-two year history.

By early November, the pound had fallen to its lowest level against the dollar since the late 'fifties, and even though well-publicised discussions were being carried on with the Bank of International Settlements over refinancing credits to bolster sterling, talk of another devaluation intensified. A further rise in Bank Rate on 11th November to 6.5% came just days ahead of the announcement of the October trade deficit, which at £107 million was the worst on record. Then on 20th November, the pound was devalued by 14.3% to $2.40. The act was accompanied by a Letter of Intent to the International Monetary Fund (IMF) under-taking that home demand would be reduced by £750/800 million almost immediately, but the aim, said Chancellor Callaghan, was not to deflate total demand and create more unemployment, but to curb consumption and investment at home in order to make room for additional exports that devaluation should make it possible to sell. To this end Bank Rate was hoisted to the record level of 8%, bank advances were to be strictly limited, hire

James Callaghan resigned as Chancellor of the Exchequer after devaluing in November 1967.

purchase deposits on cars were raised and repayment periods shortened. In addition, 2.5% was added to corpora-tion tax, SET premium payments were withdrawn together with export rebates and dividends were to be subject to a "strict watch". Ten days later James Callaghan resigned on the grounds that having broken so many pledges about not devaluing, he could no longer continue as Chancellor of the Exchequer. He was succeeded by Roy Jenkins.

The market's reaction to the devaluation package was one of extreme volatility. The index touched a new peak of 420.7 on the eve of the event, lost 5.2 on the day of the announcement, another 11.9 the following day, and promptly rebounded to 420.6 over the next two days. It then lost 17.5 in a single session on fears that severe restraint in the home market would be necessary to enable the shift of resources into export production to take place, and that a tough budget had to be in prospect for 1968. This view was apparently confirmed by the November trade deficit, which at £153 million was the highest monthly figure ever, and the FT 30 closed the year at 389.2, down 7.5% from its November peak but up 20.2% on the year. The Government Securities index lost 2% to 76.56, depressed by an 8% Bank Rate, but gold shares once again benefited from devaluation and revaluation hopes, their index gaining 26% to 65.6. Given all the excitement in November, General de Gaulle's further veto on Britain's entry into the EEC, already well signposted, passed almost unnoticed.

Nickels continue to shine

1967 was an eventful year for Australian nickels, which continued their apparently inexorable rise with **Western Mining** topping the £10 mark while **Hampton Gold** did even better, moving above 60/- against a starting price for the year of just 4/-. **Great Boulder** now joined in the fun and became the year's best performing share with an advance of 1370%. It is interesting to note that none of these companies had actually produced any nickel as yet, and more cautious investors had started to buy the larger diversified groups like **RTZ** and **BHP**.

Slater Walker wins a following

The soon to be famous **Slater Walker** now began to make its mark. The company had begun life in 1963 as a partnership between Jim Slater, a 35-year-old accountant and protégé of Lord Stokes at Leyland Motors, and rising young Conservative politician Peter Walker. In mid-1964 they took control of a tiny quoted "shell" company called H. Lotery and began to make some minor acquisitions.

Greengate & Irwell Rubber, bought in January 1967 for £2.3 million, became their most important acquisition to date. It was a typical Slater deal, adding 46% to profits and only 29% to equity. Four more acquisitions during the course of the year led to the forecast profits for 1966/67 of "not less than £750,000" being revised to an indicated £1.3 million for a P/E of 18 at 27/6. (The practice of expressing share prices as a multiple of earnings had been long established in America, but did not come to the UK until March 1966 with the introduction of a flat rate Corporation Tax in place of income tax and profits tax.) The share price had practically doubled and Jim Slater was attracting growing support from both private and institutional investors. Meanwhile, James Hanson had become chairman of Wiles Group, and Gordon White vice chairman, and in February they made their first major bid, acquiring Scottish Land Development for £655,000, a deal which enabled them to forecast profits of "at least" £550,000 for 1966/67 after just £200,000 had been realised in the first half. James Hanson was also building up a following and Wiles Group featured among the year's top performers with a gain of 152%.

Among new issues during the year, perhaps the most interesting was **Ladbroke** which, in September, made an offer for sale of 1.35 million shares, 35% of its equity capital, at 10/- a share. The issue attracted applications for no less than 120 million shares, and opened at a premium of 2/6.

GEC buys AEI

There was no doubt that the bid of the year was by **GEC** for **AEI** (Associated Electrical Industries). The initial offer was worth £120 million, but after a spirited defence by AEI this was raised to £151 million and in November AEI conceded when GEC's acceptances topped 50%. At the time, this was the largest successful contested bid on record, and marked the crowning achievement in the career to date of Arnold Weinstock. The IRC was active in promoting the bid, much to the annoyance of the board of AEI.

1968

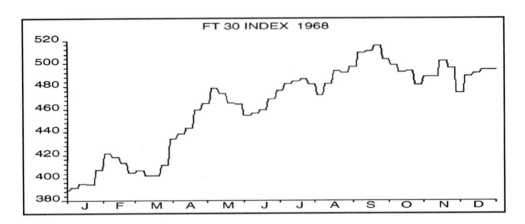

FT 30 INDEX 1968

A year of bids and mergers

There were two key questions at the start of 1968. One
was about where the promised cuts in public expenditure
would fall and to what extent they would need to be reinforced by further restrictions on consumer demand. The
other was whether the government would be able to
combat the inflationary effects of devaluation by means of
an incomes policy which relied solely upon voluntary
restraint. Both questions presented the new Chancellor
with a major political problem which went to the root of
Labour's philosophy in that he was forced to acknowledge
the practical impossibility, when actually in office, of
reconciling a policy of full employment and expansion with
a payments surplus. His position was further aggravated
by the fact that the reflationary measures of the previous
August had sparked a retail sales boom that had led to
increasing pressure on wages and prices, and that any
countermoves would have to be made against a background of high and rising unemployment.

Equities began the year hesitantly under the influence of US measures to reduce their own balance of payments deficit, which were calculated to affect the UK balance of payments to the tune of about £100 million in a full year. Even evidence from industry of sharply higher export orders since devaluation and a December trade gap halving that of November, failed to enthuse the market, and it was not until the public spending cuts were announced in mid-January that the FT 30 came to life and crossed the 400 level again. That it did so in one bound of nearly 20 points owed a great deal to the absence of any simultaneous action against consumer spending, but sentiment was also greatly helped by a rash of major bids in January, more indeed than in any month since 1945. **RTZ** bid £55 million for **Borax**, **Schweppes** £44 million for **Typhoo**, **BMC** and **Leyland**, with the blessing of the IRC, had agreed to merge to create Britain's fifth largest company with a market capitalilisation of £400 million, and **Westminster Bank** announced that it was linking with **National Provincial Bank**, to produce the largest ever bank-merger in the UK.

The last day of the month saw **Thorn** make a £155 million bid for **Radio Rentals**, and the index surpassed its post-devaluation peak to reach a new record high of 422.9 with heavy private and institutional buying – the unit trusts in particular were very active – further encouraged by a continuation of the upward trend in profits that had emerged during the final quarter of 1967.

George Brown resigns

Despite another sharp reduction in the trade deficit for January and more mammoth mergers, including a proposed £530 million alliance between Barclays, Lloyds and Martins to create the fourth largest bank in the world (instantly referred to the Monopolies Commission), equities were nervous ahead of the budget and reacted to 400 by the end of February. They were further unsettled in March by a doubling of the trade deficit to £70 million, a runaway gold price leading to the establishment of the two-tier market, and the resignation of George Brown from his posts of Foreign Secretary and Deputy Prime Minister because "of the way the government is run and the way we reach our decisions". In the event the budget took £550 million off demand, mainly by raising indirect taxation, and imposed a 3.5% limit on wages, salaries and dividends. It was widely regarded as tough but fair and was described in an *FT* editorial as "a budget admirably suited to the present situation and one which the sternest observers will find it hard to criticise". The index responded by rising nearly forty points or 10% in the week following the budget to top 440 by the end of March helped by a half-point cut in Bank Rate to 7.5%.

The rise continued with the FT 30 eventually crossing the 500 mark for the first time in the last week of August, a month which had seen another sharp increase in the trade gap, the Russian invasion of Czechoslovakia and more dire warnings from the National Institute for Economic and Social Research (NIESR) about the state of the economy. It was clear that devaluation had made more and more investors conscious of the advantages of equity investment and that they now regarded them as an each-way bet. If government policy succeeded, they were bound to rise, and if it failed and another devaluation was seen to be on the cards, then equities would win again. As a result, after a day or so bad news was brushed aside and the scramble for stock continued unabated. Obviously investors were not impressed by Mr Wilson's argument that "the pound in their pocket" would be unaffected by devaluation. There were more rumours of bids than actual bids – although there were plenty of them – and new issues were hugely oversubscribed. A notable feature was the offer for sale of 720,000 shares in **H. Cox & Sons Plant Hire** at 8/9, which attracted applications for no less than 102 million shares to the value of £44.5 million.

FT 30 reaches another new peak

At the same time there was one fundamental prop for equities in the dramatic improvement in company profits since devaluation. Much of this rise was attributable to productivity gains, but to the extent that they stemmed from post-merger rationalisation and the ensuing redundancies – the GEC/AEI merger almost immediately led to

5000 job losses following the cessation of telecommunications equipment production at Woolwich – they proved a major source of embarrassment to a Labour government supposedly dedicated to a policy of full employment. As a result the Wilson administration found itself attacked as much, if not more, by its own side than by the opposition, a situation which induced a degree of paranoia in government circles. The "Wilson must go" campaign waged by the *Daily Mirror* had led to the sacking of the editor, Cecil King, and not that of Mr Wilson, but the pressure remained unrelenting. In July, John Gunter, the Minister of Power, had resigned on the stated grounds that he "no longer desired to be a member of a government led by Mr Wilson". This obvious political instability, coupled with an apparent lack of progress towards achieving a balance of payments surplus, did not help the pound during a period of world-wide currency disturbances, and in September, Mr Jenkins obtained a $2 billion stand-by credit facility from the BIS to help quash devaluation fears arising out of the pound's role as a reserve currency. This did not stop Mr Wilson from fulminating against the "gnomes at home" as well as the "gnomes of Zurich" for conducting a campaign to undermine sterling, and Labour left-winger, Eric Heffer, demanded that the former should be arrested. Encouraged by this evidence of international support and by sharply improved August trade figures, the Chancellor cut Bank Rate by 0.5% to 7% on 20th September. The index promptly added 6.6 to 521.9, a new peak which was to remain a record until 1972. Within a week, the FT 30 fell below 500 again in anticipation of a further round of HP and consumer credit controls in the wake of indications of a continuing boom in consumer spending to a degree which could jeopardise the balance of payments objective.

A touch of the brakes

The first of these restrictions duly came in early November, and principally involved an increase in the minimum deposit for car purchase and a shortening of the repayment period. Mr Jenkins was quick to point out that his actions should not be regarded as a sign that anything had gone wrong, but simply as a move to ensure that an incipient boom was channelled towards exports and industrial investment rather than towards domestic consumption. The index staged a recovery to over 500 again, but relapsed into the 480/490 range when a new set of deflationary measures was introduced at the end of the month. Purchase tax was upped by 10%, bank lending to the private sector was further restricted, and an import deposit scheme was introduced. The object was to cut home demand by 0.5% and private consumption by 1%, but by adding 1.5% to the cost of living an additional strain was imposed on the incomes policy at great political cost to the government.

In the autumn, **GEC** announced that it had agreed merger terms with **English Electric**, having pushed **Plessey** off the scene, again with the help of the IRC. There was another flurry of bids in December. **Consolidated Goldfields** won **Amalgamated Roadstone** with a £37 million bid, **Ranks Hovis** bought **Cerebos**, **City Centre** accepted a £65 million offer from **Land Securities**, **Beechams** bid £14 million for **Horlicks** and **Unilever** proposed a merger with **Allied Breweries**. All this frantic bid activity, coupled with the reporting of a November trade deficit of only £17 million, helped industrials to end the year at 506.4 for a gain of 30%. Wall Street was no hindrance either. It had begun the year badly, influenced by the intensification of the war in Vietnam following the Tet offensive, but perked up decisively on the announcement that President Johnson would not run for a second term. Subsequent peace moves and then the Nixon victory in November saw the Dow by 31st December at 943.7, up over a hundred points on the year. Gilts, on the other hand, were down 6% at 71.75, a new low, affected by continuing currency uncertainties, high interest rates, and a growing disillusionment among investors about the investment merits of fixed interest stocks in an inflationary environment that was obviously here to stay. Golds continued to move ahead as the bullion price topped $40 and the index closed the year at 79.3, up 21%.

Hanson begins to expand

1968 was an important foundation building year for James Hanson and the **Wiles Group**. A modest rights issue in

January raised £705,000 net "to finance continuing growth in existing activities and to provide cash for future acquisitions". Part of the sum was also earmarked "to reduce bank indebtedness", a policy demonstrating an early aversion to high gearing. At the same time, a profits forecast for 1967/68 was made of £675,000 along with the promise of a raised dividend to leave the shares at 28/- yielding 4% and with a P/E of 15. In April, a successful £2.9 million bid was made for **West of England Sack**, a deal which added 18.5% to equity and no less than 50% to earnings. By this time the shares had advanced to 34/- and of the 4 million in issue Hanson had a direct holding of 1.6 million and a similar number in Hanson Trust, which he also controlled. The immense benefits of the West of England Sack deal soon became apparent and in September profits for 1968/69 were widely estimated to top £1.2 million. Wiles' share price was now over 50/-, and on a prospective P/E of 27.5, the market was clearly expecting more acquisitions. **Butterley Brick** was the next target at £3.7 million in cash and loan stock.

Hanson and Slater join forces

Now came the much lauded link with **Slater Walker** via a share exchange deal which resulted in Slater Walker taking a 14.4% stake in Wiles. At the time Slater Walker had a market capitalisation of £120 million compared with one of just £20 million for Wiles, and the rationale of the link was that the latter would undertake acquisitions which, though attractive, were too small for the larger group. James Hanson and Jim Slater had become acquainted when Slater was a director of AEC, the commercial vehicle maker for which Tillotson, the original Hanson transport company, had been a distributor. In an interview for the Men and Matters column of the *Financial Times*, James Hanson recalled that in those early years, Slater was telling him what companies he ought to be buying when at the time Hanson wanted simply to consolidate. "We were slow starters," he added.

Slater Walker goes from strength to strength

Meanwhile **Slater Walker** was also having an active year. April saw the hugely successful launch of its first unit trust, **Invan**, as well as its biggest bid yet in the form of an £18 million offer for the UK's leading window maker, **Crittall Hope**. On the assumption that profits from Invan and earlier acquisitions would take Slater Walker's pretax total for 1968 up from £1.16 million to nearer £2 million, Crittall Hope was estimated to add 37% to equity and an immediate 40% to earnings with the further benefit of a high asset value and a low return on capital providing scope for a quick turnaround. By early August the forecast profits cum Crittall Hope were raised to £3 million for a P/E of 41 on a share price which had now reached 73/-. A week later, when the purchase of a small Bahamian bank was announced, the forecast was raised yet again to £3.25 million. Then in September an agreed £33 million bid was made for **Drages**, part of Sir Isaac Wolfson's empire, which with its large hire purchase interests and its Ralli Bros. merchant banking subsidiary, brought Slater Walker closer to achieving what was widely perceived to be its ultimate goal of becoming a major force in the investment banking world.

Devaluation favourites

Among the likely gainers from devaluation to find favour with investors in 1968 was **Racal**. By the end of the year, the shares had risen to 146/- for a prospective P/E of 33.5 on forecast profits of £950,000 pre-tax for 1968/69 against £855,000, and analysts took the view that with R & D expenditure almost on a par with this figure, then it would produce more profits post-devaluation than it had before.

Another was **Lesney Products**, the maker of die-cast toys, about 70% of which were exported. So popular were the toys that despite annual increases in capacity, overseas buyers were actually "rationed". The company had enjoyed an apparently unassailable competitive position throughout the 'sixties, and investors who had been lucky in the offer for sale when the company came to the market at 20/- in 1960, had seen a £100 investment grow to something like

£10,000 in the wake of an original prospectus forecast of pretax profits of £300,000 turning into an actual figure of £3.64 million in 1967/68.

Pass the parcel

The year's big disappointment, especially for the small investor, was the demise of **Headquarters and General Supplies**, a speciality stores and mail order group. It was launched in July 1963 with an offer for sale of 600,000 2/- shares (out of 1,650,000) at 9/3, and was oversubscribed a record 177 times. On the first day of trading it opened at 15/9 and eventually touched a peak of 37/- in 1964 on expectations that the prospectus profits forecast of £160,000 would be exceeded by at least £100,000, and that a raised interim dividend indicated a 40% payment for the year against the original 27.5% forecast. Chairman and owner of 57% of the shares, Major Collins, enthused shareholders at the company's first AGM by saying, "I can see nothing but going forward. The sky is the limit." – a view which seemed to be confirmed by the report of a rapid sell-out of a stock of 25,000 Beatle wigs! The actual profit figure for the first year turned out to be £273,000 but it marked both the peak for profits and for the share price. After a mediocre performance over the next three years, in July 1967 Major Collins resigned from all his positions on the board of Headquarters and General and sold the bulk of his shares at around the then current price of 10/9 to the new Chairman, Jack Harrison. In March 1968 he sold the rest at 8/-, at a time when the new management had just forecast a profit of around £90,000 for the year to 31st March 1968 after a first half profit of £43,000. Then in July the company announced that "a substantial loss" was now in prospect for the year just ended instead of a profit of £90,000, and the following month the company was declared insolvent after the auditors had restated the first half profit figure as a loss of £125,000. Fortunately, Jack Harrison had managed to pass on his holding to Ionian Bank at 8/- a share, and hopes that the bank would stage a rescue kept the shares at around the 2/6 mark for a time. In late September, however, they were declared valueless and subsequently the quotation was cancelled.

Cyril Lord's empire collapses

One of the best known names in retailing in the 'sixties was Cyril Lord, who tried to do for household textiles what John Bloom had done for washing machines. He lasted longer but still failed for much the same reason. Vertical integration combining the role of manufacturer and retailer in a wide range of products left him with the necessity of maintaining a consistently high throughput in order to be profitable. Despite heavy and costly TV advertising, his range of products proved too wide to be economic and there was too much competition both from manufacturers and from specialist retailers. Launched at 10/- in 1964, the shares peaked at 18/6 two years later, and collapsed in a wave of rumours in November 1968 after reporting a £766,000 loss and exceeding bankers' limits. When a bailout by Courtaulds at 1/- a share had to be abandoned, a receiver was appointed.

Australians boil over

Australian mining stocks peaked in early 1968 but though down, they were by no means out and as some of the early favourites faded, there were plenty of newcomers to take their places. Dealing was often frenzied and the case of **Metals Exploration** in January was not at all unique. Reuters had mistakenly added a nought on to the estimated tonnage of nickel ore at the company's Greenvale site, and as a result the share price rocketed from 37/- to 85/- only to relapse to its starting point when the mistake was corrected!

Western Mining also helped to restore some sanity to the market by coming out with a large rights issue and at the same time detailing its production plans. Analysts now had some facts and figures to work with and once the shares could be judged on solid investment merits, they lost much of their speculative "blue sky" appeal, practically halving by the end of the year. **Hampton Gold** followed a similar pattern, closing the year at 40/9 against an all-time high of 130/- in March. A new name began to appear in the mining columns in May. It was that of a tiny Adelaide-based company called **Poseidon**, reporting that nickel values had been found at its Bindi Bindi prospect, 100 miles north of Perth. In order to raise additional exploration funds it had placed A$157,000 of shares at A$1.30 with a London institution. Less than two years later, it was to be called the "share of the century".

1969

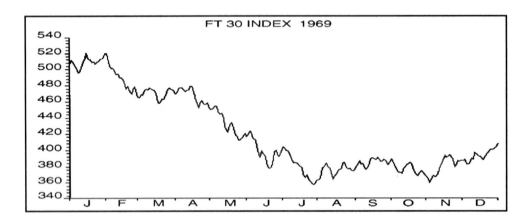

FT 30 INDEX 1969

The bear market begins

Equities began the New Year in fine form, managing on two occasions in January to get within a couple of points of the September 1968 high of 521.9 on turnover topping the £1 billion mark for the first time ever. Sentiment was helped by a sharply improving trend in the balance of payments in the final quarter, a continuing merger boom and evidence that the strong rise in industrial investment and consumption in 1968 was paying off in terms of productivity gains and corporate profitability. Contrary to earlier expectations, a high rate of growth had been achieved at the same time as an improvement in the balance of payments.

None of this meant that the rest of the year was going to be plain sailing for the equity market. For one thing, at 520 the FT 30 was selling on a P/E of 22 and yielding 3.5% with a reverse yield gap at a new record level of 4.78%, which meant that a great deal had already been well discounted. For another, the Chancellor had no intention of throwing away the advantage he had gained, and was determined that the economy should not grow faster in the months ahead than was compatible with his planned balance of payments surplus. Now, faced with evidence that a scramble for labour was developing and that a shortage was the factor most likely to limit further growth in output, in early February he began to intensify the domestic squeeze instituted the previous November. The banks were reminded that their lending restriction requirement was behind target and that they had to trim another £150 million by the end of March, and then to underline the message, at the end of the month Bank Rate was raised from 7% to 8%.

The FT 30 had topped out at 519.2 on the last day of January and was practically in freefall throughout February, declining another 7.7 points to 465.7 when the Bank Rate increase was announced. Gilts suffered too, dropping to a new all-time low of 69.38 on the Bank Rate decision. The declines continued ahead of the budget, with sentiment adversely affected by signs of a worldwide trend towards higher interest rates and more restrictive credit policies, and also by a sharply higher February trade deficit. The gloom was alleviated briefly by a 16% swing to the Conservatives at the Walthamstow by-election, which sparked a 20-point rally, but the budget in mid-April knocked that very firmly on the head. A combination of measures which included a rise in Corporation Tax from 42.5% to 45%, a 28% boost to SET, the disallowing of interest on bank borrowing as a set-off against income, and the exemption of gilts from long-term capital gains tax, at a stroke hit company earnings, reduced the buying power of the private client, and altered the balance of attraction between gilts and equities. From 479.6 on the eve of the budget, the index was down to 452.3 within a week, and gilts also fell to yet another new low of 68.47.

IMF to the rescue

The decline gathered pace as the background continued to deteriorate. There was considerable turmoil in the currency markets with the French Franc in the front line following the departure of de Gaulle, ultimately leading to a 12.5%

devaluation in August. There was also much speculation on the prospects of a revaluation of the DMark, which duly occurred in October. Inevitably the pound came under severe pressure after the first event, with foreign sentiment not helped by the strident opposition both from the trade unions and from within the Labour party, the Cabinet included, to Barbara Castle's proposed industrial relations legislation, "In Place of Strife". An International Monetary Fund (IMF) report actually referred to "a tinge of anarchy" in Britain's industrial relations but if it did not stop them providing a $1 billion standby credit facility in May, it caused them to impose strict conditions in the accompanying Letter of Intent. The two principal conditions were for a target to be set for a £300 million balance of payments surplus by the following March, and for a £400 million ceiling on domestic credit expansion in 1969/70, or one third of that which had taken place in 1968/69. The fact that the latter provision was aimed mainly at the public sector created more political unrest within the Labour party.

The squeeze stays on

With no prospect of a let-up in the credit squeeze, given the terms of the Letter of Intent and fears that it would soon begin to affect the corporate sector and its investment intentions, by mid-June the FT 30 had slipped below 400 and gilts too were at a new low. America was showing a parallel decline. The squeeze there and fears of a recession had pulled the Dow back from a high of 963 in early May to 806 at the end of July, by which time the FT 30 had reached 357.4. These dismal performances prompted a number of commentators to speculate that the post-War period of adjustment of equities to inflation had come to an end, and some to suggest that the cult of the equity was dead. Even the optimists who argued that in percentage terms the market had now matched the declines recorded by earlier bear markets, had to admit that there was nothing very attractive or at all comparable with previous lows about a dividend yield of under 5% and an earnings yield of less than 6.5%, especially in the context of a much higher interest rate structure.

In the autumn, there were occasional rallies towards the 400 level with buyers encouraged by clear signs of improvement in the trade figures but just as in America, they faded on even clearer signs that there was going to be no softening of the government's hard line on inflation. However, even though the Dow had fallen below 800 in early December, the London market managed to stage a year end rally which carried it just above 400, largely on the suspicion that the Chancellor was unlikely to intensify the squeeze in the run-up to an election. The announcement of the proposed ending of dividend restraint was also a help. On the last day of the year, the FT 30 stood at 407.4, down 22% from the September 1968 high, and the Government Securities index at 69.04 was down 3.8% on the year but well up on the all-time low of 64.28 touched in June when the US prime rate had risen to a record 8.5% and there were fears of another rise in Bank Rate. The Dow was 800.36, having begun the year at 943.75.

Hanson and Slater pull in their horns

Neither **Wiles** nor **Slater Walker** got through the year with their share prices and ratings unscathed. James Hanson bought **Provincial Traction** for £1.5 million in January but pulled out of a £3.6 million agreed bid for **Ibstock Brick** the following month over difficulties in agreeing sales and profit forecasts. Thereafter he did nothing save for making a few minor disposals and profits for 1968/69 came out at £1.96 million, leaving the shares at 18/3 in December, down from a high of 42/-, on a P/E of 13.5. By contrast Jim Slater was much more active on the takeover front, adding **Forestal Land** and boosting his stake in **Ralli Bros**. to 75%, acquisitions which raised his 1968/69 profits forecast from £4 million to £8.9 million. At the same time he acknowledged the fact of the bear market by making a number of strategic disposals. His African interests were sold to **Lonrho** for £3.9 million, albeit in Lonrho shares, and satellites **Barclay & Sons** and **Ralli International** were floated off. His share price ended the year at 47/- for a P/E of 8.6.

Goldsmith begins to make his mark

1969 was the year when Goldsmith's master plan for **Cavenham Foods** began to pay off. In September he announced that the reorganisation begun in 1965 had been completed and that he was now looking to expand both by internal growth and by acquisition, adding that the prospectus £650,000 forecast would be exceeded. By December he was able to announce that interim pretax profits were £458,000 against £161,000 and that on turnover up by 12%, trading profits had risen by 64%. The shares were now 8/9 and standing on a P/E of 21.5 on the basis of the original forecast, a rating judged by the *FT* to "leave scope for optimism".

Two "fringe banks" make their debut

Two new issues that were enthusiastically received even in the middle of a bear market were City banking newcomers, **London and County Bank**, run by Gerald Kaplan, and **Dalton Barton**, run by Jack Dellal. Both had a five-year record of strongly rising profits with forecasts of doubled profits for 1969/70, and were hailed as filling a gap in the banking system by providing a more personal service for the smaller commercial customer. London and County came to the market by way of an introduction at 20/- and promptly attracted buyers at over 30/-, while Dalton Barton's offer for sale at 42/- saw a 13/- premium in the first dealings.

Meanwhile, in a similar line of business, Pat Matthew's **First National Finance Corporation** (FNFC) was attracting favourable investment comment as "one of the most dynamic shares in the market over the past five years with Tesco-style growth but without a Tesco-style rating". The company's lack of influential City connections was widely seen as the reason for the failure of its surprise bid for Bowmaker earlier in the year, but now with Hambros, the Crown Agents and Flemings as major shareholders, FNFC was regarded as having achieved respectability in the City. Its latest acquisition, Financings, a financial services company which specialised in guaranteeing second mortgages, was hailed as another clever financial operation of the kind it had exploited so profitably in the past. It was reckoned to complement neatly one of FNFC's other main businesses, which was the purchase and break-up of blocks of flats by sales to tenants. This activity was judged by one commentator to provide FNFC with "a very important element of flexibility" in that although it was vulnerable to sharp changes in the credit background, it could smooth out the bumps by phasing in its sales of flats! At 36/-, the shares were on a P/E of 17.

Lesney goes ex-growth

Even though Lesney beat its 1968/69 profits forecast of £5.5 million, it did so by only a narrow margin, which contrasted sharply with the previous year's £3.78 million against a £3 million forecast. The shares tumbled on the implication of a slowdown in growth, and six months later, in October, the market's worst fears were confirmed by lower first half profits. Inevitably, the company had not been able to maintain its monopoly position in the lucrative die-cast model market and Mattel was now providing stiff competition. Down from a high of 94/6, the shares ended the year at 34/6.

The Poseidon adventure

There is no doubt at all that the chief excitement of the year was provided by "the share of the century", **Poseidon,** whose discovery of high nickel values at Windarra, 160 miles to the north east of Kalgoorlie, sparked a renewed and far more intensive bout of nickel fever. The importance of the discovery for the whole of the Australian mining industry was that it indicated a possible major new mineral-bearing zone a long way from the known areas of proven reserves at Kambalda and Carr Boyd Rocks. And from the point of view of the market, it was important in that most shares had topped out in early 1968 and were still in a convalescent phase. Poseidon provided them with just the tonic they needed.

With only 2.04 million shares in issue, many of them in the hands of the directors and institutions, Poseidon was obviously going to be a thin and highly volatile market in response to any real volume of buying or selling. After a run-up in the early days of the nickel boom, the shares had relapsed to around the 13/- mark when the small placing was arranged in London in May 1968 to raise exploration funds. It then fell back again and on 3rd September a bargain was marked in London at 7/10½. In the last week of the month, a sudden flurry of buying saw the price up to 20/-, prompting a statement from the company that it knew of no reason to justify the rise. Then on 29th September it suddenly added 38/7½ to 59/4½ following overnight support in Melbourne and Sydney on reports that "nickel and copper sulphides had been encountered in a percussion drill at the company's Windarra prospect". No nickel values were available but Poseidon promised to publish assays of samples as soon as possible. On 2nd October the shares hit 130/- on publication of a bore hole result indicating continuous mineralisation in the core from surface to 185 ft, with the lowest 40 ft showing values of 3.56% nickel and 0.5% copper. The instant conclusion of the market on this evidence of a single borehole was that here was a massive orebody increasing in value with depth, which could support a cheap and quickly mounted open pit mining operation. Poseidon was now valued at £16 million compared with £20 million for **Great Boulder** and £400 million for **Western Mining**.

The next day the shares touched 170/- on reports from Australia putting Windarra into the Kambalda class and suggesting the existence of an orebody of 15 million tons grading 3.5% nickel compared with Western Mining's reserves of 15.5 million tons grading 3.7%. The fact that all this could not possibly be deduced from a single borehole was explained away by the belief that buying was coming from "those most intimately associated with the venture". By the middle of the month, the shares were 290/- ahead of the next set of assay results but their apparently disappointing values knocked them back to 170/-. They then quickly recovered on the basis of the assertion that the figures were "not representative", and on the last day of October reached 340/- on rumours from Australia that the next borehole result was going to be "a beaut"! The share price advanced to over 500/- in November but fell back on profit-taking at the end of the month on news that after 20 drill holes it was clear that the company had 20 million tons of good grade nickel ore capable of supporting a mining operation of 0.5 million tons a year.

Then in December the real rise began with much of the persistent buying being in anticipation of exciting revelations at the company's AGM in Australia on 19th December. The price crossed the £50 level on the day of the meeting and surged to £64 in hectic dealings after Chairman Tom Hutton had reported, to "prolonged applause and cheering" from the 500 shareholders attending, that "a major mining operation would be possible at Windarra" and that the Board "would try to begin operations as soon as possible", but he could not say what size of operation it would be, how soon it would start or upon what ore reserves it would be based! Another surge took the price to over £80 on Christmas Eve and the mania intensified for other nickel stocks. North Flinders, which had taken 100,000 shares in Poseidon out of a 500,000 placing earlier in the month, actually doubled from £5 to £10 in the morning's trading, and Western Mining added over £1 to top its June 1968 peak at 159/- on rumours of a big nickel strike at its Mount Clifford property. Not suprisingly, **Pan Australian** turned out to be the year's best performing unit trust.

Maxwell v. Steinberg

Takeover activity was at a much reduced level in 1969 compared with 1968, but it had its moments. Perhaps the most interesting contest, with implications and complications which continue to this day, arose from US computer services group **Leasco**'s £25 million bid for Robert Maxwell's **Pergamon Press**. Clashes over future management of Pergamon between Maxwell and Saul Steinberg, head of Leasco, caused the first approach to be abandoned but when Leasco's second offer was rejected once again by Maxwell, the outside shareholders controlling 36% of the equity compared with Maxwell's 26%, complained of lack of consultation and representation and a Board of Trade enquiry was launched. At the same time, in the US, Saul

Steinberg was not without his critics. He had recently made a $9 billion bid for Chemical Bank, an attempt which drew the Chairman of the SEC to express concern about the ambitions of "big game hunters" using debt instruments to finance takeovers and thereby producing artificial inflation of earnings. Clearly, "junk bonds" were a subject of controversy long before the 'eighties.

Robert Maxwell, head of Pergamon Press, pictured at the time of the unwelcome bid from Saul Steinberg of Leasco.

1970

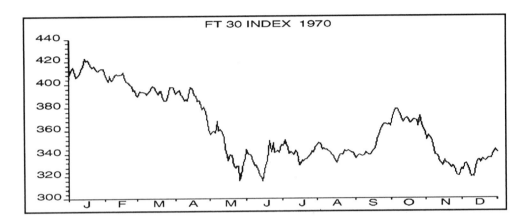

FT 30 INDEX 1970

The year began well, with many investors and market commentators convinced that the apparently decisive break above 400 had signalled the end of the bear market. Sentiment was also aided in no small part by the speculative euphoria engendered by the runaway nickel boom, and perhaps by the thought of having said goodbye to the

Prime Minister Harold Wilson with Chancellor of the Exchequer Roy Jenkins just before the election in June 1970.

'sixties. 1970 also looked very likely to be an election year and some relaxation of the credit squeeze had to be on the cards. The sudden and unexpected abolition of the £50 travel allowance limit in the first week of the New Year seemed to confirm this view, which was given a further boost by the break-even December trade figures showing that the balance of payments was entering 1970 in strong surplus. On the news the index added 7.3 to 423.4, its best level since the previous May, but already the danger signs were appearing.

The great pay rush

After four years of wage restraint, a tremendous backlog of pay claims had accumulated. Barbara Castle and the Prime Minister found this "quite serious" and "disturbing" but the TUC President, Vic Feather, thought demands for higher pay were "understandable in the circumstances". December wage rate increases turned out to be at a level of 7.1%, the highest figure in fifteen years, but in an effort to placate trade union demands, the government elected to abandon the wage freeze and concentrate on maintaining some price controls in the hope that demands would be moderated. It soon became clear that no such moderation was going to occur and with more and more claims accompanied by strike threats, the index began to crumble, slipping below 390 by the end of February. Wall Street was no help. The US economy was faltering under the impact of continuing monetary restraint, and lower earnings reports were taking their toll of the Dow. Having begun the year at 800, by the end of January the Dow was down to 748 and reckoned by many commentators to be heading for below 700.

Despite urgings by the NIESR and from the TUC to reflate, the Chancellor was well aware of the tendency of both bodies to be over-pessimistic about the home economy, leading to a resultant bias towards excessive inflationary recommendations, and contented himself with a half per cent cut in Bank Rate to 7.5% in early March. The move helped gilts more than equities but the news that the balance of payments surplus had reached £450 million over nine months, comfortably exceeding the target figure in the

IMF Letter of Intent, pushed the index towards 400 again. Further consideration of the implications for industrial costs of the wages explosion prompted a reaction to 385 but a recovery quickly set in ahead of the budget in mid-April. Another half a per cent off Bank Rate and an increase in tax allowances across the board was neatly balanced by a half per cent increase in Special Deposits in order to try to maintain restraints on bank lending. The market greeted the budget with a three point rise to 397.6, but that was the nearest it got to 400 for a very long time. A week later, it was back to 385 and then a succession of adverse developments pushed it decisively through the bottom of its trading range.

Conservatives return to power

A continuing decline in the Dow was a major influence on the London market as shock earnings reports, the Lockheed crisis, the collapse of Penn Central and the invasion of Cambodia saw the rapid approach of the downside target level of 700 and then its breach in mid-May. At the same time, there was a lot to worry about on the home front which was to have a direct impact on the stock market. Reports in April of large lines of blue chip stock on offer were widely suspected to come from the funds managed by **IOS** (Investors Overseas Services), an international fund management group rumoured to be experiencing liquidity problems. Since the group had no less than $2.3 billion under management and was a major force in markets around the world, forced selling from such a source was bound to have a serious destabilising effect on markets and on investor confidence.

A further factor affecting sentiment during the second quarter of the year was a serious dip in the Australian mining market, resulting in heavy losses for the many UK participants. And uncertainty was compounded by the pending election which Mr Wilson had called for 18th June, following a series of opinion polls which had given Labour a convincing lead. Unfortunately for Mr Wilson, the May trade figures released just two days before the election showed an unexpectedly sharp swing into deficit. In the event and contrary to all expectations, the Conservatives won with a 30-seat majority and Edward Heath became Prime Minister with Ian McLeod as Chancellor. Mr Wilson's "100 days" had lengthened to over 1,500, but thanks to a remarkable coincidence, or perhaps to his well-known sense of history, they too ended on 18th June, the anniversary of the Battle of Waterloo. Having touched a low of 315.6 two days before the election, a week later the index was back to 350, despite the inherited problems of stagnant production, sagging capital investment and high unemployment, all accompanied by a rapid increase in earnings and prices. The plan of the Heath government for dealing with what was rapidly approaching a crisis situation, was not to impose a statutory incomes policy, but to try to break the wage/price spiral by acting primarily on public sector prices and by cutting taxes affecting costs, like SET. With this in mind, a review of government spending was promised by the autumn.

Barber becomes Chancellor

Unfortunately for the Chancellor, with a growing number of wage awards fuelling cost inflation, any relaxation by cutting taxes or easing of the credit squeeze would risk adding a further element of demand inflation. Mr McLeod was prepared to hold the line by postponing tax cuts until the following spring, a policy decision which seemed more than justified by the June trade figures. The gap had jumped to £51 million as imports leapt ahead of exports, which were growing much more slowly in the wake of the recession in the US and also because of the drop in car deliveries from the strike-torn motor industry. Then at the end of July, Mr McLeod unexpectedly died after less than a month in office and his mantle passed to Anthony Barber.

The new Chancellor inherited a dock strike and a string of high percentage wage claims, all accompanied by strike threats. Unwilling to risk further disruption in such a key sector, he settled the dockers' claim on not especially onerous terms, but with unemployment topping 600,000 for the first time, and the production index falling for the third month in succession, he came under increasing pressure to reflate.

Given that the money supply was increasing at over three times the official guideline rate envisaged in the April budget, and in the absence of a statutory wages policy, the Chancellor had no scope for administering any additional stimulus to the economy, but rather the reverse. Despite this obvious impasse, the market broke through the 350 level in late September into the 370/380 range ahead of the autumn mini-budget. A 2.5% cut in corporation tax, 6d off income tax and

Anthony Barber, Chancellor of the Exchequer from 1970 to 1974, was architect of the dash for growth that came to be known as the Barber Boom.

generous depreciation allowances, balanced by a wide range of public expenditure cuts and increased social services and welfare charges, were measures enthusiastically greeted by the market as evidence of government determination to check inflation. However, a reaction set in almost immediately when Special Deposits were raised by 1% to 3.5% in order to curb bank advances and within a week the index was back to 350 again with gilts losing over a point on fears of a rise in Bank Rate.

The decline now gathered pace with sentiment adversely affected by strike after strike as the TUC resolutely set its face against any moderation of wage demands as well as showing its unrelenting opposition to the proposed Industrial Relations Bill. But an even more serious worry for investors were signs of a growing number of companies suffering from a liquidity crisis, thereby further hindering the government's plan of checking inflation by intensifying the credit squeeze. In the first week of November, **British Leyland** warned that the financial position of Austin Morris was "serious" and the index slipped below 350. The following week, **Rolls-Royce** reported a shock loss of £48 million due to cost escalations on the RB211 engine, and was rescued by a £60 million cash injection. By then the FT 30 had fallen below 330 on rumours of problems at **Vickers** and **Alfred Herbert**, as well as at Australian brokerage houses, and it was only a meteoric rise in the Dow on US recovery hopes that helped the index to end the year at 340.6, down 16.7% on the year.

Australians on the move again

The first two months of 1970 witnessed increasingly frenetic activity in the Australian mining market. **Poseidon** had greeted the New Year with a £12.50 rise to £106.50, but after touching £120, it slipped below £100 by the end of January when it was given some competition – and a new lease of life – by **Tasminex.** This 2 million 25 cent share exploration company had started life in November 1969 at 60 cents (5/7) with a clutch of leases near Mount Venn in the Cosmo Newberry area about 55 miles to the north west of Windarra. Reports at the end of January that it had struck massive nickel sulphides while putting down an exploratory bore hole to look for water for its drilling crews, sent the shares rocketing from just under £3 to £40 in London before closing at £21 to value the company at £42 million. Chairman Bill Singline was quoted as saying that the find "could be better than Poseidon and bigger" but less attention was paid to his rider that he "thought it was there but didn't know because he hadn't got on to the geologists yet"! This was the highest price Tasminex ever reached and within six weeks it was back to where it started from as later reports made it increasingly clear that the "massive sulphides" were in fact "disseminated sulphides", including nickel and copper with "minor values". Both the Melbourne Stock Exchange and the Attorney General of Tasmania ordered a probe into Tasminex "in all its aspects", and the London Stock Exchange entered into urgent discussions with its Australian counterparts over the question of establishing a common policy on the release of information to shareholders. As matters stood at the time, the strict London rules were not enforceable on overseas companies.

Poseidon takes a dive

Poseidon was eclipsed only temporarily by the Tasminex affair and in early February it shot to a new peak of £123.50

in London on rumours that drilling was going well at Windarra and that chairman Tom Hutton, his chief geologist and his chief mining engineer had been observed at the site, "all three wearing smiles". Brokers, Panmure Gordon, also came out with a report that Poseidon was conservatively worth £140 and more optimistically £178 on a present value discounted basis. All eyes were now on the drilling report due towards the end of March, but by then a wave of selling had hit the Australian mining market, knocking Poseidon back to £88. The report, when it came, was good, but not good enough to sustain the price which instantly reacted to £67.50. A week later, it took another knock as mining expert Tom Nestel of Mineral Securities observed that it was impossible on the basis of the data so far released by Poseidon to obtain any idea of exactly how much ore was in the ground, adding that there were indications of a "far narrower width, lower grades and some lack of continuity" in the ore body. Down to £44 on this news, by the end of April the price had fallen below £30, only to rally to over £60 again in June ahead of director Norman Shierlaw's trip to London scheduled for early July and widely expected to herald good news preparatory to a fundraising operation.

The meeting was very much an anti-climax with the bulls disappointed at the lack of the expected massive upgrading of ore reserves. The shares fell back into the £30/£40 range as investors were forced to recognise that the company had moved into a less exciting preproduction phase devoted to raising working capital. Things were never the same again. By the time of the eagerly awaited quarterly report in December, the shares had fallen to £27 and on the unexciting news that ore reserves totalled 29 million

Norman Shierlaw, Adelaide stockbroker and promoter of Poseidon, on a visit to London in July 1970.

tons averaging 1.5% nickel, they slipped again to end the year at £19.

Enter the "Nickel Queen"

Tasminex had stretched the credibility of the Australian mining market and the gullibility of investors, but there was still room for one more. In August a new "star" emerged in the shape of **International Mining Corporation**, chaired by Millie Phillips, reporting a near-surface strike of 2.2% nickel at Trough Wells, 135 miles to the west of Kalgoorlie in an area where Western Mining was exploring. The news doubled the price of the 5.57 million shares (with 5 million options) to 10/-. By the end of the week it had topped 20/- and then paused to await the first assays. Reports of nickel values of up to 3.74% sent the price soaring to over 90/- at one point in October despite Mrs Phillips stating that it was "too early to tell" whether or not a major ore body existed. By the end of the month, the price was back to 30/- and with no exciting news forthcoming save for a temporary suspension following a breach of Stock Exchange rules, IMC ended the year at 8/9.

Mineral Securities feels the pressure

A new wave of selling hit the Australian mines in the closing weeks of the year, and even the highly regarded **Mineral Securities Australia** (MSA) began to come under pressure. The company had built up a portfolio of mining stocks for investment and for speculation and had prospered during the boom years under the administration of chairman, Ken McMahon, and thanks to the share trading skills of top mining expert, Tom Nestel. It had also taken stakes in a number of established and profitable mining operations and was widely recommended in the mining columns as a "safe" way to take a stake in the Australian mining market. The share price topped out at 91/- in line with the rest of the market, but by the time the Poseidon excitement came along, it was heading back towards its peak and soon surpassed it, reaching a high of 172/6 in 1970. In November 1970, while most of the supposedly more speculative stocks were collapsing, MSA announced a tenfold increase in profits and a one-for-one scrip issue "in recognition of its finest year to date", adding that profits were expected to improve "significantly" with share trading continuing to make its contribution. It was mentioned that no less than A\$1 million had been made as a result of trading in Tasminex. The shares were then 120/-, but succumbing to the general weakness in late December, they had slipped below the £5 mark by the end of the year.

The rise and fall of IOS

Investors Overseas Services (IOS) was the financial phenomenon of the 'sixties and its creator, Bernie Cornfeld, tried to do for banking and investment what Hugh Hefner and his Playboy empire did for sex and style. The group had begun life in Paris in 1956 when the 29-year-old Bernie Cornfeld had conceived the idea of selling mutual funds to US servicemen. Early success had prompted him to build up a sales team selling funds to the many other expatriate Americans all over the world. IOS salesmen turned up everywhere, from drilling rigs in Alaska to mining sites in Brazil, selling the benefits of American-style capitalism on a save-as-you-earn basis. There were two vital driving forces behind this initial success. One was the great post-War bull market which provided the ideal background. The other was IOS's marketing technique whereby each salesman recruited his own sales team which then repeated the process almost ad infinitum, with everyone up the scale benefiting from the achievements of those below. While this sort of pyramid selling, or multilevel marketing, can have its place in the distribution of domestic appliances, there is clearly enormous scope for ethical problems to arise where financial products are concerned. As IOS expanded, growth went hand in hand with controversy, as regulatory authorities all over the world tried to curb the activities of this offshore colossus, which by 1969 had grown into the largest fund management group in the world handling funds totalling \$2.3 billion. It was also building up a sizeable banking business as a result of sharing in brokerage commissions, in undertaking foreign exchange transactions for investors buying into dollar and sterling funds, and providing loans to clients to give them funds to invest.

There is no doubt that this degree of vertical financial

integration sparked feelings of envy in many bankers, but it is also true to say that IOS carried within itself the seeds of its own destruction. Many of its sales operations involved

Bernie Cornfeld, former head of IOS, the biggest fund management group in the world, leaving London Heathrow with two companions.

breaching the exchange control laws of countries all over the world, and a great deal of investors' money was lodged in unmarketable shares and assets, the valuation of which was notional and highly vulnerable to any crack in confidence. Furthermore, the lavish lifestyle of Mr Cornfeld and his top aides meant that IOS figured in the gossip columns more often than in the business pages. In March 1970, the group reported that sales were up by 25% over 1968/69 and that it was planning to spend $44 million on expansion into new and potentially major market areas like Japan and South America. Yet a month later, in response to rumours of the dumping of large lines of stock to meet redemptions, and of sales, earnings and fund performance falling below target, top IOS executives were attending a two-day strategy meeting at the Geneva HQ to see what could be done to restore public confidence. A statement was issued to the effect that IOS was "sound" and that although 1969 earnings were substantial and still ahead of 1968, they were likely to fall short of projections. This did nothing to restore confidence, and the pessimists' fears were confirmed in the first week of May when break-even was reported for 1969 against a forecast of profits of $20 million, together with a loss of $5 million for the first quarter of 1970. Offers of help now became almost a daily event with the names of

Rothschild (Paris) and King Resources particularly prominent. The latter company was run by John M. King who operated IOS's Natural Resources Account and had been responsible for "investing" $11 million of investors' cash in a half share of 22 million acres of highly speculative oil permits in the Arctic. The attraction for a rescuer was the fact that IOS still controlled perhaps the largest pool of fund money in the world. Rothschild were prepared to offer $1 a share for 51% control, but only on the condition that Bernie Cornfeld and all his top management team resign from the board. John King, on the other hand, was prepared to offer $4 and let them all stay. Even though the prestige of the Rothschild name would have saved the company, the vote was in favour of King. It soon became apparent that while Rothschild had the money, King had not and soon had no choice but to drop his bid, by which time Rothschild had walked away in disgust.

Robert Vesco takes control

In May, Bernie Cornfeld was forced to give up his post as chairman and while talks were being carried on with an international banking consortium, former UK Treasury official Sir Eric Wyndham White took over. Negotiations were not helped by revelations in June of IOS's "unusual corporate generosity" to directors, officers, employees and friends in the form of loans totalling over $30 million, and then in September when it was announced that the first half loss for 1970 had swelled to $25.8 million. Salvation of a sort ultimately appeared in the unlikely form of Robert Vesco, the controversial 34-year-old head of International Control Communications, with a $15 million loan package. Bernie Cornfeld's initial opposition was overcome when he was allowed to remain on the board, but the deal was the end of IOS as he knew it. By the following May, he had disposed of his personal holding to ICC which transferred all IOS assets into a single holding controlled by ICC and its institutional backers.

E.J. Austin and the "crock of gold"

Although operating on not quite such a global scale as IOS, another American-run company demonstrated once again that there are a lot of gullible investors out there. In 1967 and 1968, **E. J. Austin**, a small builders' supplies company, had been busy acquiring a number of similar businesses, but in May 1969 it abruptly changed direction when control passed to a Mr J.K. Howarth. He then began to make investments in chrome ore mines in Cyprus and in copper, gold, silver and platinum deposits in Nevada, and after suspension in August the company came back as E.J. Austin International, an international mining concern. The transformation benefited the share price, which rose from 15/6 to 18/9, at which level it was suspended yet again in January 1970 on the announcement that it was about to acquire the El Sobrante Mining Corporation of California for shares valued at £6.5 million. It was a complex deal in that El Sobrante, which was 51% owned by Mr Howarth, held the other half of the 40-acre ore body that E.J. Austin had already purchased, and the plan was to run the two properties as a single mining venture. Great excitement was generated by the deal when it was claimed that the mine was capable of producing annual profits of not less than £10 million when the plant was complete and in operation by the end of 1970. Since the earlier forecast for the current year had been no more than £500,000 pretax, the shares were soon changing hands at between 45/- and 50/- in unofficial dealings. At the AGM a week later it was further revealed that 300,000 tons of ore had already been stockpiled and that an assay report predicted a yield of $5,000 per ton, an extraordinarily high figure made possible by a revolutionary new extraction process patented by Mr Wayne Chambers, the owner of the other 49% of El Sobrante. Given that $35 a ton is reckoned to be a respectable yield for a gold mine, this claim was greeted with considerable scepticism as indeed was Mr Howarth's statement at the AGM that "there was literally a crock of gold at the end of the rainbow".

Some credence was given to these claims by brokers Spence Veitch having confirmed the accuracy of the profit forecast, but keen to convince his institutional shareholders, Mr Howarth announced that the Californian mining expert who had carried out the assays would be coming to London to hold a press conference and meet institutional investors. At this point the Stock Exchange stepped in and refused permission for the press conference on the grounds that information should not be given at such a meeting which was not immediately available to all shareholders, adding that no further announcements should be made ahead of the issue of the formal documents. To all intents and purposes, that was the end of the affair. On 10th March, it was announced that the El Sobrante deal had been called off, that Mr Howarth had resigned over the question of a conflict of interest, and that a completely independent assessment and valuation of the mining interests in Cyprus and the US had been commissioned. A week later, a receiver was appointed, and in due course a Board of Trade enquiry was ordered. Shareholders left nursing losses were principally the fast-growing fund management group, Surinvest, unit trust group Abacus, and a number of IOS funds managed by Surinvest.

Cavenham expands on the Continent

Two acquisitions in Holland in January sparked considerable interest in **Cavenham**, pushing the share price over the 10/- mark for the first time. Then in early February, the shares were suspended at 15/- pending details of a whole series of acquisitions in Europe at a cost of £5.5 million and judged to add between 40% and 50% to equity while doubling the £650,000 pretax profits forecast. James Goldsmith hailed the deal as creating a multinational company based in the strongest European countries with the greatest growth potential. When the offer documents eventually appeared in August, the forecast had been raised to £1.623 million, which meant that at the suspension price the shares were on a P/E of 18, or 23 with a full tax charge and allowing for the deferred capital. This was described by Lex in the *FT* as "a fancy rating" for a food company given a P/E of 15.3 for the sector, and the shares closed the year at around 13/6.

Hanson and Slater take a knock

The second quarter decline in the market took its toll of the conglomerates and May saw a precipitate drop in the shares of **Slater Walker** and **Hanson Trust** (the name was changed from Wiles Group at the end of 1969) as "bull market stocks" were downgraded to suit the new market conditions. At the time of its AGM in May, Slater Walker received favourable comment for having shed many of its industrial interests to concentrate on its banking and investment business, but this did not prevent the share price dropping from 61/- to 28/- at one point in the summer before recovering to 37/9 in September. Over the same period Hanson Trust fell from 24/6 to 12/6 before bouncing back to 19/6. Both companies had exceeded their profits forecasts for 1969/70, but while Slater Walker became more deeply involved in the financial world, Hanson Trust changed direction abruptly, dropping a £3.1 million bid for Steels Garages and selling its own vehicle interests to rival bidder Lex for £5 million cash. The motor side was worth £700,000 in pretax profits historically, but it was a cyclical business and the deal transformed the liquidity position of Hanson Trust which promptly launched an £800,000 bid in loan stock for **National Star Brick**.

BTR returns from the wilderness

For many years **BTR** had been regarded as the archetypal dull share in a dull industry. Making power transmission belting and industrial rubber products is not widely seen as a glamour activity, especially when the company loses money doing so. This was the case with BTR until 1968, when it reported a return to profits and forecast an "appreciably better" current year. Greeting a 59% rise in half-time profits to £526,000 in September 1969, the *FT* commented that the company "continues to pull itself up after long years in the wilderness" but noted that its return on capital was still only 8% and sales margins 5%. By now the shares had advanced from 7/- to 11/3 and on an indicated £1 million pretax total for the year, the prospective P/E was 14. But later that month it virtually doubled its size by making an agreed reverse bid for **Leyland and Birmingham Rubber,** at a stroke complementing its own product range and providing considerable scope for rationalisation. The move had been masterminded by the recently appointed 45-year-old Owen Green backed by the IRC. A year later he was able to report sales up 16% and profits up 33% to £1.3 million for an indicated total for the year of £2.8 million, giving a prospective P/E of 12.7 with the shares at 15/-.

Sir Owen Green, Managing Director of BTR, one of the outstanding success stories of UK manufacturing industry.

1971

Rolls-Royce goes under

The New Year opened on a note of continuing uncertainty. The government faced the choice of tightening the squeeze at the risk of more bankruptcies and higher unemployment or of not tightening it enough and letting inflation get out of control. News that average earnings in the twelve months to October 1970 had risen at a rate of 14% and that companies were evading domestic lending restraints by tapping the Eurodollar market, tended to favour the former course of action, but reports of unemployment figures heading towards 700,000 and then the appointment of receivers for **Rolls-Royce** in early February, argued for a degree of relaxation. The market, which had been holding in the 340/350 range, influenced by the Dow making new highs after a succession of interest rate cuts, took the Rolls-Royce news badly. It fell rapidly to 321.9 but then rallied briefly to 335 in the next couple of weeks, only to slip below 320 at the end of the month on growing fears about company liquidity aggravated by an announcement of 1,000 lay-offs at **Alfred**

Herbert following a 30% reduction in orders for machine tools. Also adding to investors' fears had been the collapse in early February of **Mineral Securities Australia** (MSA) with its likely impact on Australian settlements.

The MSA debacle was totally unexpected, following literally within days of a fund-raising operation accompanied by a forecast profit of $3.5 million for the second half of calendar 1970. This was down on the previous half year's $4.77 million, but it was considered a good performance in the circumstances. The suspension of the shares and the revision of the $3.5 million profit to a $3.28 million loss sent a shudder through the whole Australian mining market – and through London. The Stock Exchange called for a list of outstanding Australian bargains from all its member firms, and dealings in all the shares of companies associated with MSA were suspended too. Ken McMahon and Tom Nestel both resigned and a $35 million funding operation was launched by a consortium of banks, all interested in seeing an orderly disposal of MSA's share portfolio. The problem appears to have been that MSA's long-term mining investments had been funded by short-term borrowings in the confident expectation that ever rising share prices and share dealing profits would take care of the interest payments.

Vehicle & General collapses

As if all this was not enough for the market to cope with, the first trading day of March witnessed the crash of **Vehicle & General Insurance**, leaving one in ten of the country's motorists uncovered. V&G was a relative newcomer to the motor insurance world but it had won a large slice of the market since 1960 by favouring "safe" drivers with a quickly achieved high rate no-claims bonus. It was also a member of the British Insurance Association, which the two previous insurance companies that had failed, Dr Emil Savundra's Fire, Auto & Marine in 1966, and London & Cheshire in 1967, were not. Furthermore, all this disastrous corporate news was being played out against a background of practically unparalleled industrial unrest. There was already a long-running postal strike creating considerable disruption in normal City business and the day the Vehicle & General collapse was announced coincided with a one-day strike called to protest against the Industrial Relations Bill in which 1.5 million workers were involved, making the action the biggest politically-inspired strike since the General Strike of 1926.

A new low for the FT 30

It was therefore hardly surprising that the index took another downward lurch, reaching 305.3 on 3rd March. In this instance, the FT 30 with its preponderance of large traditional industrials, Rolls-Royce included, fared worse than the broader-based Actuaries indices which had bottomed in May 1970. Even though this dip turned out to mark the precise end of the 1969/71 bear market, there were few commentators prepared to recognise it as such since inflation was coming to be seen as just as much a threat to the corporate sector struggling with falling profits and stagnant output, as to the old age pensioner on a fixed income. Clearly, profits stated in money terms now bore little relationship to the replacement cost of fixed and working capital, and provided a poor outlook for investment. It was difficult to see any way out of this impasse, given the trade unions' resolute opposition to any form of cooperation over the question of wage restraint, and the government's determination to proceed with its industrial relations legislation.

In the event, the market turned up just as things looked to be at their worst, influenced to some degree by a continuing rise on Wall Street and also by the prospect that Chancellor Barber's budget at the end of March might offer some hope of salvation. This was precisely what it was regarded as doing and the FT 30, already on a rising trend, leapt a record 20.5 points after the budget announcement, to 352.2. Among its provisions were a 2.5% cut in Corporation Tax, a halving of the rate of SET, abolition of short-term Capital Gains Tax, and increased child allowances and pensions together with concessions to surtax payers, all timed to come into effect in July. The intention to introduce VAT, albeit at an unspecified rate and not until April 1973, was also announced. And very importantly, the ceiling on bank lending was raised significantly. The whole package was considered to be "a risk on the side of expansion" but there was no doubt that it came as a welcome relief, as indeed did the 1% reduction in Bank Rate two days later. By the end of April, the FT 30 stood at a new high for the year of 386.2, apparently undeterred by money earnings still rising at an annual rate of 14%, unemployment hitting a 31-year high, and a continuing stream of bad news from the corporate sector, with Vickers reporting a sharp profits fall and the passing of its final dividend. The Dow helped to redress the balance by simultaneously posting its own new high for the year of 950 despite warnings from the Federal Reserve Board about the effects of excessive monetary expansion and a very weak dollar.

The "Dollar Crisis" comes to a head

The following month the dollar crisis broke over Europe, and although it had little immediate apparent effect on equity markets, its implications were to have a profound influence over them for the rest of the decade and beyond. The origins of the crisis go back to the end of the Second World War when the European nations, devastated and poor, looked to America for aid and the financial stability provided by the dollar, ranking alongside gold, as the ultimate monetary standard. A system of parities was devised at Bretton Woods in 1944 and it worked well for a long period. Then there was a role reversal as the European nations became richer and the US, burdened by the huge cost of the war in Vietnam and its military presence elsewhere in the world, became a debtor nation. The country's gold reserves had dwindled, as had its surplus on foreign trade, and it was now forced to meet its overseas debts in its own paper currency.

During the 1960s, this meant that huge quantities of dollars were flowing out of America and into Europe, undermining the efforts of the European nations to control their own domestic inflation and threatening the system of parities. In early May 1971 the flow of dollars became a flood as US banks which had borrowed in the Eurodollar market to beat their domestic credit squeeze in 1969, repaid the loans in order to take advantage of the greater availability of cheaper money at home now that President Nixon had taken the political decision to go for growth ahead of the election in 1972.

To the dismay of the other central banks accumulating large amounts of unwanted dollars, the US was not greatly concerned about the problems they generated. "Benign neglect" was the phrase coined to describe the US attitude formed by consideration of the facts that firstly the US economy was not heavily dependent upon external trade, and secondly the cost of US foreign policy was incurred largely in the interests of other nations.

The immediate effect of the influx of dollars in May was to force the Germans to allow the DMark to float, and of course it floated upwards. This was judged to be good for UK equities in that they gained the competitive advantages of a small devaluation without the penalty of higher raw material costs, and a strong advance took the FT 30 up to the 400 level. Gilts rose too on the expectation that a greater inflow of foreign money would lead to another cut in Bank Rate. The dollar price of gold also rose sharply, breaking the $40 barrier to reach its highest level in two years.

A monetary revolution

Two events on the domestic front in 1971 were to have a lasting impact on financial markets. One was the Crowther report on Consumer Credit, which concluded that all controls should cease and that the whole credit business be thrown open to competition. The other was the government's aim to introduce a competitive climate into the UK banking system by abandoning official ceilings to control liquidity for purposes of economic and monetary management in favour of the use of varying reserve and asset ratios. The members of the Finance Houses Association were quick to implement the recommendations of Lord Crowther, but the government's new methods for monetary control were not scheduled to take effect until September. These two measures, when allied with the Chancellor's reflation package in July, formed the foundations of what soon became known as the "Barber boom". Given the delayed effect of the March budget concessions, most serious commentators believed that no additional stimulus was required, and that the Chancellor had bowed to political pressure. Even the record level of unemployment which helped to influence his actions was seen by an *FT* editorial as paradoxically providing the best hope for the future in that it represented a once and for all labour shake-out which would have laid the foundations for productivity gains enabling the economy to accommodate a 4-4.5% growth rate without running into the usual problems of overheating and pressures on capacity. The danger was perceived that the coming recovery would be too consumer-based, leaving too little room for an adequate contribution from investment and exports.

End of an era for the dollar

Whatever the reservations about the wisdom of an expansionary budget, the stock market responded enthusiastically to measures which included the decontrolling of all HP transactions and drastic reductions in purchase tax. The FT 30 which had already crossed the 400 level again in anticipation of the package, rose to establish a new 1971 high of 413.2. Sensing unfinished business with the dollar, the Dow, however, was falling fast and its precipitate decline through the 900 mark pulled the FT 30 back to 400 again. Neither market remained depressed for long.

In mid-August, President Nixon made his move, marking the end of an era of dollar supremacy by taking it off the gold standard. This suspension of convertibility was accompanied by the levying of a 10% surcharge on all imports into the US, an action widely seen as an attempt to blackmail the rest of the world into accepting US demands for an effective devaluation of the dollar within a new and more flexible system of international payments and trading. At the same time, a 90-day wage and price freeze was imposed, offset by a formidable array of tax incentives. The Dow leapt 33 points on record volume, confident that the measures would bring the US economy back on course. When the foreign exchange markets reopened, the UK authorities had taken the decision to allow the pound to float, although at the same time reaffirming the $2.40 parity in the light of the existence of no obvious economic rationale for any significant degree of revaluation. The market greeted the news enthusiastically with the FT 30 surpassing its July peak.

Also buoying investor confidence was the acceptance in July of Britain's application to join the Common Market. After fourteen years of negotiation and three failures, this was regarded as something of a triumph, and one which would have long-term benefits for British industry. Its greatest immediate impact, however, was on the Labour Party, with Messrs. Healey, Crosland and Callaghan lining up with Harold Wilson in opposition to entry on the terms negotiated by the Prime Minister, while Roy Jenkins and Michael Stewart both agreed with George Brown (now Lord George Brown) that Labour would certainly have gone in on these terms. Labour had a three-line whip against in the entry debate while the Conservatives had a free vote. The latter prevailed with a majority of 112.

A new monetary agreement emerges

September saw a one per cent cut in Bank Rate to 5%, partly in a defensive move to stem the persistent inflow of hot money as the pound rose towards $2.50 but also in response to the chorus of calls for more reflation as the numbers of unemployed continued to climb. But if domestic developments argued for higher share prices, those on the other side of the Atlantic did not. President Nixon's August package had been well received by the market but Phase Two was a long time coming, as indeed was the new world monetary order expected to emerge from meeting after meeting of the Group of Ten. Wall Street soon began to have second thoughts and in October went into freefall, losing 70 points in three weeks with the decline assisted by prophet of doom, Eliot Janeway, forecasting a downside target of 500. The move pulled the FT 30 back to the 400 level again, but by the end of November both markets were rallying sharply on signs of progress in the latest round of monetary talks.

Wall Street was further boosted by a cut in margin requirements, and London took heart from indications of yet
another reflationary package with another half a point off
Bank Rate. Then in Washington, just a few days before
Christmas, President Nixon agreed to an official dollar
devaluation in relation to gold from $35 to $38 and to all the
major currencies, and lifted the import surcharge. The
pound's new parity became $2.6057 within the framework of
the EEC currency 'snake' which provided flexibility of
movement of 2.25% either side of that figure.

In the context of Britain's impending entry into the EEC,
this joint relationship against the dollar established by the
Smithsonian Agreement was an important step towards the
professed goal of economic and monetary union in Europe.
The news came as a great relief to financial markets with
London's FT 30 ending the year at its best level at 476.5, up
40%, and the Dow continuing its recovery to within a
fraction of the 900 level again. Gilts, which had advanced
steadily throughout the year on the trend towards lower
interest rates, were up 17% to 80.32. Only the FT Gold
Mines Index disappointed with an 11.6% fall to 47.1 on
fears that the new monetary agreement had diminished the
role of gold.

Leopold finds nickel — and loses it

The Australian mining market was down but there was yet
more excitement to come on the nickel front to show that it
was by no means out. In March **Leopold Minerals** (6
million shares) leapt from 48p to 230p on news of a strike in
Nullagine, near Pilbara, of 5.33% nickel over 25 ft at a
depth of 665 ft. Three days later, the price touched 440p on
talk that a second hole had come up with values as good as
the first. Two days after that the shares were suspended
following the resignation of one of the founder directors who
had complained about "unauthorised statements" and the
fact that the original drilling core could not be found. A new
drill hole was put down in May at the same site, this time
under the supervision of the Western Australian police, and
came up with values of between 0.098% and 0. 103%! The
affair was widely judged to be more damaging to the

Australian mining market than Tasminex, and effectively marked the end of what was probably the greatest speculative mining boom of the century.

Jimmy Goldsmith's masterstroke

Until June 1971 Jimmy Goldsmith's considerable achievements in building up **Cavenham** into an international food and pharmaceutical empire had been treated with a degree of scepticism. The event that changed all that and made the City columnists really sit up and take notice was his £9.5 million bid for **Bovril**. With Bovril's net assets two and a half times those of Cavenham, this was a bold bid by any standards, and remained so even though Rowntree's subsequent intervention led to Cavenham eventually having to pay £14.5 million to secure its prize. Given the scope for rationalisation and integration, this was a case where dilution paid, and three months later Cavenham managed to recover almost half the purchase price by selling Bovril's dairy interests to Grand Metropolitan for £6.3 million. By December, Moores Stores and Wrights Biscuit with combined net assets of £10.5 million had been acquired after an initial bid of £6.5 million, and the intention was announced of spending another £12.7 million on an unspecified European foods and pharmaceutical group. By this time the share price had begun to respond, and at 185p had more than doubled on the year to give a market capitalisation of £51 million.

Hanson and Slater Walker make further headway

Hanson eventually had to raise its bid for National Star Brick to £1.39 million after Ibstock had entered the fray, but the potential rationalisation benefits when put together with Butterley were considered great enough to overcome its well-known reluctance to pay up for acquisitions. That was practically Hanson's only major move in 1971, until November when he entered into talks with **Costain** with a view to a merger. Both companies were capitalised at around £25 million, but whereas the asset backing of Costain's shares was not far short of that figure, Hanson's represented barely 30% of it. On this simple comparison the Costain board was not happy with Hanson's proposed equal standing in the new group or with the idea of James Hanson at the helm. Ten days later the merger plan was dropped. By this time Hanson's pretax profits for 1970/71 had risen 21% to £2.87 million which, at 180p, meant the shares were selling on an earnings multiple of a modest 15.3.

Meanwhile, **Slater Walker** continued with its policy of cashing in its industrial chips and turning them into assets comprising mainly cash, investments and property. In March an £8 million bid was made for property-rich **Solicitors Law**, and then in October the last of the group's major industrial interests, Crittall Hope's metal window business, was sold for £9 million. The shares were now at a new high of 307p and, said Lex in the *FT*, a group "like any other to be judged on solid performance". However, in August the first serious rumblings of discontent with Slater Walker's aims and methods were heard. They originated in Singapore where the takeover of **Haw Par**, a leading local company and makers of the famous Tiger Balm, had angered Premier Lee Kuan Yew who did not want to see key economic interests falling into foreign hands. He also complained that Slater Walker's takeover practices bordered on the illegal, a charge vigorously defended by the local managing director, Dick Tarling.

The secondary banks had a busy year, and their often spectacular profit increases prompted equally spectacular rises in their share prices. **First National Finance** continued to find new supporters, adding ICI Pension Fund and Royal Insurance to its shareholder list following its acquisition of Spey Finance in a £9 million cash and share deal. It also boosted its property dealing potential by buying 114 blocks of flats from Metropolitan Estates for £33.5 million. Pretax profits had risen in 1970 to £5.36 million from £3.55 million, and then the first half figures for 1971 weighed in at £3.25 million indicating a total of at least £7.5 million for the full year. At 336p, the shares had practically doubled during the year and were selling on a prospective P/E of 20, very much in line with the market average. **Dalton Barton** recorded an even bigger profits rise, making £820,000 pretax in the first half of 1970/71, or more than the whole of the previous year, but even at 640p, up nearly threefold, the P/E was a modest 13.3 on the forecast total for the year of £1.7 million. Gerald Kaplan's **London & County** also did well but it had to swallow a disappointment early in the year when after acquiring a 25% stake in the newly floated merchant bank, **Leopold Joseph**, the target rejected any idea of a bid or indeed of any form of association. The shares ended the year at 180p.

Racal gains status

1970 was a bumper year for **Racal**. Interim profits were up by 68% to £769,000 against a modest 15% rise the year before, and the forecast for the full year was "in excess of £2 million". That forecast turned into an actual figure of £2.23 million, and at 141p, the P/E was a not very demanding 20 in the light of the recent acquisition of Amplivox which added 9% to equity and 11% to earnings. Racal, according to Lex, had become "one of the more reliable electronic growth stocks", and after its forecast for 1971/72 of £2.9 million, it was described as approaching "high-grade investment status".

Bids and deals

1971 was a very active year for bids and mergers, but one distinguished by the fact that so many of them failed. The biggest and the most acrimonious was **Allied Breweries'** £500 million proposed merger with **Trusthouse Forte**. It led to a split in the THF board, with the Trusthouse faction under Lord Crowther in favour of accepting, and Charles Forte resolutely opposed to the idea. The bid failed but Allied Breweries was left holding a 25% stake in THF as an "investment". Then in December, **Beecham** took advantage of **Glaxo's** recent announcement of a dip in profits to launch a £290 million bid. It was instantly rejected and a month later Glaxo agreed a £346 million deal with Boots. Beecham quickly countered by upping its offer to £385 million, but fortunately for Glaxo shareholders over the next two decades, both offers lapsed following a reference to the Monopolies Commission. **Readymixed Concrete** failed in its £75 million bid for **Redland, Grand Metropolitan Hotels** lost **Truman Hanbury Buxton** to **Watney**, but **Trafalgar House** managed to win **Cunard**.

An early warning

The year also saw the result of the DTI's investigation into the affairs of **Pergamon Press** and the associated International Learning Systems. The report ended with the following words: "We regret having to conclude that, notwithstanding Mr Maxwell's acknowledged abilities and energy, he is not in our opinion a person who can be relied upon to exercise proper stewardship of a publicly-quoted company."

1972

FT 30 INDEX 1972

The Chancellor's dilemma

In his New Year statement, the Chancellor referred to the economy having "a unique chance for expansion" and then added that "no government had ever before taken so much action in the space of one year to expand demand". It was a statement that was to haunt him forever after, but to be fair to Mr Barber many of the voices which had been critical of his reflationary moves in 1971 were now urging him "to take a risk on the side of expansion". Influencing this volte face was the fact that there was remarkably little evidence that the economy was responding to earlier stimuli. Unemployment was still rising, crossing the million mark in January, and retail sales, after signs of a revival, were running out of steam. Industrial profits, on the other hand, were beginning to improve but again not enough to relieve worries about the eventual impact of soaring wage/price inflation. In late January even the usually cautious OECD urged the Chancellor to produce a new stimulus in his impending budget, while as usual the National Institute demanded £2.5 billion in tax cuts. The latter insisted that Mr Barber had to exercise a value judgement in his budget and should give priority to the earliest possible reduction in unemployment over the risk of accelerating inflation "some years hence". Essentially, the problem was that if a 23% annual rate of growth in the money supply was necessary to accommodate a 5% growth rate, it was already accommodating a much faster rate of inflation.

Another reflationary budget

In the event, influenced by the unusual combination of a very high level of unemployment, a large balance of payments surplus and impending EEC entry, the Chancellor opted for an expansionary budget. If the tax cuts were less than the National Institute had called for, they were still substantial at £1.2 billion, taking 2.75 million people out of the tax net altogether and leaving the rest £1 a week better off. And as an incentive to investment, there was free depreciation on new investment and 40% allowances on industrial building, along with a range of help for the regions. If the Chancellor was later criticised for being too lax in the budget, in retrospect many of the economic numbers would have been distorted by the long-running labour disputes which dominated the first half of the year, causing the level of consumer demand to be under-played. The year opened with a coal strike which ran for over five weeks leading to power cuts, the declaration of a State of Emergency and a three-day working week in mid-February. There was also a rail strike and a dock strike, and settlements were on terms which served to raise expectations in other industries.

Towards a new record high

The reaction of the markets to the economic situation at the beginning of 1972 was better than might have been expected. Gilts continued their advance in the New Year to reach a seven-year high of 81.86 in late January on expectations of a cut in Bank Rate, but perhaps sensing accelerating inflation and a reversal in the downward trend of interest rates, they topped out well in advance of equities. Fuelled by the growth in money supply, easier and cheaper credit, and encouraged by a high level of takeover activity, equities as represented by the FT 30 crossed the 500 level in early February. They reacted sharply on the three-day week and then rallied after the settlement of the miners' strike with the 30 per cent pay rise recommended by the Wilberforce Report, to end the month at 520.9, just one point short of the previous record of 521.9 in September 1968. The index dipped briefly below 500 on profit-taking but picked up again ahead of the budget and then surpassed the historic peak in intra-day trading the day after. It was not until April that it finally broke through decisively into new high ground. Then in late May, under the influence of apparently good economic news in the shape of a 31% rise in industrial profits in April, a CBI survey showing growing confidence in the industrial outlook, a sharp drop in the numbers out of work, and further encouraged by the Dow hitting a three-year high of 969, the FT 30 surged ahead to 543.6. That level was not to be matched for another seven years.

The turn of the tide

Thereafter, the implications of accelerating cost inflation began to dominate the market to the practical exclusion of all else. Even the National Institute urged tougher anti-inflation policies in the wake of the miners' pay settlement, believing that the government was relying too much on hopes of effective voluntary action emerging from the latest round of talks between the CBI and TUC. Within a fortnight, the FT 30 was back below 500 again and gilts were falling fast in anticipation of higher interest rates as Bank Rate was raised to 5% again. The deteriorating situation was not lost on the foreign exchange markets, where a strong run on the pound developed, despite concerted intervention by the other EEC member states. Given the background, the parity proved impossible to defend and although, as usual, "speculative forces" were blamed for the pressure, the Chancellor's own statement earlier in the month that he saw "no reason for the country to be frustrated in its determination to sustain sound economic growth in order to retain an unrealistic exchange rate", must have provided a clear signal to the markets.

The exchange rate, which had risen as high as $2.65 after the December 1971 dollar devaluation, was already back to $2.57 when in late June, Bank Rate was raised a full point to 6% and the decision was made to let the pound float freely for the first time, although it was stated to be a "temporary measure" ahead of EEC entry on 1st January next. The move provided a very short-term boost to the index on thoughts that the crisis had been very neatly defused by providing the opportunity of improving the trade balance at the same time as pushing up company profits. However, devaluation to an undetermined level soon came to be seen as no solution to a situation where money supply growth was approaching a 30% annual rate and wage awards were well into double figures, not to mention the possibility of other countries opting to follow the pound down and risking US retaliation on the trade front. All the post-flotation gains were quickly lost and by the first week in July, the FT 30 had slipped to 480 and the exchange rate to $2.42 as the inflation rate rose towards 10%.

The talking stops

Statutory action on wages and prices was now seen as inevitable, and initially equities rallied on the prospect, believing that if a wage freeze held down costs, the impact of a price freeze on profits would be offset to some degree by the higher volume trend promised by the continuing rapid rate of expansion. However, Mr Heath persisted in trying to get some sort of voluntary agreement out of tripartite talks with the CBI and TUC and the market crossed and recrossed the 500 level as the progress of the talks ebbed and flowed. Then in early November the talks finally broke down. The sticking point came when the CBI was prepared to accept a freeze on prices as well as on wages but would not have one without the other, and the TUC refused to accept a freeze on wages. Within days the government had brought in emergency legislation imposing a 90-day freeze on pay, prices, rents and dividends with the prospect of an extension for a further 60 days. The move was reinforced by the Bank of England making a 1% call on Special Deposits designed to mop up £220 million in the banking system, and preceded by a two-stage rise in Minimum Lending Rate (MLR) to 7½%. In October, Bank Rate had been dropped as the main signpost of Government policy towards interest rates in favour of Minimum Lending Rate, based directly on the average rate of interest ruling on Treasury bills. MLR was supposed to provide a more flexible instrument for influencing short-term interest rates, free from the drama associated with Bank Rate changes.

Managing the boom

Encouraged by this evidence that the government was at last taking a firm line on inflation, the market began to prepare for an end-year rally but its scope was limited by a continuing rise in interest rates and growing industrial unrest, factors which served to counterbalance the spirit of optimism which might otherwise have been engendered by the sight of the Dow Jones index soaring through the 1000 level to reach a new peak of 1036.37 in mid-December. Then three days before Christmas, the Bank of England, seeing another sharp drop in the numbers out of work as a clear indication that industrial growth was strongly established, added another 2% to Special Deposits, thereby taking a further £450 million out of the system, and lifted MLR by 1½%. The move came as a complete surprise to the market but the FT 30 still managed to end the year at 505.4, up 6%, while the Government Securities index at 71.11 was down 11%. Given that the reverse yield gap was now at a near record 6.6% and the average P/E around 19, both at a time when money was getting dearer and tighter, in retrospect it looks surprising that the market managed to hold its level during the second half of the year. The reason was that most commentators looked at a 5% growth rate and saw the Chancellor as managing the boom rather than strangling it, contrasting his actions with those of Roy Jenkins in 1969. It was also widely believed that although MLR had risen from

4.5% to 9% during the course of the year, interest rates were fast approaching a plateau from which they would fall in due course, thus enabling the government to fund its borrowing requirement.

This generous interpretation of events also owed a great deal to the fact that the system had been awash with liquidity in the first half of the year – London clearing bank advances had increased by 40% in the year following the abandonment of qualitative and quantitative monetary controls – and that inevitably there was a hangover effect into the second half. The remarkable performance of Wall Street was another major contributory factor, its rise fuelled by Vietnam peace hopes, the apparent success of Richard Nixon's anti-inflation policy and then his landslide re-election in November. Since the peaks of neither market were to be seen again until the end of the decade, the extra-ordinary performances of London and Wall Street in 1972 might be seen as a sort of "folie à deux".

Going for gold

Top marks for the year went to gold and to gold shares, both making up drastically for their dismal performances in 1971 in the wake of the dollar devaluation. It soon became apparent that when the dollar broke its links with gold it was not gold that had been cast adrift but the dollar. The gold price quickly recovered from an initial setback when the suspension of convertibility was announced, but the gold share index continued to languish on cost pressure fears until January 1972 when it suddenly began to move, adding more than 25% on the month to 50 with the gold price approaching $50. For the rest of the year the advance was practically unbroken, accelerating in the second half as anxieties grew over the stability of the new monetary order, to achieve a 101% overall gain at 95.3. Gold ended the year at $66.20, boosted by strong French demand. Gains of 100% were common among the big South African producing mines like **Western Holdings** and **East Driefontein** but the really spectacular rises were among the older, high cost mines, the so-called "marginals" like **Durban Deep** which went from 58p to 250p as profit projections soared.

Goldsmith buys Allied Suppliers

January was an active month for Jimmy Goldsmith. After strong rumours that he was about to make a reverse bid for **Spillers**, he surprised the market by offering £82.5 million for food stores group **Allied Suppliers**. Although **Cavenham's** market capitalisation was some £60 million, its net worth was no more than £10.5 million, a discrepancy which prompted Lex to refer to the proposed deal as "the reverse bid to end them all". Allied Suppliers accepted marginally improved terms and, having more than doubled the size of Cavenham at a stroke, Goldsmith wasted no time in reorganising and rationalising his new acquisitions. In July, the biscuit interests were sold to United Biscuits for £4 million cash, and in the same month the first property disposals were made from Allied Suppliers for £3.9 million to Argyle Securities, Slater Walker's property arm. In November, a 75% stake in a leading Swedish food company was bought for £6 million, and in December it was announced that Cavenham was making its first move into America by entering into negotiations to buy Squibb's baby food division for $30 million. The interim figures to November were announced a few days before Christmas, and did not disappoint. Pretax profits were £11.16 million against £5.2 million for the whole of 1971/72, leaving the shares at 200p on a P/E of 15 assuming a total for the year of £21.5 million.

Hanson goes for Costain again

The collapse of the planned merger with **Costain** did no harm to Hanson's share price, and in February, with the shares at 237p on the back of a "not less than" £3.6 million forecast for 1971/72, Hanson returned to the fray with a £28.5 million hostile bid. Costain put up a vigorous defence arguing that the bid undervalued the company. Hanson, however, was not prepared to raise its offer and walked away, answering critics who queried where the future success of his group now lay, by affirming that it was built on the fact of never having paid too much for any business and would remain so. Interim profits of £2 million were announced in June, accompanied by a raised forecast for the year of £4 million together with a 1 for 4 rights issue raising £8 million "to reduce gearing". The actual outcome for the year was £4.47 million.

Slater Walker approaches its zenith

1972 was a boom year for the financial sector and **Slater Walker** was very much the leader of the pack. Pretax profits for 1971 were up by a third to £16.3 million and with the shares at a new peak of 412p, the market capitalisation had grown to £225 million. Recently floated **Ralli International**, run by Malcolm Horsman, one of Jim Slater's original management team, reported profits up by 61% to £5.6 million as its move into overseas earnings situations began to pay off. Then in the autumn, Ralli acquired "instant blue chip status" by

Jim Slater, Chairman of Slater Walker, at the peak of the company's popularity with investors.

accepting a £200 million bid from **Bowater** in a planned marriage of assets and management. The move was not without its institutional critics, but it had enough going for it to defeat the intervention of Trafalgar House, which put in a bid of £126 million for Bowater on its own. **Vavasseur**, once an overseas trader but now transformed by the injection of foreign exchange dealers Harlow & Meyer into a fast-growing financial conglomerate, reported a 38% advance in profits for 1971 and forecast a 60% gain to £2 million for 1972.

Pat Matthews' **First National Finance** won bank status and in accordance with its new "image" sold the bulk of the flats bought the year before from Metropolitan Estates, netting a £26 million profit in the process. First half profits for 1972 weighed in at £5.63 million, up 73%, and in November there was no problem in raising £13 million with a rights issue in loan stock. Jack Dellal's **Dalton Barton** was not far behind and after reporting a 109% boost to 1971 profits at £2.61 million, an agreed merger with merchant bank Keyser Ullman left him running a group capitalised at £175 million with the potential for making £12 million in its first full year of operation. Once again, the property element was strong since earlier in the year Keyser had merged with the

Pat Matthews, Managing Director of First National Finance Corporation (FNFC), while it was still riding high in 1971.

£70 million Central and District Properties. Gerald Kaplan's **London & County** won considerable critical acclaim as a result of trebling its asset base for an addition of 42% to equity by acquiring industrial/financial conglomerate **Drakes**, built up by Christopher Selmes (27), the financial "whizz kid" reputed to have made a fortune after starting with £200 as a 15-year-old schoolboy. After reporting interim profits in 1972/73 of £1.58 million, up from £412,000, Lex commented that the bulk of this gain had come from growth in the traditional banking business, not from dealing profits, and that the current climate looked favourable for the "high risk/reward make-up" of the group. At 300p the shares were on a prospective P/E of 16 on the likely total for the year of £3.5 million.

BTR and Racal prosper

Meanwhile back on the apparently less glamorous industrial scene, **BTR** managed to make up for the first half slowdown in 1971, beating its forecast of a maintained £2.84 million total for the year by planned cost reduction moves involving a 15% cut in the workforce. The outcome of £3.55 million for 1971 was handsomely beaten at £4.1 million in

1972 with BTR's management skills evident in this 15% increase in pretax profits being achieved on no more than a 1.5% boost in turnover. At 105p, the historic P/E was 14.8. Thanks to the remarkable success of its latest product line, the Clansman VHF manpack radio, **Racal** exceeded its £2.9 million profits forecast for 1971/72 with a total of £3.12 million. The shares were then 216p and by the time of the interim statement for 1972/73 in December they were 224p for a prospective P/E of 22 on a forecast £3.9 million total for the year. Racal, said Lex, is maintaining its "super-growth" status.

Bids and deals

The biggest bid of the year was that of **Grand Metropolitan Hotels** for **Watney Mann**, following hard on the heels of Watney's own £126 million bid for **International Distillers & Vintners**. The opening price was £353 million, but **Rank Organisation** countered with a £430 million on offer, only to drop out two weeks later just before Grand Metropolitan came back with an ultimately successful final bid of £435 million. Breweries were in the firing line again in August when **Imperial Tobacco** bid £286 million for **Courage**. **United Drapery Stores** failed with a £111 million offer for **Debenham's**, but Rank agreed a £43 million takeover of **Butlins**, and **Amey**, the aggregates group, went to **Consolidated Goldfields** for £58 million.

Mothercare and Comet come to market

The two most popular new issues of the year were **Comet**, the discount electrical goods retailer offering 4.7 million shares or 38% of its equity, at 110p, and the ever popular **Mothercare** raising £13.2 million by an offer for sale of 25% of its capital at 165p. Despite the issues being priced at relatively high P/E multiples of 18.2 and 28.2 respectively, they both scored runaway successes with premiums of 37p and 25p on the first day of dealing. The best performing share of 1972 was **Cape Town Gas Light & Coke Company**, an obscure South African utility whose sole real asset was a quotation on the London stock market. The share price rose by 453% when control passed to Terry Maher (37), who had resigned his directorship at First National Finance Corporation to create his own business empire using this tiny 'shell' company as his vehicle. Today, after surviving two major recessions, **Pentos** as it is now called is a specialised retailer with interests in bookselling through Dillons and Hatchards, office furniture and supplies through Rymans, and printselling through Athena. Unfortunately, the company entered the last recession with a heavy debt load and after a series of profits warnings, institutional shareholder pressure led to the departure of Terry Maher.

1973

FT 30 INDEX 1973

The cracks begin to show

During the first three weeks of the New Year, most commentators were prepared to give the market the benefit of the doubt, arguing that company profits were recovering strongly on the back of productivity gains in the context of a 5% growth rate, money supply growth was slowing and the government had no choice but to bring interest rates down in order to fund its budget deficit. There were also some indications in early January of a slowdown in the consumer boom and a slight pickup in industrial investment. Wall Street was no discouragement either, reaching a new record peak of 1051.7 on 11th January on expectations of an imminent end to the war in Vietnam and the success of President Nixon's wages and prices policy.

The FT 30 managed to hold above the 500 level until 18th January, when Prime Minister Heath unveiled Phase Two of his own anti-inflation policy, described by the *FT* as "the most comprehensive set of economic controls since the War" as the government assumed powers to regulate prices, pay, rents and dividends for the next three years. The next day the FT 30 dropped 10.5 to 495.1 and was not to see the top side of 500 again for another five years. The problem was that although the market had appeared to recognise the need for a tough wages and prices policy in order to break the vicious circle of inflationary expectations, the new measures were so far-reaching that at the same time as casting doubt on the future for company profits, they also called into question the chances of maintaining the target growth rate. Industry was not at all happy, for example, with a Prices Code which permitted companies to pass on in price increases only 50% of allowable wage increases and which also stipulated that any fall in raw material and other allowable costs should be fully reflected in price reductions. The picture was further complicated by the fact that the TUC, as usual, would have no truck with any sort of pay restraint, and by the end of February the index had fallen to below 450 with the government seeming to have got the worst of both worlds, alienating industry while failing to appease the unions.

A new dollar crisis

As if all this was not enough for the market to cope with, a new world currency crisis blew up in the first week of February as billions of dollars flowed into the central banks of Europe, particularly into Germany, and also into Japan. The heart of the problem was that the realignment of December 1971 had failed as yet to produce an appreciable restoration of the balance of payments equilibrium between the major industrial countries. Even accepting the inevitable time lags, it was still disturbing to see the US trade deficit rising so sharply in 1972 with no prospect of a reduction in 1973, and capital flows to those countries with corresponding surpluses were to a large extent inevitable. By the middle of the month, a new currency package had emerged involving another dollar devaluation against gold, this time from $38 to $42.22 with a new joint float by the principal EEC currencies, excluding the pound and the lira, and with the yen floating on its own. The reaction of Wall Street to this new devaluation was to slip below the 1000 mark again, seeming to heed President Nixon's warning that it was "no substitute for discipline in the economy".

Still gambling on growth

To some degree the fact that the pound was already floating had served to absorb the shocks that would otherwise have overwhelmed it had parities remained fixed, but the latest currency upheaval still managed to provide an unsettling background to the Budget scheduled for 6th March. Interest rates were rising again, the trade surplus was disappearing rapidly, and clearly it was no longer possible to pursue an abnormally rapid growth path and sustain a large public sector deficit, without fear of the external consequences.

Despite these caveats, the Chancellor still opted for an expansionary budget with the avowed aim of maintaining a high growth rate while keeping up the fight against inflation. And there were to be no cutbacks in public expenditure commitments, which involved an increase in the borrowing requirement from £2.8 billion in 1972/73 to one of £4.4 billion in 1973/74, arising not from this budget but from the spending boosts and tax reductions implemented in 1971/72 when the Chancellor was responding to the sharp rise in unemployment. Despite having implemented his promise to impose VAT on a wide range of goods and services at a standard rate of 10%, it was increasingly difficult to see how this greatly enlarged borrowing requirement could possibly be funded without a background of falling inflationary expectations and rising gilt-edged prices, but even Lex in the *FT* called this an imperative rather than an objective, seeming to believe in the Chancellor's ability to do what had to be done. Gilts knew better as usual and the Government Securities index fell 1.54 to 69.71, its lowest point in two years.

Riding the tiger

During the second quarter of the year, the magnitude of the task facing Mr Barber became increasingly obvious. The trade balance deteriorated sharply thanks to a soaring import bill in terms of volume and price even before the expected revival in industrial stockbuilding and capital investment had begun to get underway. At the same time the consumer boom showed no signs of abating and in the absence of positive measures of restraint in that area, there was little scope to shift resources into investment and exports at a time when shortages of labour, materials and productive capacity made it vital to do so. A freak April trade surplus, together with a £500 million cut in public spending, indications of a slightly more cooperative attitude by the TUC and a rather contrived reduction in Minimum Lending Rate back to 7½% sparked a rally to just over 480 in mid-June, but once again gilts were less easily influenced and failed to respond. In retrospect this rally provided the equity investor with the last chance to sell before things began to get really difficult. But at the time it all looked very different. The National Institute for one confessed to being 'remarkably optimistic' and to believing that fears about overheating were exaggerated in the context of a prices and incomes policy coupled with a floating exchange rate.

The US was having not dissimilar problems. Output was surging ahead, but so were prices and President Nixon had no easy task in implementing an effective wages and prices policy against a background of a weak dollar, a soaring gold price, and the Watergate scandal which cast doubt on the standing of his administration and its ability to regulate the economy. Sentiment on Wall Street was further upset by the sudden and unexpected collapse of Equity Funding Corporation, a popular growth stock, following revelations that roughly two thirds of its $3 billion in life policies were fictitious and that $25 million had been obtained by reinsuring them with other insurance companies. As a result the Dow was back to the 900 mark by mid-June, unimpressed by a 60-day price freeze which, with its system of audits and price reporting requirements, looked positively damaging for corporate profits.

Interest rates start to take off

The third quarter of the year was marked by renewed currency turmoil with the trade-weighted depreciation of sterling reaching a level some 20% below the point at which it stood at the time of the Washington agreement in December 1971. The size of this depreciation had tended to be obscured by the fact that the pound was floating and also by the habit of measuring it against the dollar, which was also weak, but it is true to say that the floating pound under Mr Heath had sustained a bigger fall than under Mr Wilson after three years of desperate rearguard action. It was doubly unfortunate that a depreciation of this magnitude happened to coincide with a worldwide boom in commodity prices, which meant that UK imports of food and raw materials became very expensive. Exports were rising strongly but not enough to compensate for this adverse shift in the terms of trade, and in any case, they were being held back in volume terms by labour and capacity shortages aggravated by the persistence of the consumer boom.

Despite urgings by most economic commentators, including top government adviser, Lord Rothschild, but not of course the National Institute, Messrs Heath and Barber insisted that no curbs on domestic demand were necessary. Their pledge was to "go for growth" and to pay no attention to the "prophets of gloom", but knowing that they could not allow the pound to float down any further without causing an unacceptable deterioration in the terms of trade, they decided to protect the pound by letting interest rates rise. In late July, there was another 1% call on Special Deposits taking £260 million out of the banking system, and simultaneously MLR was hoisted 1½% to 9%. Within days it was up again to 11½%, putting the finishing touches to the FT 30's sixty-point decline from its mid-June level and leaving gilts friendless and struggling to find a floor as the Government Securities index slipped to the lowest level recorded since its compilation in 1924.

Waiting for "something to turn up"

In retrospect it is clear that the Government was putting too much reliance on commodity prices topping out and actually falling, and on some sort of agreement being worked out over wages and prices in Phase Three. Indeed it was as puzzling then as now, why Mr Heath should have expected any cooperation from the unions over pay. They had made no secret of their outright opposition to any sort of freeze and to be fair to their leaders, it would have been practically impossible to carry their members against a background of soaring retail prices, especially food prices. Delegates were being withdrawn from pay talks, strikes were a daily occurrence, and the miners, after raising some hopes earlier in the year by returning a "no strike" ballot, in July announced that their latest pay claim would be pursued by a policy of confrontation, not negotiation. Neither did commodity prices show much sign of turning down to any significant extent, and with oil prices still rising and supplies tight, there was even talk of petrol rationing being introduced in August. Thus with both pay and commodity prices largely outside the government's control, most responsible economic commentators continued to stress the need for direct action by making substantial cuts in public expenditure and by keeping the money supply under much stricter control. Indeed, they argued that such action would actually help business confidence whereas the indiscriminate use of the interest rate weapon posed a threat both to growth and to the Government's electoral chances.

The oil drama takes centre stage

All the while this debate was going on, another drama was being played out around conference tables in Geneva and Vienna. This was the confrontation between the Western oil companies and the producing states, now organised in OPEC (Organisation of Petroleum-Exporting Countries), over the question of raising the return to the latter to compensate for the recent dollar devaluations. In fact the dispute went much deeper than that, involving both the matter of economic relationships between the industrial world and the developing world, and that of the former's attitude towards Israel. It was also only too obvious to the producers that while prices of practically every other commodity were soaring, the price of oil was effectively pegged.

There was nothing new about the idea of using the "oil weapon" to put pressure on the West. In August 1967, just after the Six-Day War, Iraq had tried unsuccessfully to get its Arab neighbours to support an oil sales ban and a boycott of Western goods for a period of three months. Then in February 1971, after further talk of an embargo, OPEC members signed a five-year agreement with the oil companies for a considerable increase in revenues to the producing nations. However, in the wake of the subsequent dollar devaluations it was hardly likely to hold. A 6% increase was agreed at Geneva after the first devaluation, but when demands for an 11% rise were rejected by the oil companies following the second devaluation, the "oil weapon" began to be brandished in earnest.

Libya takes the lead

Libya had already nationalised all BP's interests in the country in 1972, in May 1973 pumping operations were halted in Libya, Iraq and Kuwait, and then Libya proceeded to expropriate 51% of the assets of all the US oil companies. In September, President Nixon warned that Arab action could lead to a Western boycott of their oil, but in the absence of adequate alternative sources of supply, it must have seemed an empty threat. All eyes were now focused on the OPEC meeting in Vienna in September. There had been speeches by the Arab delegates referring to the "scandalous" profits being made by the Western oil companies at the expense of the producing nations, and unofficial indications were that OPEC would demand a straight oil price rise in the 15-20% range. No one was prepared for what was to follow.

Egypt and Syria attack Israel

The trigger was the so-called Yom Kippur War which broke out in the first week of October when Egyptian and Syrian forces simultaneously attacked Israel on two fronts.

Remarkably, markets were undeterred by the event and equities and gilts both extended their recovery from the September lows, more concerned with hopes that interest rates had peaked and news that industrial profits for the first nine months of the year were up 24.3% than another war in the Middle East. Wall Street's reaction was much the same and for the same reason, with the Dow extending its advance to 978 even though Iraq promptly seized US oil interests in the country the day after the war had started. The element of surprise in the initial attack had led to some early Arab successes, and the US began an airlift to Israel to replace the military equipment lost in the first days of the war. By the end of the week Israel had regained the initiative, stabilising the Syrian front and launching a devastating counterattack against the Egyptian forces in the Sinai. Egypt immediately called for the Arab producers to use their oil weapon against the "friends of Israel" by stopping exports at once. The Gulf States were the first to act, breaking off talks on the renegotiation of the five-year agreement and unilaterally raising the price of their crude oil by 66%, taking it from $3 to $5 a barrel.

The FT 30 exhibited some nervousness during the first week of the war, pulling back from 441.6 to 428.2 when commentators pointed out the dramatic implications for industrial costs and for the balance of payments of a rise in the price of oil of this magnitude. However, it rallied to 437.7 on news of a quarter per cent reduction in MLR, seemingly rating the event as more important than Libya adding $4 to the posted price of its oil, double the increase just imposed by the Gulf States, and the start of the embargo with a 5% cut in oil supplies. Wall Street, too, had its head in the sand, actually reaching a new recovery peak of 987 on 27th October, the day that Venezuela decided to go along with the Arab producers and raise its own oil price by 56%.

The moment of truth

Whatever the efficient market theory may say about all the news being discounted in the market at any given point, there can be no argument about the fact that if in October

1973 all the news was known, its significance was not appreciated for some days. The moment of truth arrived on the last day of the month when the Arab producers announced that oil supplies to the West might be cut not by 5% but by 20%, with nothing at all going to the Netherlands, because of its overtly pro-Israeli stance. Within a week the Dow had lost 67 points to 919, then rallied briefly to 930 on the acceptance by both parties in the conflict of the Kissinger peace plan, before plunging below 900 again after a belated awakening by investors to the serious consequences for the economy of the cutback in oil supplies and the increase in prices. London had even more problems to contend with. The power workers had been taking industrial action throughout October and then in November the miners imposed an overtime ban in pursuit of their pay claim which was well above the Phase Three limits. Nevertheless, the Chancellor insisted that there would be "no slamming on of brakes" and that the use of Special Deposits would be adequate to control the expansion of bank credit to the private sector.

Action at last

It was not until the middle of November that both the government and the market got the message and on the same day the October trade figures came out showing a record £298 million deficit, Mr Heath declared a State of Emergency over the oil and coal crisis. Simultaneously a major credit squeeze was inaugurated by lifting MLR to a record 13% and by adding another 2% to Special Deposits bringing them up to 6% to take £600 million out of the banking system. The FT 30 plunged 17.4 to 405.5, gilts lost as much as 4.5 points, knocking the Government Securities index back to 62.39, and only golds gained. Rumours that these measures would soon be followed up with a mini-Budget, the threat of industrial action on the railways, and the first manifestations of the secondary banking crisis, all against the background of Wall Street sliding towards the 800 level, took the FT 30 back to 365 by the end of the month.

The first half of December brought no respite.

Distribution problems created by the rail dispute deepened the energy crisis, and in a televised address to the nation on 14th December, the Prime Minister announced the immediate introduction of a three-day week to conserve fuel supplies. There were by now real signs of distress selling and with sentiment further disturbed by the collapse of London & County Bank and the November trade gap indicating that the total deficit for the year was going to be close to £2.3 billion even before the oil price rise had taken effect, the index touched a seven-year low point of 305.9 by the middle of the month. Then a few days before Christmas, a new package of measures was unveiled. Public spending was to be cut by £1.2 billion, consumer credit was to be severely restricted by the reimposition of HP controls, and the overheated property sector was singled out for special treatment in the form of a development tax and a clampdown on the granting of office development permits. Most commentators thought the moves were not drastic enough, but the market rallied strongly to end the year at 344 on hopes that they would serve to cool the economy without tipping it into recession. Once again, domestic considerations obviously carried more weight than the news released on Christmas Eve that the Gulf States had increased the price of their crude yet again, this time from $5 to $11.50, or four times the pre-War level in early October.

On the last day of the year the FT 30 was down 32%, gilts had lost 14% with the Government Securities Index at 61.05, and only golds gained with a 117% rise to a new peak of 207.1 in response to a bullion price up 73% to $112.50. Once again it was the shares of the marginal producers which benefited most, and while **Western Holdings** and **East Driefontein** doubled, **Durban Deep** more than trebled to 780p.

Goldsmith goes for cash

The unexpected developments towards the end of the year had a major impact on the fortunes of a great many companies. In some cases it was to be a fatal impact. Jimmy Goldsmith, however, was to enhance his reputation in 1973 for always staying at least one step ahead of the game by

selling two of his City properties for £11.7 million in March,
and then by disposing of some 1600 shops, mostly acquired
via Allied Suppliers, to Guardian Properties for £17.5
million in May. In the meantime, he had bought another
30% of French food giant, Générale Alimentaire, taking his
holding up to 48%. In June Cavenham announced pretax
profits of £22.5 million, comfortably exceeding most forecasts, leaving the shares at 151p on a P/E of 15. Market
capitalisation was now £135 million with £50 million represented by cash. Goldsmith, like Hanson, had his eye on the
US and in December he made his first successful deal there
by making a $62 million cash bid for 51% of Grand Union,
an East Coast supermarket group with a billion dollar
turnover and a poor earnings record. Half year profits were
announced just before Christmas but even a 45% gain at the
pre-tax level to £16.2 million was not enough to stop the
shares ending the year well down at 147p.

Slater Walker and Hill Samuel plan to merge

Pretax profits of **Slater Walker** in 1972 were up by only 8%
at £17.6 million but earnings per share rose by 22% to give
a P/E multiple of 16 at 250p. Gross assets in commercial
banking and in property had doubled and with a net worth
of 160p with probably another 30p surplus on book value of
quoted investments, Lex saw the rating as taking into
account "precious little goodwill" regardless of the group's
one-man image. Then towards the end of April, the City was
stunned by the news that Slater Walker was to merge with
Hill Samuel.The result would have created London's
biggest merchant bank with a market capitalisation of £260
million and £1.5 billion of gross assets, £1 billion under
management, £230 million in insurance funds, and
combined net profits of £17.5 million. The initial reaction
from the financial establishment was favourable. The Bank
of England was ready to give its support and Jim Slater's
readiness to defer to Sir Kenneth Keith by acting as his
deputy and to agree to the name of the Hill Samuel Group
was seen as a welcome move to "depersonalise" the
business. The *FT* referred to the move as marking the
phasing out of "one of the truly great financial innovators".

The government decided that no reference to the Monopolies Commission was called for and joint statements were made professing the international ambitions of the new group, particularly with an eye to Europe, the US and the Far East. Then on 20th June, two days before the closing date of the offer, it was announced that the merger had been called off because of "differences of workstyle and personalities" between the two companies.

It was at this point that the formerly fairly muted criticism of the proposed deal became overtly hostile, largely on the grounds that the incompatibility of the two groups had always been obvious. It was not good news for Sir Kenneth Keith who, under institutional pressure, had been forced to abandon a proposed merger with Metropolitan Estates in 1970, and neither was it for Jim Slater, in that it appeared that his ambitions had been thwarted for the first time in his meteoric career. Supposedly as part of an "image mending" exercise, Slater Walker offered to buy back shares at a premium in the relatively disappointing Dual Trust originally formed to hold stakes in the group's satellite companies and as a result nicknamed "Dustbin Trust". Strategic stakes in companies were also detailed as part of a new disclosure policy, and they were seen to include Spillers (10.8%), J. Bibby (24%) and British Ropes (11%). Despite the Hill Samuel setback, Slater Walker still looked to be ending the year in good shape despite a share price practically halved to 140p in reaction to the secondary banking crisis.

London and County Bank collapses

The other financials began the year in fine form but ended it in very different shape, affected in varying degrees by the credit squeeze and soaring interest rates. Gerald Kaplan's **London & County**, for example, proceeded to beat its 1972/73 profits forecast by reporting a total of £3.58 million, indicating a pre-tax figure for the current year of probably £7 million, which would drop the P/E from 16 to 10 with the share price at 250p. The company announced that it planned to set up a chain of regional offices to service industrial and commercial borrowers, and with deposits having trebled in the past year to £76 million, the future was widely judged to be bright. Fears that it was about to darken became very evident in November when the share price fell dramatically from 200p, to 58p. The company put out a statement saying that it knew of "no reason for the extreme fluctuations in the share price", but the market paid more attention to the abrupt resignation of the recently appointed head of the banking department reputedly because of a "clash in operating style" with Mr Caplan.

On 1st December the shares were suspended at 40p, valuing the company at £4.67 million, and urgent rescue talks were reported to be underway with London & County's bankers, National Westminster, and large shareholders, Eagle Star, First National Finance and Keyser Ullman. United Drapery Stores was also involved as a result of having granted London & County a licence to operate banking departments within many of its stores. Within days a rescue plan had been devised by a consortium led by Pat Matthews' FNFC which bought 25% of the capital from some of the major shareholders (including Mr Caplan) for a nominal £1, and pledged to make up to £30 million available in order to overcome the liquidity crisis.

Other secondary banks under pressure

The troubles of London & County cast a shadow over the rest of the financial sector, prompting a run on some of the smaller ones which were then caught out as a result of their dangerous mismatching of short-term borrowing with medium and long-term lending. **Cedar Holdings**, a banking and second mortgage specialist, was the next to fall to the great embarrassment of its prominent institutional shareholders.

Save in terms of share price, the more highly regarded **FNFC** and **Keyser Ullman** continued to forge ahead. First National Finance turned in almost doubled profits in 1972 of £13.23 million, excluding property dealing gains, mainly stemming from a massive increase in banking profits as lending volume expanded sharply. The first half of 1973 recorded a further substantial gain to £9.02 million indicating a probable total for the year of around £19 million on the back of hugely expanded advances mainly to "non-bank borrowers". In December, the company was applauded for having pulled off something of a coup by striking a deal with British Rail to provide banking services at up to forty mainline stations over the next four years. Significantly, the shares demonstrated relative weakness within the sector, ending the year 60% down at 42p. **Keyser Ullman** also appeared to be well on course, reporting profits of £8.69 million for its first part-year together with Dalton Barton, compared with £4.06 million, and then selling Central & District Properties to Town & City for £97 million, realising a handsome profit on the original acquisition price. At the time of the London & County collapse, Keyser Ullman was widely congratulated on its timely property sales, and as a cash-rich group with a net worth of some £130 million against a market capitalisation of £96 million, it was judged as unlikely to be disturbed either by stock market weakness or the recent softness in property values.

Vavasseur bails out Barclay

Just like the other financial groups, **Vavasseur** had been keen to expand its asset base in 1973, and in January it made a surprise £17 million bid for John Bentley's **Barclay Securities**. John Bentley, one of Jim Slater's early lieutenants, then 28, had taken control of Barclay in mid-1969 when it was refloated with the aim of reorganising and rationalising a chain of wholesale chemists and expanding the business by making further acquisitions. This he managed to do very successfully and then began to branch out into other areas. In November 1971 he bought

John Bentley (32), Chairman of Barclay Securities, sold out to Vavasseur in 1973 and neatly avoided the Crash of 1974-75.

the Lines toy business from the liquidators for £5.3 million, a deal which made Barclay the biggest toy maker in the UK. It was his rationalisation moves there and again at Shepperton Studios following the takeover of Lion International that began to give the whole Slater-inspired "asset stripping" technique a bad name, not least because at Shepperton John Bentley ran up against the outspoken left-wing union leader, Alan Sapper. In the event, having reputedly exclaimed "Vava ... who?" when told of the bid, John Bentley accepted the offer after getting it upped to £18.5 million, placed his new Vavasseur paper with institutions and neatly avoided the financial holocaust that was soon to follow.

More excitement for Hanson

After a quiet 1972 in the wake of the abortive Costain bid, **Hanson** began 1973 with an agreed £12 million offer for BHD Engineers, simultaneously making a forecast of a 34% rise in pretax profits to at least £6 million. In May a £4.8 million bid was made for unquoted specialist pumps maker, Sykes Lacey-Hulbert, and the following month a 140% rise in interim profits prompted a full-year forecast of a minimum of £7.5 million. Then in mid-June **Bowater** cum **Ralli** bid £51 million for Hanson, offering fourteen of its shares for fifteen of Hanson's. Hanson shares jumped 20p on the news to 172p, and it was announced that the Hanson interests controlling 13.4% would accept, as would Slater Walker with between 5% and 7.5%. It was vigorously denied by the Slater camp that this was in any way a contrived marriage created by Jim Slater "moving the pieces around the chess board". In any case, the objection became academic when five weeks later the proposed merger was referred to the Monopolies Commission and Bowater bowed out. Then in September, Hanson sold two of BHD's principal divisions for £13.6 million cash, retaining a rump worth £2 million earning £500,000 a year, and the market wondered why Hanson would have wanted to accept a bid from anyone. The shares now stood at 121p, backed by net assets of 100p of which 50p was in cash and were on a 1972/73 P/E of 9. In December it became clear where Hanson's ambitions lay. Two acquisitions were made in the US. The first was a 24% stake in building materials group, Gable Industries, for £4.5 million, and the second was Howard Smith, a producer of edible oil and animal foodstuffs, for which £13.7 million was paid. Vice Chairman Gordon White justified this substantial move into America on the grounds that the country was "better equipped to withstand crisis than any other", adding that it would not be long before at least 50% of the group's earnings would be coming from overseas. Full year figures announced at the same time came out at £8.25 million, handsomely beating the £7.5 million forecast, and leaving the shares at 90p on a modest P/E of 6.7.

Sainsbury comes to market

One of the most popular new issues of the year, and the biggest one to date, was **Sainsbury's** offer for sale of 27% of its equity at 145p for an overall valuation of £117 million. There was no forecast for the coming year and the P/E on the 1972/73 figures was a lofty 20.6 compared with Tesco's 17, but the offer was 14.5 times oversubscribed, pulling in a record £495 million. The shares opened with a premium of 17p in very active trading. Frozen food group **Bejam** also attracted an enthusiastic response when it offered 25% of its equity or 2.75 million shares at 72p. The P/E was a relatively modest 16.5, and on the first day of trading the shares opened at 118p. 1973 was also the year in which Asil Nadir (29) made his first public appearance in the role of Chairman and Managing Director of **Wearwell**, a "cash and carry" wholesaler of mens' wear from stock. Out of an equity capital of 8 million shares, 3.2 million were offered for sale at 46p on a P/E multiple of 10.9. The issue was well received and after opening at 53p, the shares quickly settled down to around the 50p level.

1974

FT 30 INDEX 1974

Into the abyss

Wall Street saw a New Year rally which carried the Dow up 37 points to 880, boosted by a flurry of Prime Rate cuts, a reduction in margin requirements and President Nixon's so-called "oil initiative" designed to promote co-operation between the oil-producing and the oil-consuming nations. London, on the other hand, took a gloomier view, influenced by estimates that the oil price rise would add another £1.8 billion to the UK's already soaring import bill. There were also no signs of the miners or the railworkers moderating their demands, lay-offs topped the million mark as energy-starved industries cut production, and there was renewed anxiety over sterling, which by the middle of January had plunged to a new record low against the dollar at $2.18. The decline in industrials was slowed to some degree by a 0.25% reduction in MLR leading to an easing of liquidity fears and by increased oil supplies heightening prospects of a move to a four-day working week before long, but they caught up with a rush in the last days of the month when it became clear that a full-scale miners' strike was inevitable, and the FT 30 crashed to a seven-year low of 301.7. The fall made history in that the level of 305.3, which had marked the end of the 1968/71 bear market, had been breached, the first time that such a reversal had occurred since the introduction of the index in 1935. With a fall of 44.5% from the May 1972 all-time peak of 543.6, the decline had exceeded the extent of all previous post-War bear markets. Simultaneously, gilts achieved a new record low, losing nearly four points in January to 57.45, with yields topping 13%.

Mr Heath seeks a fresh mandate

Pressure now began to intensify for the Conservatives to call a General Election. The dramatic change in external circumstances created by the oil crisis seemed to be largely unappreciated by the miners, and the whole of the TUC, and since it was clear that the government would be forced into taking drastic measures to deal with the new situation, it was clearly vital to seek a stronger mandate. National Union of Mineworkers' Vice President, Mick McGahey, heightened the political tension in the country by calling for the TUC to "mobilise support for the miners, to burst Stage Three, to defeat the Tory government, and to elect a Labour government committed to the progressive policies of the Left". The index reacted by penetrating the 300 level, thereby wiping out all the gains since late 1959, and then rallied on the announcement that the election date was to be 28th February.

Expectations of a Conservative victory carried the FT 30 up to 337.8 on the eve of the declaration of the poll despite the miners' strike having begun and a TUC statement to the effect that it had reached an "understanding" with the Labour Party. The shock result with Labour five seats ahead of the Conservatives, but with no overall majority, caused the market to achieve yet another record, this time with a 24-point one-day fall (after 32.8) to 313.8. Mr Heath's failure to retain office with support from the minority parties, led to the return of Harold Wilson to Downing

Street with Denis Healey as his new Chancellor, asserting that their immediate priorities were to get the miners back to work and the rest of industry back to normal working, the repeal of the Industrial Relations Act, and the introduction of a budget as soon as possible. Henceforth, industrial relations were to be regulated by a strictly voluntary "social contract" whereby both sides of industry would work together in the national interest.

The miners go back to work

After a further dip to 309.6, the market rallied to 321.6 and sterling gained nearly 5 cents to $2.33 on relief that a period of uncertainty had ended and on hopes that the miners' strike would be quickly settled. The miners did indeed return to work, but only after winning a generous pay award that drove a coach and horses through Stage Three, but the uncertainty remained thanks to the inflationary fears rekindled by the settlement terms with its almost immediate impact on coal, steel and electricity prices.

It soon became clear that the "social contract" was destined to be a very one-sided affair when two days after the NUM had accepted the new pay award, the Yorkshire miners demanded another £20 per week, their leader Arthur Scargill adding that the only "social contract" he recognised was the one between him and his members. If Prime Minister Heath had called the election to decide who ran the country – the government or the trade unions – the answer was now clear. It was not the government of the day, whether Conservative or Labour, and with "their" government in office, the unions were determined to have their say. Furthermore, with Michael Foot as Minister of Employment, Anthony Wedgwood Benn as Minister for Industry talking of planning intervention in the country's top one hundred companies, and Denis Healey promising to squeeze the rich until "the pips squeaked", they were not going to be seriously opposed.

No help from Healey's budget

The market was becoming increasingly unsettled by these developments, and the new government's first budget at the end of March confirmed its worst fears. Admittedly, Chancellor Healey's task was not an easy one. He had to curb home demand and turn round the balance of payments without generating massive unemployment, restrain the monetary printing presses without

Chancellor of the Exchequer from 1974 to 1979, Denis Healey failed to gain the cooperation of the trade unions.

producing a new wave of bankruptcies, placate the IMF and foreign bankers without alienating his own followers, and at the same time reconcile his avowed aim of squeezing the rich without creating a crisis in the capital markets. In the event, he chose to let private industry and higher income groups bear the brunt of his deflationary measures. The basic rate of income tax was increased by 3p while the top rate went up from 75% to 83%, and to 98% for investment incomes. Corporation Tax was raised to 52% with an advance payment element, employers' National Insurance contributions were increased, and sanction was given to a broad range of price increases for the nationalised industries. And of course there was the Green Paper on the Wealth Tax. Coming on top of the price curbs introduced immediately after the election involving a 10% reduction in gross margins for all retailers, the first of the threshold pay awards, and another record trade gap, this was too much for the market to bear. Already bumping along just below 300, equities assessed the impact of these new impositions on company liquidity and promptly nosedived to 267.4 by the end of March, their lowest level since October 1962. Gilts followed suit, falling to a new low of 54.2 with yields at the long-end nudging 15%. Once again, gold shares were the only bright spot, approaching the 400 mark as the bullion price soared.

The calm before the storm

Adding to investor anxiety was a new wave of rumours about many of the secondary banks, and the hammering of stockbrokers Mitton Butler & Priest. The US economy was also becoming a source of worry as Prime Rates began to rise again, threatening the downtrend in UK domestic rates. However, with sterling holding up well at around the $2.40 mark, thanks to a $2.5 billion foreign loan arranged through the clearing banks and a $3 billion swap agreement, the government continued to reduce MLR in quarter point steps and to release Special Deposits in an effort to ease industry's liquidity problems. Encouraged by the prospect of further cuts in interest rates and by the belief that after an unprecedented 50% decline the bear market had to have run its course, the FT 30 quickly regained the 300 level by mid-April and managed to hold it, give or take a few points, until the third week of May. Gilts rallied strongly over the same period, with buyers taking heart from evidence that the money supply was at last being strictly controlled. This phase of relative optimism failed to last out the month.

No way out

By the end of May it was no longer possible to ignore what the CBI referred to as the "horrifying rate" at which industrial costs were rising and the implications for company profits at a time when world trade was declining and the government was dedicated to a policy of strict price controls. Any chance that the Labour government might have had of stabilising the situation was doomed to failure by its inability to impose any degree of wage restraint on the trade unions. As the retail price index rose, the timebomb of threshold pay awards left behind by the Heath administration now began to be triggered, pushing wage inflation up towards an annual rate of 30%. Furthermore, those unions that had not had the foresight to sign threshold pay agreements were threatening strike action in order to obtain them now.

Against such a background, there was no prospect that

industry, the powerhouse of the economy, could achieve the shift of resources into exports and capital investment necessary to correct the balance of payments deficit and to maintain it in surplus. Sentiment was further damaged by a renewed wave of collapses in the finance and property sector. **Vavasseur** was suspended "pending reorganisation following a substantial fall in the value of its assets", the £130 million **Lyon Group** was taken over by its creditors, and the £200 million **Stern Holdings**, one of London's biggest residential property groups, announced that it was having "cash difficulties". **Guardian Properties**, the group that had bought the shops from Jimmy Goldsmith, was suspended. **Keyser Ullman**, itself the subject of rumours about property lending problems, was forced to take over management control of **Grendon Securities** to protect the £17 million it had lent to Christopher Selmes to buy it, and **FNFC**, now down to 22p, yielding 12.5% and on a P/E of 3, admitted that its provisions against losses had probably been inadequate.

Cash is King

Already back into the 280/290 range by the end of May, the FT 30 paid less heed to further interest rate cuts than to Jim Slater's much publicised speech at Slater Walker's AGM when he announced disposals so far in 1974 totalling some £50 million, adding that "cash is the best investment now". Wall Street was also no help at this stage. Hopes that interest rates had reached a plateau were dashed as the Federal Reserve Board made it clear that the control of inflation would take priority over expansion, and Prime Rates began to rise again. Other countries' problems also made themselves felt with the collapse of Germany's Herstatt Bank, and on the last day of June the FT 30 was close to 250, gilts were challenging their all-time low, and the Dow was barely holding the 800 level in the wake of the collapse of the Franklin National Bank. There were now real fears that the fall in markets could become self-feeding.

The £500 million 'lifeboat' for the secondary banks created by the Bank of England in the wake of the London & County collapse plus another £50 million pledged by the

Crown Agents, itself a heavy property lender and a major shareholder in FNFC, was beginning to look woefully inadequate. As for the private industrial sector, there seemed to be no hope of solving its liquidity problems. The fall in share prices and the huge rise in interest rates had effectively killed off the new issue market and the bond market, and banks were in no mood to lend money, especially to those companies which really needed it. The suspicion of the Lex column voiced on 25th May that "something nasty is about to happen" appeared to have been very well founded.

Heading for below 200

A few commentators wondered whether staying on the sidelines after such an unprecedented fall in equities would in due course be seen as a classic case of lost opportunity. However, their views lacked conviction in the context of a corporate sector caught in the trap of excessive taxation, sharply rising production costs, strict price controls, and the almost daily evidence of its results with its devastating impact on confidence soon came to be known widely as the "Doomsday Machine".

There was a modest rally in gilts and equities, ahead of Chancellor Healey's minibudget on 23rd July, but despite his announced intent "to attack inflation at its source", the measures, which included a reduction in VAT from 10% to 8%, a slight easing of dividend controls, doubling of regional employment premiums and more food subsidies, did not impress the market. It was much more concerned with rumours of further trouble in the finance and property sectors, talk that even tighter price curbs were under discussion for inclusion in the Labour manifesto, and a fall in the Dow towards 750 as Dr Burns of the Federal Reserve Board warned of yet higher interest rates to counter inflation, with sentiment further unsettled by the moves to impeach President Nixon. By the end of July the FT 30 was back to a 16-year low of 236.4 and gilts had lost all their pre-budget gains. August was even worse. The month saw the country's premier HP company, **United Dominions Trust**, forced into degearing with a £30 million rescue package; once high-flying **Triumph Investment Trust** reporting a near £20 million loss after provisions against loans and write-offs; and the collapse of **Court Line**, the country's second largest tour operator.

On the political front, Minister for Industry, Anthony Wedgwood Benn, unveiled his plans for intervention in industry, designed to greatly increase the degree of State control, and with an eye to a likely October election, President of the powerful engineering workers' union, Hugh Scanlon (later to become Baron Scanlon of Davyhulme), called the Tories and the Liberals "enemies of the working class" and warned of industrial chaos if Labour lost. The July trade gap was a near record £478 million thanks to a fading of the export boom and a growing non-oil deficit, causing concern about sterling and severely restricting the scope for any sort of reflationary budget in November. And in America, the resignation of President Nixon and his succession by Gerald Ford failed to help markets there and the Dow lost another 100 points to 656 by the end of August. This atmosphere of universal gloom pushed the FT 30 to 199.8 on 19th August, wiping out 16 years of gains. With a decline of 63%, the 1972/74 bear market was now the worst on record, beating that of 61% from November 1936 to June 1940, and the 52% drop from 1929 to 1932. The Government Securities index also hit a record low of 53.13 during the month as yields on undated stocks topped 16%, thereby maintaining a very large yield gap with equities returning an average 9.62%.

The Arabs start buying

September opened with the news that wage rates had doubled during the first seven months of the year and were now rising at an annual rate of 19%, and an FT Business Opinion Survey which revealed that fears about the impact of rising costs and controlled prices upon profit margins and earnings on capital employed were now widespread throughout industry. There was also another hammering on the Stock Exchange, this time of brokers Tustain L'Estrange, making the fifth this year; an unconvincing denial from another HP company, **Mercantile Credit**, that it was in financial difficulties; and **Lloyds Bank** reporting a loss of £33 million due to "irregularities" at its Lugano branch. The only bright spot of the month was a Kuwaiti bid of £107 million for **St Martins Property**.Coming so soon after Abu Dhabi's £36 million payment for a 44% stake in Commercial Union's head office building, this raised hopes of further reinvestment of Arab oil money bearing in mind that at their current valuation, all the constituents of the FT 30 could be bought by Saudi Arabia out of six months of oil revenues.

The setting of the election date for 10th October immediately ushered in a new period of uncertainty and there was little comfort for investors at a time of national crisis to read in Labour's manifesto that the Party's main objective was "to bring about a fundamental and irreversible shift in the balance of wealth and power in favour of working people and their families". Meanwhile Wall Street was fast heading towards the 600 level, destroying the myth of the "glamour stock" and the two-tier market in the process. Thus Avon and Polaroid were now down by 50% on the year, Fairchild and Dr Pepper by 30%, and even such proven growth stocks as Xerox and IBM had lost 25% and 15% respectively. The Dow ended the month at 607 with the FT 30 similarly depressed at 188.4, and markets around the world down by an average of 40%, seeming to heed Dr. Kissinger's warning that the strains on the world economy were threatening "to engulf us all in a general depression".

The "Doomsday Machine" rolls on

In the days ahead of the election, the market steadied in the belief that whichever party won would have no choice but to take urgent action to ease the corporate liquidity situation and to restore profitability as well as keeping wages and personal consumption under strict control. This view gained credibility from the news that corporate profits, which had risen 30% during the first nine months of the year, were now falling sharply, but the more cynical thought that industry was being deliberately weakened to the point where it would fall into the outstretched arms of Mr Benn and his National Enterprise Board. There was also no evidence that if Labour won, as seemed likely, it would use anything stronger than exhortation to get the unions to live up to their side of the social contract and moderate their wage demands.

In the event, Labour retained office with a majority of 3 and the FT 30 rallied to over 200 on Mr Wilson's promise that he would take measures to help industry and stimulate investment. However, the Queen's Speech made no mention of any such priority while nationalisation plans figured largely, and by the end of October the index was below 200 again with gilts hitting new lows in reaction to the inevitable increase in the borrowing requirement and the latest inflationary pay awards. All eyes were now on the budget scheduled for mid-November, but its £1.6 billion of relief to industry failed to offset the huge prospective increase in the PSBR, now quantified at £6.3 billion compared with the March forecast of £2.73 billion. Even the Chancellor admitted that the figure was "disturbingly large", and equities, gilts and sterling all fell sharply on fears that overseas confidence would be upset, making a continuation of high domestic interest rates necessary to attract capital to finance the trade deficit.

National Westminster in the firing line

During the remainder of the month, the decline accelerated. The FT 30 fell into the 160/170 range to a 20-year low, the All Share index went into new low ground, the gilts index came within a whisker of the 50 level and the pound reached a record 20.8% weighted depreciation against its December 1971 benchmark. Adding to the gloom were the triggering of the latest threshold pay increases, this time for another 10 million workers, serving to push the rise in wage rates up to 26.4%, and indications that the miners were preparing another huge pay claim with no regard for the social contract or a productivity deal proposed by the National Coal Board. Confidence was further damaged by the collapse of **Triumph Investment Trust**, the suspension of **Jessel Securities**, and renewed fears over the financial stability of **Slater Walker**, **FNFC** and **Keyser Ullman**, as well as practically every property company, all accompanied by falling share prices. But most damaging of all were the rumours about the clearing banks, and **National Westminster Bank** in particular.

By the end of the month, NatWest and Lloyds were both below their par values and the Bank of England took the unprecedented step of issuing a denial that the former had requested or been offered large-scale support. Apart from talk of foreign exchange dealing losses, the principal source of anxiety was over property lending. It was plain to see what bad debts in this area had done to the secondary banks, and the clearing banks were estimated to have lent well over a billion on property in the context of capital and reserves of the Big Four and the two Scottish clearers of £2.7 billion in total, all at a time when their normal lending to industry was looking none too secure.

The last lap

No one was looking for a pre-Christmas rally in London or indeed in New York where the Dow had just crashed trough the 600 level for the first time in 12 years on growing signs of a deepening recession. The first week of December saw the publication of an FT Business Opinion Survey showing that industry expected the trend of costs and prices to worsen; British Leyland, the country's biggest exporter, going cap in hand to the government for financial assistance; and the National Institute forecasting a 25% inflation rate in 1975 and for once offering no solutions. The Stock Exchange called for monthly returns from its member firms in order to detect any liquidity problems as early as possible.

Almost the last straw was the November trade gap which, at £534 million, was the highest ever, and the FT 30 slumped to 150 while the Government Securities index slipped below 50 for the first time. Above all, there was no sign whatsoever of any action by the government to produce a credible anti-inflation policy which relied upon anything more than pious and obviously misplaced hopes about the value of the social contract. The vanity of these hopes was underlined by the strike record for the first 11 months of 1974 which with 13.9 million lost working days was rather more than twice that for 1973 under a Conservative administration. Not surprisingly, against such a background, 1974 turned out to be the worst performing year ever for the stock market. The FT 30 at 161.4 was down 53% and no less than 70% from the May 1972 high of 543.6, while the Actuaries indices were all down 54%. At 49.8, the Government Securities index had lost 18.4% in 1974 following a 14% drop in 1973. Consols now yielded 17% while equities returned a strictly historic 12.5%. Only gold and gold shares gained, beneficiaries of anxiety over monetary stability, and bullion closed the year up 65% at $186 with the FT Gold Mines index adding 117% at 353.5.

What went wrong?

There was no shortage of postmortems on 1974 but at its most fundamental level the problem was simply a massive erosion of real corporate profits at a time of accelerating inflation when rigid price controls coupled with a penal tax system made it impossible to earn a real return on investment. Lex attempted to put some figures on it by calculating that between 1968 and the second quarter of 1973, trading profits of the corporate sector before depreciation and tax expressed as a percentage of Gross National Product net of stock appreciation, fell from 12.7% to 10.1%. By the second quarter of 1974, the figure had fallen to 5.7%. In the space of a year, cash flow of industrial and commercial companies had dropped from an annual rate of £4 billion to £1 billion while capital spending had been slow to respond, still running at an annual rate of £5 billion.

Disappointment with this drop in real profitability led to the collapse of the new issue market and the long-term bond market, and while in 1972 new issues in each category were £300 million, in 1974 redemptions of long-term debt were greater than both of them together. This resulted in a huge increase in the importance of bank finance and in the year to November 1974, advances to manufacturing industry rose by £2.7 billion or 40%. If this unhappy combination of inflation and recession triggered by the massive and unexpected cost in the price of oil was a worldwide phenomenon as evidenced by the collapse of stock markets everywhere, the impact in the UK was that much worse thanks to the coincidence of political factors. Thus the monetary free-for-all unleashed by the revolution in credit and competition introduced by the Conservatives, clashed head on with Labour's free-for-all policy on wages coupled with one of strict control on prices.

The "X" factor

Even though the market was just days away from its biggest rise in history, at the turn of the year few authoritative commentators were prepared to venture a forecast. Lex did not feel confident enough of the sort of climate that 1975 would bring to list any New Year selections. It should not be forgotten that at the time there were real fears that Britain was heading for social and political chaos. Official indulgence of the ugliest elements on the left of the Labour Party and the unions was causing great concern in the Establishment, and there was an "unofficial" resurgence of potential counter-movements by the Right. Harold Wilson publicly denounced "smear" campaigns against him and there was serious speculation about a coup. Colonel David Stirling, the war hero known as the Phantom Major for his exploits behind enemy lines, formed "Great Britain '75" made up of former professional soldiers who were ready to infiltrate picket lines to keep essential services going in the event of large-scale trade union disruption. Condemned by Labour minister, Reg Prentice, for his "provocative" action, Colonel Stirling assured the country that he would not deploy his team unless requested to do so by the government of the day.

Financials count the cost

In 1974 the chickens came home to roost for the finance and property sector. The year began with **Cornhill Consolidated** admitting to liquidity problems at the same time as it was being sued for $8.5 million by an American insurance company for conspiracy to defraud. Also in

January, **P&O** bailed out **Bovis** with a £25 million bid, or one fifth of what it had been prepared to offer two years earlier, all thanks to the problems of finance subsidiary, **Twentieth Century Banking**.In early March, FNFC reported profits up from £13.23 million to £18.42 million despite heavy exposure to property sector lending, but at 37p with estimated net worth of 40p a share, the group was widely considered to be stable, especially bearing in mind its 50/50 share with the Bank of England over the London & County rescue operation. Nevertheless the chairman referred to the group's "uncertain outlook", adding that the emphasis in the coming year would be more on consolidation than expansion, and immediately began disposing of some of its industrial interests for cash. The interim figures were well down at £3.8 million against £9 million, after provisions out of profits, and it was pointed out that a large part of the £5 million contributed to the consortium loan for London & County would be "irrecoverable". The share price was now in single figures as investors worried about the apparent lack of provisions against losses on the group's £400 million loan book.

By contrast **Keyser Ullman** was judged to be a model of conservatism, having made provisions of 12% against total loans in 1973/74 with £17 million, or an effective 30%, against the property element despite having made a profit of some £30 million on the sale of Central & District. A press conference had been called in July to announce the results and at the same time the resignations of the two principal Dalton Barton directors largely responsible for the property book, Jack Dellal and Stanley van Gelder. Nervous ahead of the press conference, the shares rallied to 115p on news that the Prudential had increased its stake in the bank by buying shares from the resigning directors. The shares continued to weaken during the rest of the year in common with those of other secondary banks, and at the end of December were back to 34p on the interim statement that further provisions would have to be made against property lending and that profits in the first half of 1974/75 were substantially lower with the trend not likely to be reversed in the second six months.

Doubts grow about Slater Walker

There is no question that Jim Slater was quicker to sense trouble ahead than were his fellow bankers, primary as well as secondary. In February he sold his remaining 50% stake in Crittall Hope Engineering to Norcros for £6.3 million in Loan Stock, and it was clear from the 1973 results announced at the end of March that banking and money market profits had taken over from those formerly supplied by dealing. Profits were only marginally higher after adjustments at £23.4 million, but it had been a difficult year and, having reduced much of the group's equity exposure before the worst of the market slide and with a £50 million cash pile, Slater was considered still to be in a position to weigh up his options rather than be forced to concentrate on survival like some. The shares then stood at 140p, selling on a P/E of 8, and were regarded as a bid target for one of the larger banking groups looking for innovative management. In quick succession, the satellite companies in America, Australia and South Africa were all sold off to local interests. The half share in South Pacific Properties, a leisure development venture, was sold to P&O, the other partner, and the German interests comprising an industrial holding company and a small merchant bank were sold to Bowater for £3.5 million. Jim Slater explained the rationale behind his move into cash in very striking terms at his AGM on 30th May, saying: "Many people in recent months have found you cannot always turn property into cash, you cannot always turn large lines of shares into cash, you cannot always turn pictures into cash. Cash you can always turn into other things." Privately he is reputed to have used even more forthright language, recommending investment in gold coins and tins of baked beans, all to be tucked away in a mountain hideout with a machine gun to protect them!

In July he sold his controversial stake in Singapore-based Haw Par for around £10 million, but despite all the disposals to date, the interim figures announced in August showed that even though short-term loans and creditors had been reduced by a third to £205 million, the group was still highly geared with £142 million of unsecured loan stocks and long-term loans. Rumours about the group's liquidity position in the context of a share price that had fallen dramatically to 50p, prompted a statement from the company in October reaffirming its "inherent financial strength" and making reference to "completely uncharged free assets" of £65 million or 86p a share. Lex concluded that there was "no reason to be concerned" about the financial state of the Slater Walker Group but expressed some puzzlement about the decision to inject another £5 million into the insurance side given that it was reported to already have £21 million in cash.

In November Slater completed the withdrawal from the Far East with the sale of Slater Walker Overseas Investments to Hutchison for £4.4 million. The deal was described as a "further movement in the retrenchment of the group". Later that month the first acquisition in over two years was made with the purchase for £1.58 million cash of Jessel's Unit Trust Management Company, thereby doubling Slater Walker's funds under management to £80 million. Some saw this as Slater going back to what he did best. Then just before Christmas, the 20% stake in Costain was sold to a group of Arab investors for £4.17 million, albeit at a £3.2 million loss on the original purchase price. Still, Slater had never been averse to taking a loss when he thought it necessary, a policy given point a few days later when Bowater announced that it was winding up the German merchant bank bought from Slater in June. Despite these disposals, the share price continued its relentless decline, ending the year at 35p.

Property shares become "penny stocks"

Among the worst performing stocks in 1974 were those of the highly geared property companies. Huge development programmes embarked upon with borrowed money at low rates of interest at the top of the market, had become disaster areas. Rising interest rates coupled with collapsing property values wiped out profits, generated staggering losses and uncovered loans on an almost heroic scale. John Ritblat's **British Land** ended the year at 9.5p, down from a 1974 high of 122p, **English Property Company** fell to 32p from a high of 112p, and even Jeffrey Sterling's **Town & City**, into which he had merged his **Sterling Guarantee** in a £34 million reverse bid in April, dropped from 59p to 11p despite a string of very timely disposals by the new chairman. Even the blue chips in the sector suffered. **Land Securities** fell from 212p to 89p and **Hammerson** from 470p to 175p, but they were in the vanguard of the recovery while the position of some of the most highly geared companies actually continued to deteriorate.

No problems for BTR and Racal

BTR may have suffered in share price terms in 1973 and 1974, but this reflected no disappointment with the group's performance. Despite a difficult year in automotive products because of rising raw material prices and the price freeze, pretax profits for 1973/74 were up 38% at £6 million on sales only 20% higher overall but 46% higher overseas. The first half of 1974 continued this remarkable trend with pretax profits up two thirds at £4 million on sales 42% greater at £50 million. £10 million was considered to be the target for the full year and at 52.5p the shares were yielding 9.1% and selling on a prospective P/E of 3.7. Thanks to its electronics tag, **Racal** always had a more glamorous image than BTR and a higher rating to match. The £3.9 million forecast for 1972/73 had been comfortably exceeded at £4.27 million, and then in 1973/74 the forecast of £5.3 million was beaten handsomely again with a total of £6.25 million. At this point overseas sales and exports represented 50% of the total and, at 137p, the shares were selling on an historic P/E of 11.7. By December, when the interim results were announced, the share price was back to 100p despite a 46% advance in pretax profits and a forecast of "in excess of £8 million" for the full year. Racal's equity market capitalisation was now £24 million, the dividend yield 4% and the historic P/E 9.4.

US acquisitions pay off for Hanson and Goldsmith

Rising overseas sales, especially in the US, served to more than make up for **Hanson's** problem areas in the UK and first half figures for 1973/74 showed profits up 11% to £5.5

million with £10 million in prospect for the full year. Seacoast, a fish-farming operation and the biggest US purchase yet, was acquired in January, and its contribution in the second half of the year brought the year's total to £10.4 million. In spite of holding cash balances of £22 million, Hanson's share price was not spared the widespread declines of the second half of the year, and at 55p with an equity market capitalisation of £17 million, the yield was 14%.

Cavenham suffered much more in share price terms than the other proven growth stocks. To a large extent this was due to the complex nature of the group's controlling companies, and to the close links with Anglo-Continental, Goldsmith's banking arm, itself very much involved with Slater Walker's financial and property interests. After reporting 1973/74 pretax profits of £30 million, the interim figures for 1974/75 showed only a modest increase at £16.4 million after sharply higher interest costs, but sales were swelled to £800 million by the inclusion of Grand Union. The shares ended the year at 40p to yield 13.8% on a P/E of 2.8.

Brent Walker makes its debut

May 1974 saw the stock market launch of what was to become the **Brent Walker** leisure empire following the merger of the original business set up by George and Billy

George and Billy Walker laid the foundations of what was to become the Brent Walker leisure empire with the takeover of Hackney and Hendon Greyhound Stadium in May 1974.

Walker with Hackney and Hendon Greyhound Stadium. The company had begun life in the mid-'sixties selling baked potatoes from four sites in the City under the name Billy's Baked Potato, and then quickly acquired some restaurants in the West End. Profits had risen from £16,000 in 1968/69 to £180,000 in 1972/73, and the shares of the combined group were floated at 38p on a P/E of 10 based on a forecast of profits of not less than £615,000 in 1974/75. The market capitalisation at the offer price was £3.42 million.

1975

No bell rang

The first trading day of the New Year opened inauspiciously with the suspension of **Burmah Oil** at 100p when the company was forced to call for government assistance to help service its huge US loans. This came as a shock to the market in spite of an 80% decline in the share price during the year, since first half profits in 1974 of £28 million compared with £57 million for the whole of 1973. There had been a warning about a "substantial loss" from the tanker side in the second half but no indication that it would create an overall loss.

In the event, the story of Burmah was of a gamble that failed. The two acquisitions that were intended to catapult Burmah into the major league were the huge tanker operation and Signal Oil and Gas in the US. They were financed by $650 million in loans from American banks but the resulting heavy gearing left Burmah unable to cope with the sharp down-turn in trading conditions in 1973 and the gaping hole in its balance sheet created by the fall in the value of its holding in BP from £443 million to £182 million. The Bank of England agreed to guarantee the loan but in return Burmah had to hand over 51% of its North Sea operations, its 21.6% holding in BP together with its 2% in Shell. Nervous speculation about the size of the likely loss for the year meant that the shares were changing hands at around 45p in unofficial dealings. The FT 30 lost 10.8 to 150.6 on the news and by the end of the first week had shed another 4.6 points to 146 on 6th January as **Bowater** crashed 20% to 51p after 44p on rumours of liquidity problems and losses on commodity trading. This was the bottom of the market but true to form, no bell rang. In retrospect it was argued that the market was absurdly cheap and with the FT 30 yielding 13.4% and selling on a P/E of 3.8, there was no doubt that it was discounting almost every conceivable disaster.

The recovery begins

The recovery began slowly and cautiously. Legend has it that the turn was engineered by a buying programme initiated after a lunch given by Prudential at their High Holborn office attended by fund managers from the other leading insurance companies. On 7th January the index rose 7 points to 153 with rises outnumbering gains by only 5 to 4, but significantly markings were the highest for six weeks, and Government Securities added 1.21 to 50.86 encouraged by more Prime Rate cuts in the US and clear signs that the Federal Reserve Board was moving towards a less restrictive monetary policy. The Dow had bottomed at 584 just before Christmas and had added 50 points in heavy trading during the first two weeks of the New Year. London's advance now began to gather momentum, aided by hints from the Chancellor of a tightening of the social contract and two 0.25-point cuts in MLR, bringing it down to 11%. Activity also picked up sharply and by the end of the month the FT 30 had topped 250 for a 73% gain on its 6th January low point while the Dow had crossed the 700 level on record volume. The Bank of England now had an £86 million profit on the BP shares taken over from Burmah just three weeks earlier! It was time for a pause, and it came with the publication of the White Paper on Government Expenditure which provided a reminder that its apparently inexorable rise meant that after claims on available resources had been met, there would be very little left over for personal consumption and that tax rises were inevitable.

The setback was short-lived, and encouraged by a much reduced trade deficit in January together with a compromise settlement on the latest miners' pay claim, equities surged ahead again, crossing the 300 level on the last day of February with the Government Securities index reaching 58 in the wake of a further cut in MLR to 10.5% and indications of a continuing worldwide downtrend in interest rates. One political event of great significance during the month was the ousting of Edward Heath from the leadership of the Conservative party, and his replacement by Margaret Thatcher.

Sterling passes judgement

Companies were not slow to take advantage of this new-found enthusiasm for equities to try to rebuild their balance sheets and in the three weeks to mid-March there were calls for £180 million in rights issues. They were relatively easily absorbed but kept the index below 300 until the budget in mid-April when expectations of action by the Chancellor on wages and public expenditure prompted a renewed advance. In the event a £1.25 billion increase in taxes through 2p on the standard rate and surcharges on drink and tobacco with VAT up from 8% to 25% on luxury items, was taken as evidence that Mr Healey meant what he had said about raising taxes unless the social contract was more strictly observed. There was also a promise of a £1 billion reduction in public expenditure but given that the PSBR for 1975 had more than tripled to £9 billion since he had become Chancellor, and looked like heading for £12 billion in the current year, this carried little weight. Equities received a further boost in early June from the Referendum resulting in a 2 to 1 vote in favour of the UK staying in the EEC and from further gains in the US, taking the Dow well above 800, but after peaking at 365.3, the index began to slip as investors turned their attention to what sterling was saying about the economic situation.

The momentum of the recovery in equities and gilts to a large extent had masked the deterioration in sterling, where the weighted depreciation had increased from 21.7% in early January to 28.9% by the end of June. But if the domestic market had been impressed for a time by Chancellor Healey's "tough" budget and his "tough" talking to the unions, clearly the international community had not. Now, thanks to the plight of sterling, the message had got through at last to the domestic market, Mr Healey and the TUC included. To cure inflation by demand reduction alone would cause such severe unemployment that there was seen to be no alternative but to introduce a workable incomes policy combined with a reduction in public expenditure enabling government financing to get back on a sound footing and to leave room for resources to be diverted for the improvement of the trade balance and for productive investment. The demotion of Mr Benn from his post as Minister for Industry to the Department of Energy was another step designed to rebuild business confidence.

Biting the bullet

Even the TUC saw which way the wind was blowing and came up with its own plan to fight inflation which TGWU General Secretary Jack Jones referred to as necessary "to avoid the destruction of the Labour movement". Chancellor Healey seized his opportunity and introduced a voluntary 10% (or £6 per week) pay limit backed up by a veiled threat of statutory action, the latter to the great dismay of Employment Minister Michael Foot. The aim was to reduce inflation from 24% to 10% by the time of the next pay round in September 1976 and to single figures by the end of that year. This new mood of realism by the Government and its grudging acceptance by the TUC, marked a turning point for the market. The FT 30, which had fallen below 300 in July, stayed there throughout the first half of August, recrossed that level before the end of the month, encouraged by the first signs of a slowdown in the rate of wage rises and a consequent pick-up in business confidence. Even a continuing rise in unemployment and a further decline in sterling failed to dent the market's recovery as investors saw each new shock as likely to push the government further into following the unaccustomed path of financial rectitude. A rise in MLR to 12% in October prompted some nervousness, but taken in the context of hints of a request for an IMF loan, this was seen as further evidence of the government facing up to its responsibilities, and the market surged into the 360/370 range on rising volume.

The IMF takes a hand

In early November, Chancellor Healey made formal application to the IMF for a $2 billion loan and a team from that international body flew into London to "look at the books". Another rise in unemployment had prompted calls from the TUC for the imposition of import controls and rumours of a pre-Christmas reflationary package embodying such controls were seen as a possible threat to the granting of the loan. But with sterling now close to a 30% depreciation level and to a $2 exchange rate, Mr Healey could not take any chances. His package involved only very selective and temporary import restrictions in the textile sector together with an easing of HP curbs on consumer durables, cars excepted, but most important of all, he had won Cabinet agreement to public spending cuts of up to £3 billion. This was widely seen as the most important area of all given that the unplanned and out of control growth in public expenditure since the Government took office, meant that the public sector had become the chief engine of inflation. It was here that the deficit ran riot and where inflation was financed. The bailing out of Chrysler with a £180 million package designed to avoid embarrassing job losses indicated that the public purse was still open for really hard luck cases, but the huge operating losses in the coal, rail and steel industries had begun to drive home the lesson that overmanning and inefficient operation in the public sector could not be allowed to continue, whatever the trade unions might say. As Mr Healey had said at the Labour Party conference in October, capital investment in industry, public or private, is simply wasted in situations where there is persistent overmanning and constant strikes, adding that such laws of arithmetic are not changed by elections, an observation prompted by the fact that he had just been voted off the National Executive for these unsocialist views.

The year ended with the equity indices very close to their November highs, the FT 30 at 375.7, up 133%, and the All Share at 158.08, up 154%. Gilts, not surprisingly in the light of the obvious temptations for the government to keep spending, closed below the year's best, but at 59.83 the Government Securities index was still up 20%. Golds had a very see-saw year, with the FT Gold Mines index hitting a new peak of 442.3 in May, then relapsing sharply following the abolition by the IMF of the "official" gold price, to end the year at 243.2.

FNFC and Keyser Ullman clear the decks

Welcome though the upturn in the market was, it could do nothing to help the secondary banks and reflex gains in share prices in January were quickly lost as it became clear that their problems persisted. In May, **FNFC** provided some idea of the extent by reporting a loss of £8.3 million for 1974 after provisions of £33 million had wiped out trading profits of £27.3 million, but even after such drastic write-offs, a question mark still hung over the loan book totalling £390 million. The figures for the first half of 1975, released in October, provided a partial answer when the loss rocketed to £73 million after £91 million was provided against the loans. The shares were back to 2p by the end of the year with the Bank of England "lifeboat" continuing to provide support to avoid the further shocks to the banking and property sectors which would come from a forced liquidation. In fact almost half the £1.3 billion of support funds was taken up by FNFC and by leading HP company, **United Dominions Trust**. In the case of **Keyser Ullman**, too, it soon became obvious that there were still problems to solve and that provisions made at the time of the departure of Messrs Dellal and van Gelder had not been adequate. In July, with the share price now down below 50p, directors Ian Stoutzker and Roland Franklin announced their resignations, and two weeks later the company reported a loss of

£61 million after provisions of no less than £82.5 million. This was very much a deck-clearing operation and in December the bank announced operating profits for the first half of 1975/76 of £2.4 million, which translated into a £1 million loss after provisions. The share price ended the year at 45p after touching a low point of 32p.

Slater Walker begins to fade

Slater Walker staged a remarkable recovery on the back of the turnround in the market that began on 7th January, and from 27p on that day the shares rocketed to 79p five weeks later. Disposals totalling £5.75 million were made in March alone and after the 1974 results released later that month showed a £9 million drop in pretax profits to £14.5 million, the group was widely judged to have weathered the storm remarkably well. Net worth, which had fallen from 81p to 60.8p in the course of 1974, was now up to 83.6p, a performance that practically no other financial group could even approach. Disposals over a 15-month period now totalled £140 million and despite book losses of £40 million, bank balances still comprised a third of current assets, but a warning was given at the AGM in June that profits in the current year would be 'very low indeed'. The big question was in what direction Jim Slater would now go, and there was some speculation about the identity of the "new and attractive" investment areas he had recently mentioned.

Unfortunately, it was at this point that the Haw Par issue, first raised in Singapore in 1971, came live again. Investigations by the Singapore authorities had led to allegations that there might have been "misappropriation of company funds" and illegal share dealing for the personal benefit of the Slater Walker directors, including Jim Slater and Dick Tarling, through the medium of a company allegedly specially formed for the purpose, namely Spydar Securities (Hong Kong). If this hint of a scandal muddied the waters more than a little, the interim results released in August did nothing to help matters. Profits were down from £10.1 million to just £2.2 million thanks to the absence of dealing profits and to losses in the property portfolio. Sentiment was further unsettled by news that Jim Slater was selling some of his other shareholdings and his agricultural land investments in order "to reduce personal borrowings". Farmland had been a great favourite of Slater and there is a story that his agent, after querying just how much land he was expected to buy, received the answer, "Stop when you reach the sea"!

Jim Slater resigns

By October the share price was back to around the 50p mark, and then on 24th October Jim Slater stunned the City by announcing his resignation, not just from the company he had created but from City life, in order to devote more time to his "family and other interests". The share price lost 11p to 35p and the market fell 10 points on the news but recovered for a loss on the day of 2.7 at 354. Slater's friend and business associate, Jimmy Goldsmith, took control of the group and Lord Rothschild and Charles Hambro joined the board. Goldsmith announced that a "close scrutiny" of Slater Walker would be undertaken over the next three to four months, and the share price fell back to 20p on fears of what might be revealed. In December, the new board decided to cancel the interim dividend declared in October, and the shares fell back to a new low of 17p.

Just to complete the picture of an end of an era, a month earlier Malcolm Horsman had relinquished his executive appointment at Bowater which he had taken up when it had merged with Ralli International in 1972. Ralli's diverse interests had failed to fulfil their early promise and the combined group had put in a creditable performance only by virtue of Bowater's traditional activities.

Hanson and Goldsmith consolidate in the US

1975 was the year **Hanson** made his major move into the US. Former Vice Chairman, Gordon White, had already set up office in New York with the purpose of looking for suitable acquisitions. Those he had found so far proved their worth at the time of the interim results for 1974/75 when their contribution more than offset the downturn in property and building materials in the UK. As a result pretax profits were up from £5.5 million to £5.7 million and a total of at least £11 million looked attainable for the full

Lord Hanson (right) transformed a tiny Yorkshire-based company over twenty years into a multinational giant. Lord White (left) began to search out acquisitions for Hanson Trust in the US in the late 'sixties, and later embarked upon some of the biggest takeovers the country had ever seen.

year. Then in July, an £8.6 million rights issue was announced with the aim of facilitating further expansion in the US. On the back of a forecast doubled dividend, the shares jumped 22p to 162p, although one leading commentator described the move into the US as a "high risk strategy". Before the end of that month a $35 million deal had been agreed to purchase the textile interests of Indian Head. This was a cyclical business being bought very advantageously at the trough of a recession — 1974 profits had just halved to $6 million — at a 40% discount on net assets. Then in November, $7.5 million was paid for a 27% interest in Hygrade Foods, the well-known meat-packers, and when the 1974/75 results were announced in December, two thirds of the £12.1 million profits were seen to have been made in the US. With the shares at 122p, the market capitalisation was now £82 million and the group still had £21 million in cash.

Cavenham had not scored quite such an immediate

success with its US acquisitions as Hanson, and Grand Union, the East Coast supermarket chain, needed a $9 million write-off which resulted in a drop in 1974/75 profits from £29.5 million to £25 million. A significant improvement was forecast for 1975/76 and interim profits duly came in 18% up at £19.9 million, indicating a total for the year of £33 million for a prospective P/E of 8 with the shares at 130p.

BTR and Racal ignore the recession

BTR's overseas sales rose 74% in 1974/75 to represent 60% of total sales producing a pretax profit of £9.9 million. A further improvement was forecast for the current year, and the interim results in September showed that it was well on target with profits up 60% at £6.3 million on sales 50% higher. There had been a rights issue in July to raise £5.7 million but the object of the company's ambitions did not become clear until 1976. **Racal**'s profit forecast of "in excess of £8 million" turned out to be £9.5 million, a gain of 56% on sales up by 45%. There was also a one-for-one scrip issue. In December, first half profits weighed in at £6.24 million as against £2.8 million for the previous period, and a full year forecast of £15 million was made. Like BTR and Hanson, one of the secrets of Racal's success was the large overseas sales content which was now roughly 70%. The other was the absence of borrowings of any kind. BTR ended the year at 153p and Racal at 235p.

1976

FT 30 INDEX 1976

A flying start

The year opened on a high note. The FT 30 crossed the
400 level and reached 417.4 at the end of January, joining
in the worldwide rally led by Wall Street on expectations
of a continuing decline in interest rates. There was a lot
for the London market to be hopeful about. Industry was
more confident than at any time since November 1973.
Inflation was under some degree of control, thanks to the
pay and prices policy and the recession, and there were
real signs of an export-led boom developing. This latter
point seemed to be fully confirmed by the December trade
deficit, which at £79 million was less than half that of
November, bringing the 1975 total to £1.7 billion, or half
that of the previous year. The coming oil bonanza was
another major bull point. Only eleven years had passed
since drilling in the North Sea began and despite much
earlier scepticism, the area had proved to be one of the
most productive oil and gas basins in the world. By the
end of 1974 oil was flowing at the rate of a million barrels

a day, just when it was most needed, and oil shares were booming.

Company profits had risen just 4.3% in 1975, down from 33.1% in 1974, but for 1976 expectations were of a rise of around 20-25%. Unemployment was rising fast but while the TUC's response was to call for a £2 billion reflationary package, the Prime Minister avowed that the Government's anti-inflation drive would not slacken, hinting at a tough Phase Two. The aim, he said, was to reverse the UK economy's 30-year decline in order to enter the coming economic upturn with inflation under control and domestic resources not overstretched by an excessive rise in public spending. Any major reflationary moves were out of the question. Just to underline this tough message, the Chancellor's White Paper on public expenditure referred to his planned £2.4 billion "cuts" by 1978/79, as a "long, harrowing, but necessary process", and Jack Jones pressed for a continuation of the £6-a-week limit against strong opposition from his TUC colleagues. Equities had also been boosted by a rapid succession of cuts in MLR which by the end of January had fallen to 10%. Significantly, while the Government Securities index responded positively to this last reduction, rising 0.82 to 65.21, it took no notice of subsequent cuts and was back to 62.47 when MLR reached 9% on 5th March.

The problem was sterling, which had just fallen below $2. By the end of the month it was down to $1.93, with the authorities making no attempt to stem the decline in line with the then policy of accepting depreciation as long as the rate of inflation in the UK remained substantially higher than that ruling in other industrial countries. France blamed its withdrawal from an already very shaky "snake" that month on the UK's "uncontrolled devaluation" of the pound and also on Germany's adamant refusal to revalue the DMark. The aim of the policy was to stimulate export-led growth and keep interest rates down to encourage investment, thus buying time for an excessive rate of monetary expansion to be adjusted gradually to inflation goals.

Confidence begins to wane

Overseas holders of sterling seemed to be taking the view

that whatever a Labour Government might say about cutting public expenditure, it was neither willing nor indeed able to do so. Furthermore, plans for funding the public sector deficit looked certain to run into problems as the economic recovery picked up and industry began to compete for funds. In any case, the much-vaunted "cuts" announced so far were not immediate but only reductions in future planned expenditure, which was already more than the economy could bear. Overseas opinion was also influenced by the chaotic state of the UK motor industry, especially British Leyland, which had become a symbol of the country's industrial weakness and of the Government's inability to cure it. In receipt of Government funds and run by Government appointees, the company was still a hotbed of industrial unrest, crippling the country's principal export earner. Two factors now added to the uncertainty. One was the surprise resignation of Harold Wilson and doubts about the succession. The other was the April budget where tax cuts were rumoured to be linked to acceptance by the trade unions of a 3% pay norm. The election of James Callaghan two days before the budget removed one uncertainty and provided some relief even though the enhanced position of Michael Foot in the new cabinet continued to cause anxiety. The budget, however, did not help in that the trade-off between tax cuts and pay restraint was seen to accord to the trade unions a pivotal role in the formation of economic policy.

Sterling continues to slide

A flood of rights issues, including one for £200 million from ICI, helped to subdue the market in April and May, but also keeping it in check were real doubts that the Chancellor could persuade the TUC and its members to agree to a Stage Two incomes policy. After all, incomes restraint at a time of recession when the connection between the wage explosion of 1974 and the sharp rise in unemployment in 1975 had become obvious to all, was one thing. Quite another would be to gain acceptance for such a policy when an upturn was underway. There were also doubts that the Government's newfound enthusiasm for the role of the private sector could be maintained in such circumstances.

The budget had provided some useful concessions in the form of tax relief on stock appreciation and promised revisions of the Price Code, but the idea that industrial investment was a precondition for the eventual ability to indulge in social expenditure was totally lost on the left of the Labour Party. Relief that the TUC had agreed to compromise on a 5% pay norm helped to keep the FT 30 above 400 until the end of May, but the sight of sterling continuing to fall despite a 2.5-point rise in MLR, now began to erode investor confidence.

The problem was now seen to be a lack of monetary or fiscal support for the pay policy, hampering its present effectiveness and in due course ensuring its demise as well as that of the inflation reduction targets. There had been further talks with the IMF about a loan but the inevitable and predictable conditions attached to the granting of one were bound to cause such political problems for the Government that it was reluctant to endanger the delicate rapport that it had achieved with the TUC. Instead, in June, it opted for a $5.3 billion stand-by credit from the Central banks for six months, effectively buying time to put its house in order and thereby avoiding the necessity of going to the IMF. Sterling rebounded 5.5 cents to $1.77 on the news but gilts and equities remained largely unmoved, staying in the 62/63 and 370/390 range respectively until late August.

Public spending cuts become a priority

The Central bankers might have expected the implementation of a tighter fiscal policy in return for their loan, and coincidentally the BIS in a European report added that Britain should set money supply targets and cut back on its PSBR. Unfortunately, however good the Chancellor's intentions may have been, his resolve was soon to be severely tested. Jack Jones responded to hints of a Stage Three wages and prices policy by asserting that he would not support it and wanted an "ordered return to free collective bargaining". Then the monthly trade figures began to deteriorate alarmingly in May and June, forcing Mr Healey to look again at the idea of public spending cuts. Unfortunately just when he and the Prime Minister had steeled themselves to pushing them through, the unemployment figures soared to a new post-War record at 1.46 million. Their conviction that priority must be given to the strengthening of the country's industrial base and that the Party's supporters must "accept the cuts or see Labour driven from office", appeared to have moderated somewhat by the end of July when the first definitive cuts were announced. A planned £1 billion cut in the PSBR from the expenditure proposed in 1977/78 was to be offset by raising the employers' National Insurance contributions by £910 million.

The reaction of the markets was to believe that the Government once again was looking to the corporate sector's developing surplus to fund its public spending ambitions, and a month later the index was down to 350 with the pound coming under pressure again. The picture was complicated further both by a drought so severe that a three-day week was on the cards, and a challenge to the pay policy by the National Union of Seamen which served to undermine the whole accord between the Government and the TUC. Activity in the equity market was abysmally low at this point and of three new issues in July, **Hambro Life, Molins** and **Borthwick**, all were trading at a substantial discount to their offer price. Oils were a firm exception on North Sea exploration hopes.

Trying to square the circle

The problem for the Government was that it had a huge public spending programme to fund and that to do so, it needed to sell an equally huge amount of gilts. Its relative lack of success in doing so had led to a succession of interest rate rises, but as MLR rose another 1.5 points to 13% in mid-September, the question began to be asked whether the reliance on high interest rates alone to fund the Government deficit did not serve to perpetuate the recession which the burgeoning deficit was intended to offset. In fact, by this time it seemed clear that what lay behind the Government's difficulty in funding the PSBR had less to do with the level of interest rates, than with simply a lack of confidence in the stability of the pound and the Government's whole economic strategy. Thus a high rate was not going to prove attractive to investors if it sparked fears of a still rising trend. The policy of pushing up rates to a level from which it was hoped they would be expected to fall, known as the "Grand Old Duke of York" strategy, did not work for Mr Barber in 1972, and there was much less reason to think that it would work for Mr Healey in 1976. After all, everyone now knew what heights inflation could achieve under a lax monetary and fiscal regime, and there were no guarantees that the recent decline from those heights was going to persist. Indeed, the present policy actually threatened to reverse that decline.

In early September it was announced that the Government would apply to extend the $5.3 billion credit facility for a further three months but markets were not impressed at this further attempt to buy time and by the middle of the month the FT 30 was back to 335, Government Securities to 60.03 and sterling to $1.7350. The feeling was that the Government was simply waiting and hoping for "something to turn up".

"Crisis? What crisis?"

With yields at the long end of the gilts market now topping 15%, the Government launched a new tap stock with a 14.5% coupon, the highest ever. It was comfortably oversubscribed at an issue price of £96.50 and there were hopes that this modest success in funding a rapidly accumulating deficit would continue.

A week later, the Government's funding programme lay in tatters. A wave of selling from across the world had driven sterling below $1.70 and the new tap stock was now at a one-point discount as yields neared the 16% level. The spark for this new slide in sterling had been a "special case" treatment of the National Union of Seamen's claim which they had won by the simple expedient of threatening to strike, knowing full well that this was the last thing the Government wanted at such a critical juncture in its fortunes. An inflationary settlement, however, was almost as dangerous and a 4 cent fall in sterling on 28th September prompted Mr Healey to abandon his trip to Hong Kong for the Commonwealth Finance Minsters' Conference, while the

Prime Minister countered reporters' questions with "Crisis? What crisis?" as his Chancellor returned to Downing Street to formulate an emergency package preparatory to the now inevitable application for a $3.9 billion loan from the IMF. The timing was particularly unfortunate for the Chancellor from a political point of view in that the Labour Party Conference was in full swing, and while the delegates gave his policy their backing, they insisted that no strings should be attached to the loan, especially those concerning cuts in public spending. On the same day, they also voted over-whelmingly in favour of a resolution to take over the banks and the insurance companies!

Markets now began to take fright and by the end of the first week of October, the FT 30 breached the 300 level as MLR was raised 2 full points to a record 15% and £700 million of Special Deposits were called for. Gilts fell by between 3 and 4 points and the 14.5% tap stock now stood at a 4-point discount to its offer price just three weeks earlier as yields edged over 16%. Home loans soared to their highest ever level of 12.25% and a new tap stock with a 15.5% coupon was launched.

Grasping the nettle

The Government now had no choice but to grasp the nettle of public spending cuts regardless of the threat to Party unity, but it still took one further panic at the end of October to make them decide to do so. The Prime Minister appeared on the Panorama television programme, warning of the grave political consequences if the IMF were to try to force the Government to adopt policies which would be so harmful to the economy that it would go into a downward spiral. The next day there were rumours of an imminent rise in MLR to 18%, a devaluation to $1.50, and a split between the Chancellor and the Prime Minister leading to the resignation of the former. The Treasury took the almost unprecedented step of formally denying the resignation story, but by then sterling had fallen to $1.57, Government Securities to 56, and the FT 30 to 265.3. The Chancellor promised an economic package for late November, and on the bold assumption that it would contain the necessary

measures, markets began to recover, seemingly on the idea
that the worse the news, the more effective the package was
likely to be. By this time Mr Healey was perhaps influenced
more by the Conservatives winning two of the three by-elections in November, than by his own National Executive
voting 13 to 6 to oppose any cuts in public spending and a
motion to the same effect tabled by 100 Labour MPs. Within
a week the FT 30 was over 300 again and gilts and sterling
had risen sharply as talks with IMF representatives got
underway. News that the 15.5% tap stock had been sold out
gave a boost to the gilt market, as did a new squeeze on
bank lending in an attempt to bring the growth of money
supply under stricter control. The first stage of the
Government's monetary restabilisation programme had
been judged in the market to be a relative success, and
before the end of the month, MLR was reduced by a quarter
of a point to 14.75%.

Going straight

The gains in sterling, gilts and equities were consolidated
and then extended as December progressed, gathering pace
after the IMF-tailored package in the middle of the month.
There was an initial but short-lived disappointment with its
provisions which were thought to be half-hearted and likely
to make no more than a marginal contribution towards
correcting the fundamental imbalances in the economy.
However, second thoughts concentrated on the novel sight of
a Labour Government actually agreeing to cut back on its
public spending programme by £1 billion in 1977/78 and by
£1.5 billion in 1978/79, targeting such sacred cows as food
subsidies, roads, new housing and school buildings. This
would mean reducing the PSBR by £2 billion in 1977/78 to
£8.7 billion, and by another £3 billion in 1978/79 to keep it
at that level. Furthermore, the rate of growth of the money
supply, which had crept up to an annual rate of 27% in
September, was to be firmly controlled within a 9-13% band.
And perhaps most important of all was the fact that the
Government was now firmly in hock to the IMF and subject
to its supervision. Another quarter point off MLR just before
Christmas gave another boost to sentiment and the year

ended on a high note, further encouraged by the Dow breaking through the 1,000 level on expectations of the newly-elected President Carter providing a major stimulus to the economy. The FT 30 ended the year at 354.7, down 6% over the period but up 34% on the October low. The Government Securities index was practically unchanged on the year at 60.27 but this was up 8% on the October figure. Golds were the worst performer of all, with the FT Gold Mines index practically halving to 119.8 on fears about the long-term effect of demonetisation and the new official sales policy for physical gold.

Slater Walker — the final chapter

In January Slater Walker's new chairman, Jimmy Goldsmith, arranged for the transfer of Jim Slater's personal holding of 2 million shares at 23p to his own stable of interests. This deal effectively ended Jim Slater's relationship with the company he had created. The company, however, continued but despite drastic job cuts the new management was unable to turn the operation around. The share price began to weaken significantly in September and later that month a loss for 1975 of no less than £42 million was announced. Insolvency was only avoided thanks to the cooperation of the Bank of England, which not only made available a £70 million borrowing facility but also guaranteed £40 million of potential bad debts in the loan portfolio. The price dropped 9p to 7p on the news, and little encouragement was provided by the accountant's report. The banking side of the business was described as "inherently weak with too high a proportion of loans to 'in house' companies and their affiliates" and the insurance investment portfolios were criticised for having too high a property content and too many shareholdings of questionable value. There was also criticism of loans to directors, and loans to affiliated companies allegedly for the purpose of share support operations contrary to Section 54 of the Companies Act. Only the investment management and unit trust side, run by Brian Banks as a largely independent operation, received a completely clean bill of health. Slater eventually was charged on six counts, but all were dismissed on the basis that there was "no case to answer", and Singapore's application for extradition was rejected. Dick Tarling was not so fortunate and had to serve some months in Changi jail.

In August 1978 it was announced that the Bank of England was going to buy Slater Walker Limited, the banking operation, together with some properties and "other group assets". All the prior charge holders assented to the terms, and the ordinary shareholders agreed to a change of name to **Britannia Arrow Holdings** for their equity interest. Thus ended, not without some dignity, perhaps the most remarkable financial phenomenon of the post-War years.

Hanson boosts its US interests

Hanson's first move in 1976 was to make a tender offer for the balance of **Hygrade Foods**. Despite some legal obstacles the offer was successful, doubling group sales to £350 million, 80% of which now arose in the US. The acquisition focussed more attention on the group's US activities and in particular on the role of Gordon White whose 10% interest in Hanson Industries, the company controlling US operations, had not been disclosed to shareholders despite the fact that it had come to account for four fifths of total sales. Furthermore, given his obvious importance, the fact that he was not a director of the UK company also caused some concern. Later in the year, it was disclosed that Gordon White had bought his 10% stake for £265,000, or just £265 on the basis of 0.1% paid, and that a formula was being devised to buy him out. The fact that he had been practically solely responsible for the creation of the US side of the business and its remarkable contribution to the success of the parent company, now received less attention than the huge profit he would make on his modest investment. Interim profits were comfortably ahead at £7.8 million and a "substantial increase" was forecast for the full year which resulted in a figure of £19.2 million, establishing the group firmly among the top 300 US companies.

The final act of the year was an £8.5 million bid for the 75% of **Whitecroft Industries**, the Midlands based conglomerate, that it did not already own, the original stake having been purchased from Slater Walker. The bid was rejected by the Whitecroft board and its supporters as inadequate and, unwilling to pay up, Hanson dropped the bid. The shares ended the year at 108p.

Control of Cavenham shifts

1976 saw the first step in Goldsmith's plan to move control of Cavenham into French hands. His master company Générale Occidentale bought out the balance of shares in Générale Alimentaire publicly held, and passed them on to Cavenham in return for Cavenham shares, thus bringing its holding in Cavenham up from 39% to 51%. The 1975/76 results came out in June and showed expectations of £33 million comfortably exceeded at £34.7 million. The interim figures for 1976/77 recorded a 14% improvement at £22.7 million, but by then the share price had slipped back to 93p to yield over 9%. In Goldsmith's eyes this was too modest a rating for a company which had grown in ten years from practically nothing to become an international food giant, and the second stage of his plan began to take shape.

BTR and Racal go from strength to strength

Two weeks after revealing pretax profits for 1975 up by 62% to £16 million, **BTR** took its first step along the path of expansion into the US market with a £15.5 million bid for SW Industries, a leader in elastomeric roll coverings and web control systems. The acquisition came too late to have a great effect on the interim results for 1976, but on sales up just 19% pretax profits showed a 37% gain to £8.6 million. The shares then stood at 138p, yielding 8.1% on a P/E of 6, but by year-end had advanced to 150p. As usual, **Racal** beat its forecast of £15 million for 1975/76 by turning in a figure of £19.65 million, but it was the first half result for 1976/77 that really excited the market. Sharply rising demand for its military communications equipment and a relatively fixed cost base, sent profits soaring 85% to £11.5

million, prompting a forecast for the full year of more than
£28 million. At the time of the announcement at the beginning of December, the shares stood at 208p yielding 1.25%
on a dividend covered 17.5 times by earnings, but by the
end of the month they were up to 240p.

The secondary banks limp on

Continuing provisions still hampered the chances of
recovery at **FNFC** and **Keyser Ullman** despite the notable
absence of the sort of investigations and allegations that
had accompanied the demise of London & County and
Slater Walker. Still, the losses were equally staggering, and
while history seems to look upon the "secondary banking
crisis" as an exceptional and rather disreputable episode in
the country's financial development, it should not be
forgotten that at their peak all these companies possessed
the enthusiastic backing of the financial establishment. All
had major institutional shareholders, some of which were
represented on the board. Eminent Conservative politician,
Edward du Cann, was chairman of Keyser Ullman, leader of
the Liberal Party, Jeremy Thorpe, was a non-executive
director of London and County and Sir Gordon Newton,
chairman of the *Financial Times*, was also chairman of
Vavasseur. As top City journalist Ivan Fallon put it in a
memorable phrase in the *Sunday Telegraph* in October
1975, "At one time to be a Slater associate was akin in the
City to being a companion to Alexander the Great". Indeed,
given the huge provisions that had to be made by the Big
Four against the loan portfolios built up in the early 1970s,
it was as much a crisis for the primary banks as it was for
the secondary, with the former surviving only by virtue of
their much larger reserves.

Poseidon sinks beneath the waves

As a sad postscript to the heady days of the Australian
nickel boom when Poseidon was known as the "share of the
century", in September 1976 its quotation was suspended at

155p on grounds of "liquidity problems". The following month a receiver was appointed and the company was reported to have accumulated losses of A$16 million and debts of A$28 million. Western Mining and Shell subsequently acquired the Windarra prospect as a joint venture, and two years later Poseidon returned to the market as a gold mining company.

1977

FT 30 INDEX 1977

North Sea oil proves its worth

The New Year began with high hopes. On the external front, Saudi Arabia was acting as a moderating voice within OPEC, keeping oil prices down, and expansionary moves in the US boded well for Britain's exports. At home, sterling had recovered to the $1.70 mark after the Chancellor's November package and overseas confidence had been buoyed by the knowledge that the IMF was looking over his shoulder. There was also a growing realisation of what North Sea oil could be worth to the balance of payments given that the country was no more than two years away from self-sufficiency. It was only two years since the economy had emerged from its gravest post-War crisis and it was now clear that the policies of deficit financing intended to avoid recession, had in fact, served to perpetuate it. Even though gilt yields were high, apparently providing little incentive for investment in equities, there were grounds for hoping that the latter would be a longer-term beneficiary from the more realistic appraisal of the economic facts of life forced upon the Government since

1975. Sentiment was given another boost by the BIS agreeing to provide a $3 billion facility as security against a further rundown of foreign official sterling balances, and also by the plan to reduce sterling's reserve role by banning its use as a trading currency for transactions in which the UK was not directly involved.

News of a £21 million trade surplus in December, followed by further cuts in MLR to 12%, prompted a strong advance in equities to over 400 and in the Government Securities index to 65.5 at the beginning of February. But while capital markets responded quickly to Government action, inevitable time lags meant that neither the rate of inflation nor the numbers of unemployed could do so immediately. Thus with price rises comfortably outstripping the rise in earnings, there were going to be difficulties in negotiating a deal with the TUC over a third phase of wage restraint at a time when real incomes were being so severely squeezed. However, further falls in MLR and another trade surplus in February, ensured a rising trend in gilts and equities ahead of the budget at the end of March. Restrained by a still high rate of inflation, by the limitations imposed by the Letter of Intent to the IMF, and by the need to reach agreement over Stage Three, the Chancellor brought in a broadly neutral budget with £2.3 billion of tax cuts, £1 billion of which were conditional on a satisfactory Stage Three, and a rise in personal allowances and thresholds to help the lower paid, balanced by an £800 million boost to indirect taxation, largely on drink, tobacco and petrol duties. Markets were now subject to a two-way pull. The optimists argued that the fact of the Government observing the limitations on its actions imposed by the IMF guidelines at a time when there was so much slack in the economy, was bound to mean a continuing decline in interest rates, while the more cynical suggested that the Chancellor had been happy to introduce such a cautious budget since it left him with the scope to be more reflationary in the event of an election being called.

Time for a pause

Falling interest rates proved the more powerful influence for a time and by mid-May, after MLR had dropped by stages to 8%, the FT 30 reached a new peak for the year of

477.4, its highest point since June 1973. Meanwhile gilts had topped out with the Government Securities index at 71.48 as institutions, heavy buyers of gilts in the final quarter of 1976, had swung back to equities, seeing them as better value when the downtrend in interest rates apparently had run its course and inflationary trends had not.

But now uncertainties began to dominate both markets. The Retail Price Index in April rose by 17.5%, showing that there were still plenty of price increases coming through in the wake of the collapse of sterling in the last quarter of 1976. Short-term rates were rising in the US as the Federal Reserve Board reimposed a tight monetary policy to try to combat the persistence of inflationary pressures, and the Dow slipped below 900 to a new low for the year. And potentially most serious of all, union after union rejected the idea of a third phase of wage restraint, preferring a return to free collective bargaining in an effort to redress a situation where earnings were now rising at just about half the rate that prices were increasing. There was the further anxiety that the Labour Government's hold on office was looking increasingly tenuous. The so-called "Lib/Lab" pact had collapsed, the Conservatives had made gains of landslide proportions in by-elections and local elections, and the Finance Bill had been thrown out, upsetting a not insignificant part of the Chancellor's budget arithmetic. While a change of government no doubt would have been welcome in many quarters, the market's attitude was that with Labour following IMF guidelines and engaged in negotiating Stage Three with the trade unions, maintenance of the status quo at this stage was greatly preferable to the uncertainty of a General Election. By the end of July the FT 30 had lost nearly 50 points to 430 and Government Securities just over 4 points to 67.

Markets get their second wind

Then in August the mood of the markets changed abruptly for the better as fears about the Government's ability to secure a third stage pay deal and control the money supply without a rise in interest rates, suddenly seemed to melt away. The trigger was the decision of the authorities in the last week of July to abandon the policy of linkage with a weak dollar at $1.72, embarked upon at the beginning of the year as a rough and ready way of cushioning export margins. The support peg was now shifted from the dollar to the trade-weighted average providing a general index of sterling's value. The effect on confidence was dramatic and the result was the rapid establishment of a virtuous circle of further currency inflows, falling interest rates and booming gilt sales. £1.5 billion of gilts were sold in August as MLR dropped to 7% but equities were the biggest beneficiary. There was no "tap" to supply whatever the market wanted and a wave of buying sent the FT 30 to 500.9 on the last day of the month. Up to a point, nothing succeeds in the stock market like success and that point was still some way off. Overseas money continued to flow in, and reserves rose to a new record of £14.85 billion, reflecting confidence that the recession in the UK economy had bottomed and that with the benefits of North Sea oil already flowing, the prospects were bright.

In mid-September, the FT 30 hit a new all-time high of 549.2, on the same day a record trade surplus of £316 million was announced, and two days later MLR was reduced to 6%. However, the picture was soon upset by a run of disappointing profits statements from such industrial leaders as **GKN**, **Dunlop** and **Vickers**, and within a matter of days the index was heading back towards 500 again despite further reductions in MLR to 5%, its lowest level for five years, and another trade surplus in September indicating a probable surplus for the year as a whole.

Success brings its problems

Doubts centred on the likely difficulty of keeping the growth of money supply within the target range now that so much overseas money was pouring into the country, and fears that if this problem was countered by letting the exchange rate rise, then industrial competitiveness would suffer. The dilemma was partially resolved on the last day of October, immediately after the Autumn 'package' announcing more tax concessions and reaffirming the lower public spending targets embodied in the Letter of Intent to the IMF. The pound was to be cut loose altogether, clearly indicating that, for the moment at least, observance of monetary guidelines had priority over exchange rate stabilisation and industrial competitiveness. Sterling jumped six cents on the news to $1.8405, gilts remained steady, but equities dropped like a stone, losing 33 points on the week to 476, only to bounce back over 500 again a week later just as gilts began to weaken in anticipation of a reversal in the downtrend of interest rates.

The decision to free the pound worked to a degree. Currency inflows peaked at £20 billion, and the diversion of 'hot money' into the DMark and the yen meant that the UK's competitive position was relatively unaffected, but the market found it difficult to shake off its anxieties over the money supply and about the chances of Mr Healey managing to keep the growth of average earnings within his target limit of 10%. The raising of MLR by two full points to 7% at the end of November seemed to clear the air and at year end the FT 30 was up 36% at 485.4, gilts were up 30% at 78.09, and the FT Gold Mines index, up 11%, enjoyed a modest revival on the back of a strongly recovering bullion price, benefiting from a weak dollar and flying in the face of IMF sales.

Cavenham goes home to France

After asserting a corporate philosophy of concentrating on food companies, Jimmy Goldsmith surprised the market in January by taking a 35% stake in **Beaverbrook**, the Express Newspaper group, at a cost of some £2 million. The size of the deal was insignificant in relation to the whole group, but it still worried some investors who saw it as a perverse reaction to the blocking in the US of his attempted $350 million takeover of Schenley. By now **Cavenham** shares had an abysmal market rating totally out of line with the company's meteoric growth record, and there was little surprise when Goldsmith's master company, Générale Occidentale, made a bid of 120p for the 49% of Cavenham that it did not own. At the time the shares stood at 93p yielding 8.75% and were selling on a P/E of less than 5, and most commentators regarded the bid as woefully inadequate for a company with net assets of 150p earning 20p a share in 1977. It was an attempt, said Lex in the *Financial Times*, by the top of the pyramid to absorb the base. In the face of such adverse comment, Goldsmith dropped the 120p bid, but returned to the fray two months later with a partial bid of 155p cash designed to take his holding up to 75%. Despite further criticism, the bid was successful and then in August he proceeded to mop up the 25% rump with an offer in Cavenham preference stock valued at 127p a share against a suspension price of 81p. The net result was that for a total outlay of £40 million, the cost of the partial bid, Goldsmith had brought Cavenham, one of Europe's leading food groups making annual profits of very close to that figure, under his personal and private control. The top of the pyramid had indeed absorbed the base and it had used the latter's own capital to do so.

Racal looks to the US

In January **Racal** made its first major bid, which proved to be a double diversification, taking the group into the US and into a new product. The target was Milgo, an American computer peripheral equipment manufacturer, and after a hard fought battle Racal succeeded with a $63 million offer. Simultaneously, a £14.7 million rights issue was announced, accompanied by a full year forecast of £32 million, against an earlier one of "more than £28 million", and the shares rose 22p to 305p on the news. The actual outcome was £32.7 million, up 67% on a sales increase of 53%, there was a 1 for 1 scrip issue, and at 380p, the shares were selling on a P/E of slightly less than nine. Another foray into the US electronics market was made in October with a £3.5 million bid for Dana Laboratories, makers of voltmeters and systems counters. In December the interim figures showed a 68% jump in pretax profits to £19.4 million, and the forecast for the full year was "in excess of" £45 million. The shares ended the year at 208p after the 1 for 1 scrip, recording a 73% gain.

Another £12 million for BTR

BTR reported 1976 profits up by 51% to £24 million and at the same time announced a £12 million rights issue, the second in eighteen months. The terms were 1 for 5 at 140p, against a market price of just under 200p, giving an ex-rights yield of 7½%. The interim results announced in mid-September revealed a useful advance in profits from £10. 1 million to £13.3 million. Then in early December a £9.5 million bid was made for **Allied Polymer**, an industrial rubber products group originally formed by Slater Walker out of Greengate & Irwell, P.B. Cow and Frankenstein Group and floated in 1971. The group had run into problems in 1975/76 and BTR was making an offer at a one third discount to the original flotation price. BTR shares ended the year at 256p yielding 5.4% on a P/E of 9.6.

Hanson increases its US interests

Hanson's interim profits for 1977/78 were up by 43% to £11.23 million and a "substantial improvement" was forecast for the full year with £23 million the consensus target figure. In the intervening period, a number of tactical disposals were made in the US, cutting borrowings by $8 million. In October, an unsuccessful approach was made to **Lindustries**, a UK engineering, rubber and textiles group, and then in November a $29 million bid was launched for Interstate United Corporation, a US specialist foods group. Full year results exceeded most expectations with profits at £24.4 million, but the cyclical nature of the US operations prompted caution from most commentators. At year end the shares stood at 154p, yielding 6.2% with a P/E of 7.6 and equity market capitalisation at this point was £100 million.

The Sir Eric Miller Story

The scandal of the year involved **Peachey Property** and its Chairman, Sir Eric Miller. Sir Eric, a keen supporter of Labour Party fund-raising and social activities, knighted during the Wilson premier-ship, suddenly resigned from his position as Chairman of Peachey Property, London's largest residential property company and owners of the Park West block in Edgware Road. The resignation had been forced upon him by his three fellow directors following Sir Eric's failure to give what they considered to be a satisfactory answer to questions concerning a missing £282,000. His expla-nation was that the money had been expended in pursuit of an abortive European acquisition and

Sir Eric Miller, deposed Chairman of Peachey Property, shot himself in the garden of his Kensington home in September 1977.

that £130,000 had been deposited in a bank which then had sent a letter to the board acknowledging receipt. The three directors denied categorically that they had ever seen such a letter and Sir Eric was unable to provide evidence of its existence, as indeed was the bank concerned. As a result of his inability to refute the charges against him, Sir Eric lost a proxy fight to remain on the board, and the Department of Trade and Industry embarked upon an investigation. Just before its findings were published, Sir Eric shot himself in the garden of his Kensington house.

1978

FT 30 INDEX 1978

Trying for a pay policy

Given that the rate of inflation was coming down, that the economy was beginning to stir, and that the balance of payments was considered certain to improve thanks to the bonus of North Sea oil, prospects for 1978 were widely regarded as more encouraging than for a very long time. However, Lex in the *FT* pointed out very prophetically that the two principal dangers would turn out to be the excessive weakness of the dollar and growing domestic demand pressures.

It did not take long before the first of these dangers became only too apparent. At the end of the first week of January, it was announced in Washington that the term of office of Dr Arthur Burns at the Federal Reserve Board would not be renewed. The departure of this strict advocate of sound money was taken as a sure sign that the Administration was giving lower priority to the control of inflation and maintenance of the exchange rate, and the dollar fell sharply, taking the Dow Jones with it. A ½% cut in MLR to 6½% failed to help the London market, which was becoming increasingly concerned about export prospects as the pound rose ten cents in a month to $1.95. February brought further shocks with the release of the January trade figures showing a £179 million deficit, and banking figures which indicated that the growth of the money supply had already exceeded its upper limit. The anxiety now was that the bull position in gilts could be rapidly unwound as last year's big overseas buyers rushed to sell while sterling was still strong, thereby making it very difficult for the Government to sell gilts on a falling market. In the event, equities took fright first, following Wall Street down and hitting the year's low point of 433.4 at the beginning of March. The slide in gilts began later in the month after it became clear that the money supply was rising much faster than originally thought and sterling fell sharply. The prime concern was that sterling's fall could turn into a rout just as it had two years previously, but markets recovered and stabilised ahead of the budget in the reasonably confident expectation that the Chancellor would act positively to rebuild foreign confidence.

A confident budget

In a budget designed to "encourage the level of economic activity" and achieve a 3% growth rate, the Chancellor introduced a £2 billion package of tax concessions, raising allowances and widening bands. Simultaneously he announced a new growth target for money supply in the range of 8-12%, adding that the progress of his pay policy would determine whether it could be tightened further in the autumn. He also raised MLR to 7½%.

Markets were not impressed. They were understandably sceptical about his ability to finance an £8½ billion PSBR at the top end of the range, given the strong possibility, on past performance, of exceeding the money supply growth target and of running into difficulty selling enough gilts against a background of rising interest rates. Doubts were increased two days later when the March trade gap was announced to have been £164 million, largely as a result of another increase in the volume of imports. Clearly a great deal depended on the Government managing to continue to convince the trade unions of their mutual interest in maintaining a moderate pay policy, and in a May Day speech, the Prime Minister confidently declared that Labour had found the key to controlling wages without precipitating a trade union revolt. It was a bold claim that was soon to be severely tested. Meanwhile slow gilt sales, despite long yields up to 13%, prompted another hike in MLR, this time to 8¾%, but with money market rates already pointing to a higher figure, there was little conviction in the market that this level was going to prove a peak.

The Opposition rocks the boat

Later in May, the Chancellor's already suspect budget arithmetic was upset further by two Opposition amendments, one to knock a penny off the standard rate of income tax to 33p and the other to raise the starting point for higher tax rates by £1,000 to £8,000. Their effect was to reduce revenue by £500 million in a full year, and speculation began about where the Chancellor would look to make up this deficiency. His first move was to raise MLR to 9%, but again the market judged this level not to be one from which interest rates might be more expected to fall than to rise and selling gilts remained an uphill struggle for the authorities. News of a record trade surplus of £336 million in April and of the Retail Price index rising just 7.9%, its lowest rate for five years, helped to some degree but markets were not prepared to ignore the fact that the money supply was rising at over 16% on an annualised basis, that wholesale prices were up again and that the rise in earnings had now overtaken that of prices. Since these latter factors were capable of reversing the favourable trend of the former, it was clear that some new initiative was necessary to enable the Government to reassert monetary control.

The problem lay in the difficulty of convincing the City that public spending plans could be reconciled with monetary objectives without endangering the natural recovery of the private sector by starving it of credit, but the Chancellor's June package of fiscal and monetary measures, designed to rescue his budget strategy, demonstrated once again that the public sector took absolute priority over the private. MLR was raised to 10%, the "corset" was reimposed on the banks, limiting the expansion of their interest-bearing deposits in order to squeeze bank lending, and employers' National Insurance contributions were raised by 2½% to offset the loss to revenue resulting from the Opposition's tax amendments. It did not work. Gilts enjoyed a short-lived burst of buying enthusiasm which evaporated within days, and equities fell back at the prospect of this new tax on labour and investment driving up prices and slowing down the recovery of the private sector.

The pay policy collapses

In July and August the revival in consumer spending began to pick up sharply with retail sales heading for their peak levels of 1973/74. The buying enthusiasm embraced equities and, encouraged by Wall Street hitting a new high for the year of 888 and a similar revival by most world markets, the FT 30 rose above 500 again. Commentators rationalised the moves by pointing out that equity values were still trailing far behind the rate of inflation, retail prices having risen by 50% since 1973 in the US and by 100% in the UK, and that P/Es were less than half the figures ruling in 1973. The FT 30 peaked at 535.5 in mid-September and the All Share index achieved a new all time high, but significantly gilts, sensing dearer money on the way, failed to participate in the rally. By this time it was clear that a monetary and fiscal policy, however strictly implemented, was not an acceptable alternative to a pay policy and there was now no chance of the Government achieving the latter. Messrs Callaghan and Healey had argued hard for one but in the face of determined opposition both from the TUC and individual unions, for all practical purposes, the policy was a dead letter.

If the decision not to go for an autumn election but to postpone it until the following spring, had been a gamble on winning trade union support for Stage Four, it was one which was seen to have failed by the end of September when the Ford manual workers greeted a 5% pay offer with an immediate all-out strike. A week later the TGWU made the strike "official", and recognising a fait accompli, the Chancellor hinted at easing his 5% earnings increase guideline in an effort to avoid further confrontations. After seven weeks on strike, the Ford workers eventually agreed to accept the employer's "final offer" of a 17% increase. The miners promptly filed a claim for a 40% increase and the engineers one for 33% while the TUC contributed to the debate by proposing a change in the Government's anti-inflation strategy whereby rigorous controls would be put on prices rather than on wages. Public sector workers, who had borne the brunt of the wage restraint policy over the past three years, now looked for the promise of "comparability" to be made good. The stage was set for the "winter of discontent".

The monetary squeeze tightens

The net result of the abandonment of pay policy while monetary policy remained firm was to leave private industry squeezed between soaring credit costs and ever rising wage demands, a development which gilts seemed to suspect immediately after the April budget but equities did not. Rather than relieve the pressure on credit demand by cutting back on public spending, in November the Chancellor renewed his efforts to fund an excessive PSBR by raising MLR to 12½%, tightening the credit squeeze further and maintaining the money supply growth targets. Home loans shot up by 2% to 11¾% and base rates by 1% to 12½%. The Government broker managed to satisfy a large demand for gilts, but equities stagnated at around the 480 level as buyers held off in the face of so many uncertainties, content to collect a return of over 12% in the money market.

Events on the other side of the Atlantic provided no encouragement on the interest rate front. Worldwide concern about the continuing weakness of the dollar in the face of persistent inflationary pressures in the US economy, prompted President Carter in November to introduce an anti-inflationary package which constituted the most sweeping moves to help the dollar since those of President Nixon in 1971. The discount rate was raised from 8½% to 9½%, currency swaps with other central banks were doubled to $15 billion, gold sales were to be increased, and a $3 billion loan was obtained from the IMF. Unfortunately, the impact of the measures was largely negated by the onset of a new oil crisis as the Shah's regime in Iran collapsed. It rapidly became obvious that the event would have a profound effect on the world economy in 1979, and not surprisingly the year ended on a dull note with international investment sentiment upset by OPEC's decision to raise oil prices by 14½%, an act inspired both by a new militancy following the Iranian revolution and by a wish to compensate for the decline in the dollar.

The FT 30 closed the year at 470.9, 3% lower on balance after reaching extremes of 535.5 and 433.4, while the Government Securities index fell by 12% to 68.89. The Dow Jones index stood at 805 against 831 at the start of the year. Gold did best of all, benefiting from a growing distrust of paper currencies – especially the dollar – gaining 37% on the year to $226 but the FT Gold Mines index rose by only 3.7% to 138.

Racal buys more in the US

In April, **Racal** announced another important US purchase, this time of data communications company Vadic, for £5.4 million. Two months later, the South African subsidiary was sold to local interests for £6 million, a move emphasising the new concentration on the US, the world's biggest market for electronic equipment. Later that month, the 1977/78 results showed a 52% gain in pre-tax profits to £50 million as against a forecast of "in excess of £45 million". Sales were reported to be still booming and Lex described the company as the market's "only real remaining growth stock". At 248p, the P/E was 11 and the market capitalisation £282 million.

The interim figures in December saw another strong advance to £24.3 million, up 25% and less dramatic than the market was used to, but very creditable nonetheless for a company still in the process of digesting its recent acquisitions. Milgo was a key contributor this time, increasing its share of profits from 25% to 29%. The whole balance of the group had changed dramatically since 1976 and data communications plus electronic equipment, other than military communications, now accounted for some 45% of profits. By now the shares had risen to 332p where the dividend yield was 2% with a prospective P/E of 12 on the forecast for the full year of £57 million.

...and so does BTR

BTR continued to forge ahead in 1978, demonstrating that it too deserved to remain firmly in the growth stock category. Full year profits were up 20% at £29 million, putting the shares at 213p on a modest P/E of just 6½. Then in June, BTR made its biggest bid yet in the US with a $48 million offer for Worcester Controls, a manufacturer of ball valves, pneumatic and electric activators. Another rights issue was announced in August, the third since 1975, to raise £24 million. It was well received by a market which recognised BTR's ability to combine rapid organic growth with an aggressive acquisition policy, and looked to be well on the way to making £40 million in 1978/79.

Hanson consolidates in the US

1978 was a relatively unexciting year for **Hanson Trust** and first half profits only just managed to keep the rising trend unbroken at £11.4 million against £11.2 million as the US acquisitions began to demonstrate the cyclical nature of their businesses. However, forecasts of £25 million for the full year were well beaten at £26.1 million even though the contribution of the US side had slipped from 65% to 50%.

1979

FT 30 INDEX 1979

A year to remember

Markets entered 1979 in an uneasy frame of mind. On the domestic front, the breakdown of the Government's pay policy was a major concern giving rise to fears of increasing industrial disruption and the prospect that inflation would soon be back into double figures. Externally, worries centred on the Iranian situation and the further threat that it could pose to the stability of the Middle East as well as on the implications for the industrialised world if it led to oil shortages accompanied by a new wave of price increases. Against such a background, the Government's scope for manoeuvre was seen to be strictly limited. January quickly showed that fears on both counts were well grounded.

The first week of the New Year saw 25,000 lorry drivers on strike, virtually paralysing the nation's distribution services, and leading to speculation that the Government would be forced to declare a State of Emergency and use troops to keep essential services running. This eventuality was narrowly avoided, but the Chancellor's "peace package" promising more cash to the lower paid, reaffirming the pledge of comparability with the private sector for public sector workers, and tougher price controls, was widely judged to undermine his basic policies by granting concessions when he should have been standing firm in the face of importunate trade union demands. Meanwhile, bank lending had risen sharply as companies were forced to borrow to finance the build-up of stocks during the haulage strike, and by mid-February pressure on money market rates, coupled with the Government's need to complete its funding programme, prompted an increase in MLR to 14%.

During all this time, equities proved remarkably resilient as a result of buyers being more impressed by the UK's new oil wealth than depressed by the latest round of industrial disruption. Even the record spot prices being paid for oil and the delivery cuts of up to 45% imposed by BP, Shell and Exxon, harmful though they were, still served to emphasise how much better off the UK was than the rest of the industrialised world. Gilts were dull initially but picked up sharply as the funding operation in the wake of the boost in MLR proved a resounding success. The pound was now around $2 and a petrocurrency carrying one of the highest interest rates in the world was irresistible to overseas buyers.

Pre-election optimism boosts the market

The boom in gilts now began to instil a renewed confidence into the equity market as investors took a view of the longer-term effect of North Sea oil on the economy and on profits and dividend prospects. From 450 in mid-February, the FT 30 had recovered to 500 by the end of the first week in March. Activity was at its highest level for eighteen months, and the All Share index actually broke into new high ground, unhampered by the FT 30's bias towards heavy capital goods constituents.

At this point a new factor emerged to add momentum to the rise. This was the near certainty of a spring election and expectations of a Conservative victory. The open challenge to the Government by the unions and the industrial chaos it had caused, had effectively destroyed Labour's claim to be able to manage the trade unions better than the Conservatives. It had also hardened public opinion against the Labour Party's basic premise that the governance of the country was only possible with the advice and consent of the trade unions. Mountains of rubbish on street corners, pickets preventing the delivery of food to hospital patients and daily disruption of essential services, had made the public much more sympathetic to Mrs Thatcher's determination to place reform of the trade union movement at the top of the Conservatives' list of priorities. The announcement at the end of March that the election was set for 3rd May sparked a further advance in the FT 30 towards 540 and saw the All Share index at another new peak. Two reductions of 1% in MLR, bringing it down to 12%, helped but so did a comparison of the manifestos of the two parties. Labour's renewed pledges to seek further control over industry, to impose a wealth tax, to abolish the public schools and to extend the powers of the Price Commission, looked doctrinaire and irrelevant. On the other hand, the Conservatives' plans to pursue reform of the trade unions, to cut taxes, to control the money supply and to advocate a return to responsible pay bargaining between employers and workers with no government intervention, appeared to be not only eminently practical, but also long overdue.

Mrs Thatcher takes over

In the days immediately preceding the election, all the main indices moved ahead with both the FT 30 and the All Share reaching new records, and Government Securities topping 75. The actual result, giving the Conservatives a 43-seat majority, exceeded their most optimistic expectations. Nevertheless, it had been well discounted. The FT 30 responded with a 5-point rise to a new all-time peak of 558.6 but the reaction was swift as the magnitude of the task facing the new administration began to be appreciated. Clearly it was not going be possible to make significant cuts in public spending "at a stroke" and with money supply still growing too fast, interest rates were likely to continue to rise, putting pressure on both gilts and equities.

Attention now was firmly focused on what the new

Chancellor, Sir Geoffrey Howe, would do in his first budget on 12th June, but before then the market had to absorb three items of bad news. The first was the report that earnings were rising at an annual rate of 14.2%. The second was Iran's decision to start a new round of oil price increases, and the third was the announcement that the trade deficit for the first four months of the year was just over £1 billion. Because of a strike by Civil Service statisticians, there had been no trade figures for four months and the cumulative total came as a shock. The FT 30 was down almost to 500 on the day of the budget, and concern over the Chancellor's radical change of direction prompted a decisive penetration of that level.

The keynote of the budget was a major shift from taxes on income to taxes on spending. The basic rate of income tax was cut from 33p to 30p, personal allowances were increased, the threshold for the 40% tax rate was raised from £8,000 to £10,000 and the top rate of tax for those earning over £25,000 was slashed from 83% to 60%. All these reductions added up to £4.5 billion and they were to be offset in part by increasing VAT to a unified rate of 15% and raising the excise duties on beer, wines and spirits and tobacco. Simultaneously, the Chancellor raised MLR by two full points to 14% and announced that money supply growth would be restrained within a 7-11% target range, thereby demonstrating his urgent need to cure the current surge in private sector credit demand and to establish a new level from which funding could resume. Public spending cuts of up to £1.5 billion were promised, as well as the first in a series of asset sales led by BP. Also the first steps were taken to dismantle the system of exchange controls, a move which initially boosted sterling. The Chancellor described it as an "opportunity" budget, but the market worried about the extent and severity of the impending credit squeeze, the impact of high interest rates and a strong pound on corporate profits, and the chances of further industrial unrest. Accordingly, the FT 30 slipped into a 450-480 trading bank to await developments, an attitude that appeared to be fully justified a month later when Sir Geoffrey, in reaffirming his determination to cut public spending down to size, described the immediate outlook as "almost frighteningly bad".

The Federal Reserve Board gets a new Chairman

In July an event occurred on the other side of the Atlantic that was to have a profound effect on the economies of the US and of the world. It was the appointment of Paul Volcker as Chairman of the Federal Reserve Board. Mr Volcker had very determined ideas of how to achieve domestic price stability and restore international confidence in the dollar.

Paul Volcker, appointed Chairman of the Federal Reserve Board in 1979 with the task of restoring international confidence in the dlollar.

It was by the application of "disciplined, persistent and consistent monetary policy" which, in effect, meant tight money accompanied by whatever level of interest rates might result. His predecessor had pursued policies of relative monetary stringency, but the dollar had been undermined by a disastrous over-expansion of dollar credit through domestic and overseas channels for years, and the authorities had been slow to realise just how drastic measures to check it would have to be. Furthermore, the role of the dollar as the international trading currency meant that monetary policies everywhere were at risk unless the dollar was controlled. Hence the importance of Mr Volcker's new approach to the problem. His appointment was greeted with a ten-point rise in the Dow to 839, but one particularly prescient commentator noted that this was "like throwing a party to celebrate the arrival of your executioner".

Recognising that the source of US inflation was domestic and had to be tackled by the effective control of domestic credit growth, Mr Volcker's inaugural package in October involved a 2% hike in the discount rate to 12%, an increase in bank reserve requirements to 8%, acting rather like the UK "corset", and very importantly, a change from managing interest rates on a day-to-day basis by the so-called federal funds rate, and instead using the monetary base as a yardstick. The significance of this last measure was not only that interest rate moves would no longer be predictable but also that they could reach any level. The sky was the limit. The reaction to all this was a sharp rise in the dollar and a sharp fall in bonds and equities as prime rates topped 15%.

The Chancellor tightens the squeeze

Whatever the longer-term benefits of the new US monetary policy might be, the abrupt rise in interest rates over there posed some shorter-term problems for Chancellor Howe by effectively sabotaging his funding operations as bank lending rose and the growth in money supply strayed well above the top of the 7-11% target range. The situation was not helped by the fact that following removal of the remaining exchange controls, sterling had lost all its immediate post-election gains. Erstwhile foreign buyers were paying more attention to the UK's continuing balance of payments difficulties and the prospect of a new wave of exorbitant wage claims accompanied by the threat of industrial action now that retail prices were rising much faster than earnings as the budget increases filtered through. CBI surveys were universally gloomy, showing business confidence at its lowest level for two years and forecasting a sharp drop in corporate profitability in 1980. At least the setback in sterling had brought some relief to hard-pressed exporters, but the question was being asked whether the monetary squeeze would have its impact on inflation before it destroyed the profitability of large parts of UK manufacturing industry. At the same time, industry striving to protect its margins in a high interest rate recession by shedding labour and closing down unprofitable activities, was likely to do less damage to productivity and profits than to output and employment. However, doubts about the answer caused the FT 30 to drop below 450 at the end of October.

Against such a background, gilt-edged prices continued to be eroded until mid-November when the Chancellor acted to regain the initiative in financial markets. MLR was raised by 3% to the unprecedented level of 17% and mortgage rates promptly rose to a record 15% as the price had to be paid for the Chancellor's budget tax cuts. After some initial hesitation the tactic worked and by mid-December, gilts were rising strongly on news of a sharp slowdown in the rate of monetary growth and a run of prime rate reductions by the US banks. Encouragement was drawn also from some signs of moderation on the labour front. British Leyland workers voted not to strike over the dismissal of Communist shop steward, Derek Robinson, known as "Red Robbo", albeit under the threat of plant closure if they did, and the miners, after rejecting an 11-15% pay deal, agreed to accept an offer of 20%. On the other side of the fence, welcome signs of managerial firmness were noted in British Steel refusing to improve on its 2% offer, despite strike threats.

All in the same boat

Equities were less enthusiastic than gilts about these supposedly encouraging developments and by mid-November the FT 30 was getting uncomfortably close to the 400 level. The 20% settlement for the miners was considered by many to establish a "going rate" for future claims, giving rise to the belief that the coming recession would impinge more on profits than on incomes. It was also a reminder that there were those in the Conservative ranks who believed in the omnipotence of the trade unions and who would go to any lengths to appease the miners or indeed any other group of workers with enough muscle to bring down a government. At the same time markets took some comfort from the fact that interest rates were rising in all the industrialised countries as part of a general determination to check the growth of money and credit in an effort to conquer inflation. Furthermore, a recession endured in the cause of fighting inflation was likely not to be so deep or obstinate and once inflation began to respond, the natural forces of recovery would start to make themselves felt.

Such consoling thoughts were much needed in December, a month which had seen a warning from the Bank of England that companies were facing a financial squeeze as severe as that of 1974/75, Libya raising the price of its oil to $34.50 a barrel, Russian tanks rolling over the border into Afghanistan and the train drivers' union, ASLEF, blacking steel imports, not to mention the rate of growth of the Retail Price index practically doubling on the year to 17.4% in November. This was not the sort of background to provide much of a Christmas rally, and the FT 30 ended the year at 414.2, down 12%, while the All Share index actually managed a 4.2% rise to 229.79. Gilts, as measured by the Government Securities index, lost 5.2% to 65.10. Golds were the star of the year. Beneficiary of a growing distrust of all paper currencies, especially the dollar, and of the highly unstable situation in the Middle East, the bullion price rose by $300 to $526 an ounce, while the FT Gold Mines index gained 90% to 268.6. The Dow Jones index managed to add a modest 33 on the year to 838 despite the persistent weakness of the dollar and the political problems posed to President Carter by the Iranian hostage situation.

BTR powers ahead

In 1978/79 **BTR**'s "constellation of unglamorous but formidably efficient businesses" turned in profits of £42.5 million, a 43% advance, as contributions began to flow from its fifteen plants in the US. BTR still had acquisitive ambitions in the UK and in June launched a surprise £26 million bid for **Bestobell**, the fluid engineering and insulation group. Bestobell's record had been uninspiring in comparison with that of BTR, but its management convinced enough institutions that it could do better by retaining its independence and the bid failed, although leaving BTR with a 25% stake. Interim figures showed that BTR's growth momentum was undiminished with pre-tax profits up 50% at £27.4 million on sales just 33% higher. The shares ended the year at 287p, well down from the year's high of 347p, yielding 5% and selling on a P/E of 11.3.

Racal slows down

Iran's drastic cut backs in defence spending showed the wisdom of **Racal**'s efforts to reduce its dependence on the military communications market, and profits for 1978/79 easily topped the £57 million forecast at £61.6 million. First half figures for 1979/80, however, were much less exciting but they too underlined the management's foresight in diminishing the importance of its UK manufacturing base. Held back by strikes and the strength of the pound, profits were up by only 4% at £25.3 million, indicating a total for the year of perhaps £65 million. The shares fell sharply on the news and closed the year at 183p as against a high of 276p, yielding 2.9% on a P/E of 10.9.

Hanson consolidates

Hanson accompanied its modestly better half year results of £12.4 million, up 10%, with a £17 million rights issue, obviously with an eye to acquisitions. The terms were a deeply discounted 1 for 2 at 50p against a share price of 168p and the issue was not underwritten, thereby saving expenses in a dull market which had just seen 75% of Thomas Tilling's £57 million rights issue left with the underwriters. Then in August a successful £27 million offer was made for **Lindustries** and the following month its biggest bid to date, $163 million, was made for Barber Oil Corporation in the US, although it was subsequently dropped because of legal complications. The year also saw the settling of the terms for Sir Gordon White's 10% stake in Hanson Industries, the group's US operating arm, and he received 4.3 million shares in Hanson Trust, then valued at £5.5 million. Full year profits were £31.2 million, boosted by a cyclical upturn in the US market and a strong recovery in brick demand in the US. The shares ended the year at 123p, yielding 8.5% and with a P/E of 6.8.

1980

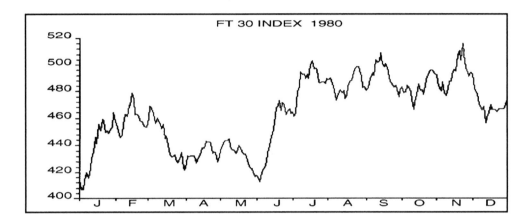

FT 30 INDEX 1980

Return to Go

The onset of the steelworkers' strike in the first week of the New Year provided a clear indication that the Government's resolve to make loss-making industries confront the reality of their situation was going to be severely tested in 1980. A gloomy assessment by stockbrokers Phillips & Drew, based on the assumption that the next five years would show average earnings rising at an annual rate of 15%, just as they had in the last ten, did not help sentiment, but after falling to 407, equities suddenly embarked upon a strong rally, adding 50 points in three weeks. With the steel strike spreading, the latest earnings figures recording a rise of 19.2% and the gold price soaring to over $800 in response to international tensions, it was difficult to believe that the market was doing anything other than looking into the distance, accepting that things would have to get worse before they got better. The hope and expectation was that the Government's efforts to contain monetary growth as a first step towards reducing inflation, would establish the preconditions for tackling the real economic challenges, principally the imbalance between the public and private sectors, and the idea that the government of the day could and should use public funds to rescue any and every hugely unprofitable industry, public and private, just because it happened to be a large employer of labour. These were challenges which previous governments had either refused to recognise as such or simply ducked for reasons of political convenience.

"Medium-Term Financial Strategy" unveiled

By mid-March the upward spiral of dollar interest rates had taken some of the heat off sterling as well as breaking the back of the boom in commodity prices, thus relieving some of the cost pressures on UK industry. However, with MLR at 17% and average earnings rising at almost 20%, such pressures remained acute, and hopes of some relief in the budget at the end of the month were soon dashed. The principal feature of the budget was the unveiling of the Chancellor's "medium-term financial strategy" (MTFS) which, in the words of an *FT* editorial marked "an historic break in economic management". Its keynote was to give total priority to reducing monetary inflation by keeping money supply growth within the 7-11% range, setting a target of 4-

Sir Geoffrey Howe, first Chancellor under the Thatcher Administration and originator of the Medium-Term Financial Strategy in 1980.

8% by 1983/84, and at the same time ensuring that the Government's own demand for credit remained consistent with these aims by planning to reduce the PSBR's share of national income from 5½% in 1978/79 to 1½% by 1983/84.

This ambitious programme would be made possible only

by using North Sea oil revenue to reduce the public sector deficit instead of distributing it around the economy. Assuming everything went according to plan, by 1983/84 debt sales would be minimal, and huge savings flows would be released for industrial investment both at home and overseas. The downside was that if it would allow only modest room for growth, industry might have a hard time surviving the transitional period, and the budget provided no comfort beyond minor concessions on stock relief and the long-term prospect of lower interest rates. The remainder of the budget was concerned with taxing welfare benefits, raising excise duties on beer, wine, spirits and tobacco, and while raising personal allowances and thresholds, still letting fiscal drag increase the real burden of income tax.

Signs of success

Disappointed at the absence of a cut in MLR, the market fell immediately after the budget but rallied on the ending of the steel strike in its thirteenth week and on renewed hopes of a cut in late April as world interest rates showed distinct signs of peaking. These hopes were encouraged by the fact that money supply growth, after hovering just above the target range all year, had at last fallen within it.

As a result, the first anniversary of the Conservatives taking office appeared to have witnessed at least a modest success in round one of the battle to contain monetary growth, while the real economy was withstanding the monetary battering it had received rather better than many had forecast. However, by July there were distinct signs that Government borrowing in 1980/81 was going to be well above target, and also that money supply growth was once again creeping above the 11% upper limit in response to the buoyant demand for credit from the private sector. But in the context of falling US interest rates, unemployment topping the 1.5 million mark for the first time, indications that both the rate of growth in earnings and in prices were peaking and two successive months of trade surpluses, the Chancellor felt he had enough leeway to take his first step to ease the credit squeeze and took MLR down one point to 16%. The market responded positively to the cut with the

FT 30 crossing the 500 level once again in mid-July while the All Share index achieved a new peak of 286.5. Gilts, too, moved ahead strongly, convinced that inflation and interest rates had topped out even though the Government's funding needs probably ruled out another reduction in MLR in the very near future. This conviction was strengthened later in the month when the rate of growth of the Retail Price index, at 21%, down from 21.9% in May, recorded its first significant fall since 1978 and the growth in average earnings was also checked.

Straying off course

Banking figures released in August showing money supply rising at an annualised rate of 22%, twice the upper limit of the target range, quickly took the steam out of gilts. They were hit again later in the month following further evidence of overshoot in the PSBR, both excesses underlining the tendency of public and private sector borrowing needs to rise with a fall in economic activity with the one undermining the other. The root of the problem was that a year ago it might have been assumed that either the pound would fall or wage increases would be sharply reduced, and that one way or another the competitive position of manufacturing industry would be restored, its financial position improved and its need for new borrowing fall. In the event, margins continued to bear the brunt of the adjustment, leading to dreadful profit figures, wholesale closures and redundancies, and reliance on the banks for day-to-day finance. As if to prove the point, at the end of the month, ICI announced a 52% fall in profits between its first and second quarters, and the unemployment total topped two million as the labour shakeout continued.

The Government was now coming under increasing pressure from both the TUC and the CBI to abandon policies, the harsh effects of which on the real economy now cast serious doubt on the validity of the whole "medium-term financial strategy". The Labour Party was too involved with its own leadership struggle to take much part in the argument, but with the TUC warning of "uncontrollable social unrest" and the CBI chairman threatening the

Government with "a bareknuckle fight" unless there were major policy reversals, equities held their ground remarkably well and the FT 30 did not stray far from the 500 mark while the All Share made new highs. Investors seemingly were less influenced by the rhetoric of vested interests than with the straws in the wind of falling pay settlements and falling inflation, albeit both recession-induced, and the dramatic improvement in the balance of payments. Furthermore, with the spot price of oil now below OPEC's "official" levels, even the outbreak of war between Iran and Iraq was not regarded as such a potentially dangerous development as it might have been. The depth of the recession, too, was not necessarily being contemplated with despair. Rather it was being seen as a measure of the scope for recovery available to companies forced to rationalise and reorganise to a point where they were now much more capable of taking advantage of an improving business climate.

Markets contrast with the real economy

Thus in the last week of October, when ICI reported a £10 million loss in its third quarter, the first in its 54-year history, the All Share index moved into new high ground. November saw money supply up sharply again but the measure (M3) was now widely reckoned to be erratic and misleading, and markets paid more attention to a record £534 million October trade surplus, another fall in the retail price index and hopes of a cut in interest rates in the Chancellor's economic package promised for the end of the month. A two-point reduction in MLR to 14% was accompanied by measures designed to put the MTFS back on course and to lighten the burden on the private sector. The savings net was widened to pull in another £3 billion for an attractive National Savings scheme, National Insurance contributions were increased for employees but not for employers, and a supplementary tax on North Sea oil profits was introduced to raise another £1 billion. The need for such fund-raising provisions became obvious when it was announced simultaneously that the PSBR for 1980/81 was likely to be around £11½ billion compared with the £8½ billion aim at the time of the last budget. After holding above 500 for just five trading days, and buoyed also by the Dow Jones crossing the 1000 level in the wake of the Republican victory, the FT 30 suddenly fell away as US interest rates began to rise dramatically after President Reagan gave Paul Volcker free rein to pursue his anti-inflation policies.

Dollar interest rates soar

The first half of December saw the FT 30 back to 460 with the upsurge in dollar interest rates dominating financial markets everywhere and prompting speculation about a new worldwide bear market after the Dow had lost almost 100 points in less than a month. Gilts fell away, too, on fears that the US rate rises - prime rates had reached 21½% – made the latest MLR cut look misjudged in the context of a still rising PSBR and could lead to another funding crisis for the Government.

The last days of December brought slightly better news with the rate of growth in average earnings at 20% slowing appreciably for the first time since 1977, another drop in the retail price index to 15.3% and US prime rates reacting from their peak levels. The FT 30 closed the year at 474.5, up 14.5%, but the All Share index at 292.22 recorded a gain of 28.5% as the stock market took due note of the huge structural changes that had been taking place in the economy over the past couple of years.

While many commentators with a political axe to grind, deplored the decline in Britain's traditional manufacturing industries, the stock market was quietly acknowledging it as a fait accompli, reflecting the shift of resources into service industries and oil extraction while so much of the burden of manufacturing was being assumed by Japan and the fast developing economic powers of South East Asia. This change of roles was both inevitable and inexorable, and as one commentator put it, there was no doubt that "the moving finger was firmly attached to the invisible hand"! The Actuaries Oil share index, for example, having crossed the 1000 mark for the first time in October was still up 35% on the year at 933, the Financial Group index was up 28.5%, while the Metals & Metal-forming sector index was down by 4%. Gilts were below their best levels but still cautiously optimistic about the outcome of the Government's policies, and at 68.69 the Government Securities index recorded a gain of 5.5%. The gold price continued to reflect international tensions and currency fears, hovering around the $600 mark, and FT Gold Mines was up by 52% at 407.5, undeterred by the collapse of the silver price following the failure of the Hunt brothers' attempt to corner the market.

Racal buys Decca

Corporate activity in 1980 kicked off with **Racal**, now capitalised at £467 million, making a bid approach to pioneer electronics company **Decca** which recently had slipped into losses. GEC was also interested but Racal still managed to win the day with a £101 million cash offer. Even though there were a few more problems than expected to sort out at Decca, there was no doubt that Racal chairman, Sir Ernest Harrison, was pleased with his prize, and after reporting 1979/80 profits up by just £2 million to £63.6 million, he confidently forecast that with Decca breaking even, the current year would be the "best for years". At the time, the shares stood at 259p yielding 2.3% with a P/E of 19, and despite considerable comment about a slowdown in earnings growth in the wake of the Decca acquisition and a worldwide recession, Racal attracted major institutional support, ending the year at 330p.

BTR also continued a "gravity-defying profits performance" in 1979/80, reporting a 43% advance in pre-tax profits to £57.2 million despite suffering industrial disruption at its UK-based manufacturing operations. As usual it was the overseas side that made the running and at the time of the interim results in September, showing profits of £36.4 million, it was announced that substantial gains had been made in all countries with the exception of the UK. Meanwhile, two acquisitions had been made in the US, carbide cutting tools manufacturer Adamas Carbide for $10 million and disposable clothing manufacturer Huyck for $143 million, but a £60 million rights issue in September was reckoned widely to be the prelude to a renewed offer for

Bestobell. Like Racal, BTR had built up a devoted institutional following and the shares closed the year at 364p, yielding 4. 1 % with a P/E of 13.6.

Hanson buys McDonough

An initial contribution from Lindustries, together with a strong performance by the UK industrial services operations, helped to offset a cyclical downturn in the US and **Hanson Group**'s first half profits came in 29% up at £16.1 million. There was still a lot of comment about the dullness and the cyclical nature of most of the group's businesses but in the context of an all-embracing recession, it was difficult to fault the achievement of a total of £39.1 million for the full year. In October a major US acquisition was made in the shape of McDonough Co. for $180 million. Makers of footwear, cement and handtools, the company was bought at the bottom of a cyclical trough after profits had halved, and funded with debt secured on its assets. The shares ended the year at their high point of 208p, although the rating was still modest with a yield of 5.8% and a P/E of 9.2.

Asil Nadir takes control of Polly Peck

In February an obscure paragraph in the *FT* reported that Restro Investments, a private company based in Jersey, was making a cash offer of £470,000, or 9p per share, for troubled ladies' fashion business **Polly Peck (Holdings)**. The directors, including the founding Zelker family, agreed to accept the offer for their 57% shareholding, and Asil Nadir, who was chairman of Restro as well as of clothing concern **Wearwell**, said that he intended to "continue and develop" the business of Polly Peck and maintain the listing. At the time Asil Nadir did not have a reputation as a stock market operator, but the shares moved strongly ahead in thin trading conditions and eventually were suspended at 83p in mid-June "pending an announcement". The following month a 1 for 5 rights issue at 75p was announced. The £1.6 million raised was to pay for the acquisition of Uni-Pac, a company owned by Mr Nadir and engaged in the production of corrugated packaging from plants based in Turkish Cyprus. As the first and only producer of corrugated packaging in the region, the company was expected to be the principal supplier to the local agricultural industry with one third of production being absorbed by Cyprus and the balance going to mainland Turkey. On the basis of Cyprus sales alone, pre-tax profits of £2 million were forecast for 1980/81 and the shares of Polly Peck returned from suspension at

Asil Nadir, Chairman of Polly Peck International, was to preside over the biggest 'boom and bust' in UK financial history.

128p. September saw a flurry of activity in **Cornell**, a small loss-making London dress company, on rumours of a bid for a controlling interest from another of Asil Nadir's companies, Jersey based Azania Investments. A bid of 19p was eventually made in December, by which time the shares were already over 50p. Polly Peck ended the year at 145p with the distinction of being the best performing share of the year, recording a gain of 2708%.

An illusion of depth

There was another interesting introduction to the stock market in 1980 in the form of **Nimslo**, the makers of a 3-D camera. Founder, Dr Jerry Nims, had raised £3 million for development finance from UK institutions in 1978 and was now looking for another £7 million to market his product. The attraction was a 30% share in pre-tax profits of $20 million forecast for 1982, rising to $98 million in 1985. On the other hand, said Lex, it could all turn out to be a "resounding flop". It did, but not before becoming the biggest company on the USM at one point.

April also saw the debut of Alan Sugar's **Amstrad** with an offer for sale of 25% of the company at 85p on a prospective P/E of 12.7 and a yield of 5.5%. At the offer price the whole company was valued at £8 million, and despite reservations about the highly competitive market in which it operated, the shares established a 10p premium on the first day of dealing.

The USM is born

The year was notable also for the creation of the Unlisted Securities Market (USM), designed to provide an easier route to fund-raising and public trading for smaller and relatively untried companies. Principally, the advantages for entrants were, firstly, a 3-year instead of a 5-year record and, secondly, a placing of a minimum of 10% of the company's equity instead of 25%, but in every case the services of a sponsoring stockbroker had to be acquired. The first two companies on the market were **Scan Data International** and **John Hadland**.

Canada Dry

The success of the oil majors in 1980 prompted a great deal of interest in the smaller exploration counters and two newcomers from Canada attracted a considerable following. **Double Eagle** and sister company **Warrior Resources** had raised C$89 million from UK institutions earlier in the year for the development of exploration targets in Alaska, Oklahoma and Texas. Dealings were permitted in London under Rule 163(1)e covering shares quoted on overseas stock exchanges, in this case Vancouver. From 120p in June, Double Eagle rocketed to 810p in October on hopes of a major find in Alaska after an announcement that "potential hydrocarbon zones" had been encountered. The excitement generated was reminiscent of the Poseidon boom but it was to prove even shorter-lived. In December a statement from the company released in Vancouver, but not simultaneously in London, reported that the find was "insufficient" and the share price of Double Eagle halved overnight to 295p. Lex commented wryly that the best discovery the companies had ever made was the London stock market!

1981

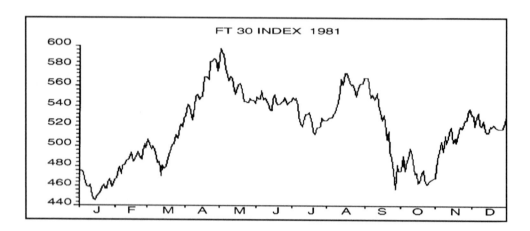

FT 30 INDEX 1981

Rationalisation and redundancies rule

Hopes for the New Year were tempered by worries about the impact on the real economy of Government policies should the recession persist, and the test that rising unemployment, together with falling investment and output, would pose for the Government's nerve. Even the most ardent supporters of the MTFS had to admit that it was a failure in the sense that the money supply, public spending and the PSBR were all growing wildly in excess of the original target levels, and that the squeeze on the corporate sector was much worse than intended. On the other hand, the objective of falling inflation was being achieved by the recession anyway with little regard for a policy that seemed to have created every kind of deflation except monetary deflation. The budget, scheduled for 9th March, was confidently expected to remedy at least some of these policy deficiencies and the FT 30 managed to struggle over 500 again just before the event despite further evidence from industry of falling profits, shrinking dividends and redundancies as ICI reported a 54% fall in profits for 1980, cut its dividend, and rationalised many of its operations with huge job losses.

At the same time, a measure of the difficulties that the Government was going to have to tackle during the rest of the year and beyond was provided by the sight of still rising US interest rates, and of striking South Wales miners forcing the National Coal Board to back down on its cost-saving pit closures programme. The more serious problem, and the more intractable in that it was totally outside the Government's control, was US interest rates with their immediate impact on the level of sterling. President Reagan had much the same free market and deregulation policy as Mrs Thatcher, and his programme of big personal tax cuts to be matched by deep cuts in public spending ran into precisely the same problem that was facing her in the UK. Taxes can be cut at a stroke but government spending cannot, and Paul Volcker had been given carte blanche to bridge the gap. That meant sharply higher interest rates to reduce domestic inflation and protect the dollar. As a result, from $2.40 in January, the pound fell to below $2.20 just before the budget. Capitulation to the striking miners also did nothing for foreign confidence in sterling and served to detract from an otherwise tough and resolute budget.

The market looks ahead

The aim of the budget was to strengthen and advance the MTFS, and at the same time redress the imbalance between the personal and business sectors, and the private and public sectors. To this end the burden of taxation was shifted to the wage earner and consumer, largely by increasing indirect taxation on petrol, drink and tobacco and also by failing to index allowances. MLR was cut from 14% to 12%; a PSBR inflated by recession, by spending on defence and by aid to state-owned industries was forecast to fall back to £10.5 billion in 1981/82; and the money supply growth target was lowered into the 6-10% band.

An early fall to 470 by the FT 30 immediately after the budget was followed by a strong recovery. This was helped by another fall in the rate of earnings growth, a trade surplus in February of £614 million, and signs of a fall in interest rates plus considerable merger activity in the US pushing the Dow over 1000 again. Gilts, too, were firm on the tightening of fiscal policy evident in the budget and the Government Securities index rose to a new high for the year of just over 70. Interestingly, the advance in markets was led by the depressed industrials, most of which were still reporting appalling results. **GKN** had just announced a loss of £1.2 million against the previous year's profit of £125 million after a second half slump, and **Tube Investments, Turner & Newall** and **Lucas** shocked the City with their figures and dividend cuts. Clearly, investors were taking the view that rationalisation and reorganisation of industries that for years had been grossly overmanned and hence low in productivity, would benefit from this once and for all shake-out of surplus labour and unprofitable operations. The celebrated letter to *The Times* from 364 university economists showed that not everyone agreed with Government policy, but their confident assertion that "There is no basis in economic theory or supporting evidence for the Government's belief that by deflating demand, they will bring inflation permanently under control and thereby induce an automatic recovery in output and employment", coincided very neatly with the announcement that ICI's first quarter profits had risen to £52 million compared with just £7 million in the last quarter of 1980, and with the FT 30 almost breaching the 600 level on the last day of April.

US interest rates call the tune

From this point on it was developments on the other side of the Atlantic that dominated the course of markets in the UK and in the rest of the industrialised world. The rise in the dollar on the back of soaring US domestic interest rates was seen as equivalent to a "third oil shock", threatening to bring both lower growth and higher inflation. On its own, this was bad news for the pound but the effect was greatly aggravated by a sharp fall in the oil price as the worldwide recession slashed consumption. The first week of June saw the pound hit by a wave of selling as foreign holders re-evaluated its role as a petrocurrency. The exchange rate fell below $2 and gilts slipped in sympathy to a 13-month low. Equities, however, remained firm on the prospect of an upturn in profits as a consequence of a sharply reduced cost base and a de facto devaluation. Even the largest rights issue ever, a £624 million call from BP towards the end of June, failed to put buyers off but by late September an almost daily catalogue of rights issues together with a sharp increase in interest rates in response to US prime rates topping 20%, proved too much to bear. In two weeks the FT 30 lost a hundred points and the fall was mirrored in stock exchanges across the world, giving point to BIS calls for the US to stop relying on a monetary policy which caused such high interest rates with their attendant damage to other economies around the world and instead do something about cutting its own huge budget deficit.

Sterling in the front line

It was now widely perceived that with sterling back to around $1.80, interest rates were likely to be at higher levels for much longer than anyone had thought likely earlier in the year. By October UK base rates were up to 16% again (MLR had been abandoned in favour of the Bank of England signalling its wishes via a less obtrusive money market intervention point), but a month later they were down to 14.5% as US short term rates eased significantly, and the FT 30 managed to climb back over 500 again. Gilts were less easily persuaded that lower interest rates were here to stay but after touching a 5-year low of 60.44, they staged a modest recovery only to relapse again as disappointing money supply figures, and the retail price index reversing its downtrend, seemed to put paid to hopes of further rate cuts. The feeling was that the authorities had given up on keeping the money supply within bounds and were now operating an exchange rate targeting policy. Despite official denials that this was the case, sterling strengthened in December, helping markets to end the year on a note of cautious optimism. This mood was encouraged further by indications that the PSBR target was being achieved, a rising trade surplus, and the first significant indications of a pick-up in industrial output.

Anxieties remained over the prospect of serious industrial disruption in the New Year by the miners and the railway workers, but the year which had seen the worst recession in half a century still managed to end with the FT 30 up 11.8% at 530.4 and the All Share up 6.8% at 313.2. This disparity in performance was accounted for by the strong recovery in the industrial stocks which dominated the FT 30 contrasting with only minor advances by the Financials and a 25% fall in Oils. High interest rates took their toll of gilts, and the Government Securities index closed the year down 10% at 62.37. Sky-high dollar interest rates plus signs that the Volcker medicine was going to work were no help to Golds either and with the bullion price down from $600 to $400, FT Gold Mines slipped 40% to 307.5. During the year Wall Street had to cope with far higher interest rates than London and the Dow Jones index ended 1981 with the loss of 100 points at 873.

Racal sorts out Decca

Problems sorting out Decca continued to hold back **Racal**'s performance in the first half of 1980/81 and profits were up by only 5% at £26.5 million. The shares fell on the news and at 310p, yielding just 2%, Lex concluded that there was "no margin for disappointment". In the event there was no disappointment with full year profits of £73.2 million accompanied by the announcement that losses at Decca were now under control and that the group was heading for "substantial profits" over the next two years. The shares rose 12p to 384p to yield 1.7%, but by the end of the year they had advanced to 435p on strong institutional support.

BTR acquires a "growth stock" rating

BTR's full year figures came in at £70.3 million, up 23%, with strong growth in the US and Australia more than offsetting a downturn in the UK. Vigorous rationalisation measures involving a 25% cut in employment in the UK factories helped the interim figures to a 20% gain at £41.6

million and a £90 million total was assumed to be within reach for the full year. Then in September, BTR showed that its acquisitive ambitions remained unsatisfied with a £25.5 million bid for Serck Radiators. By now the shares were seen no longer as a dull industrial conglomerate but had been accorded a rating in line with that of Racal, ending the year at 344p selling on a P/E of over 20.

Hanson goes for Berec

Hanson's half year profits gain of 13% to £18.2 million was suitably impressive against a background of recession both in the US and the UK, but what really pushed the group into the headlines in 1981 was its bid for the well-known battery company, **Berec**, formerly called by its much better known name of EverReady. With an asset value of more than twice the share price, a strong brand name, a costly investment programme nearing completion, and recession-hit profits, Berec looked a classic target for Hanson, and in July a dawn raid at 90p took the latter's holding to 15%. Reinforced by a £44 million rights issue later in the month, Hanson eventually launched a full bid with a £73 million offer in September. Following intervention by Thomas Tilling, Hanson had to raise its bid to £95 million, a figure which managed to secure the prize. Meanwhile, Hanson's full year figures of £49.7 million, showing a strong second half acceleration, raised hopes of what 1982 could bring once rationalisation of Berec was underway. The shares ended the year at 287p yielding 5.2% ahead of a one for one scrip issue.

Nadir beats his forecast

Polly Peck's forecast of profits of £2 million for its first year of operation in the packaging business was treated with some caution, but the shares had doubled to 325p by the time the actual figure of £2.11 million was announced. This was accompanied by an even more apparently fantastic forecast of £10 million for 1981/82. One analyst computed that there was not enough citrus fruit production in the whole world to utilise the numbers of boxes required to justify that forecast, but the shares of Polly Peck ended the year at 355p, up another 145%, on a prospective P/E of less than 2.

The transformation of W. Williams & Sons begins

In January, Caerphilly-based engineering and foundry company, **W. Williams & Sons**, hard hit by the downturn in the industry, reported a sharp swing from profit to loss in the first half of 1980. There was no improvement in the second half, but rescue for the company and its shareholders appeared in November with a 25p a share offer for 51% of the 3.4 million shares in issue by C. Price, a private

Nigel Rudd and Brian McGowan, Chairman and Managing Director of Williams Holdings, quickly turned an obscure Welsh foundry company into a major international manufacturing group.

building company operating in the East Midlands. The move attracted little attention at the time but within ten years, the company, under its new management of ex-London & Northern executives Nigel Rudd and Brian McGowan, was to rival the achievements of Hanson and BTR.

Maxwell takes control of British Printing

Following a dawn raid in July 1980, Robert Maxwell's Pergamon Press had picked up a 29.4% stake in the country's largest printing concern, **British Printing Corporation**. Then, in April 1981, he paid £10 million to take Pergamon's stake up to 77%. It was an audacious move in that Pergamon, with net worth of some £9 million and pre-tax profits of £3½ million a year, was taking on a loss-making, debt-ridden colossus. BPC had just reported a loss of £11.3 million for 1980 and its debt load had risen to £40 million. What attracted Maxwell was BPC's £200 million turnover and the scope for reorganisation and rationalisation in the leading company in an industry grossly over-manned and hog-tied by trade union restrictive practices. It was now operating under a Government committed to changing the rules of the game, and Maxwell was ready to make the most of the opportunity.

1982

FT 30 INDEX 1982

The revival begins

The resilience of equities, especially industrials, during a
recession-hit year, pointed to a more encouraging outlook
for the New Year than had been the case at the beginning of
1981. At the same time, no one had any illusions about the
potential pitfalls that lay ahead, especially those related to
the US economy which left that of the UK hostage to another's fortune. Industrial disruption too could prove to be a
major stumbling block. Admittedly high unemployment had
weakened the trade unions in 1981, but as it continued to
rise some thought it could spark a "do or die" degree of militancy, signs of which were already appearing among the
miners, now led by the redoubtable Arthur Scargill, and
among the railway unions. There was also no widespread
evidence of industrial recovery – both Laker and deLorean
collapsed in February – despite the pick-up in share prices,
and the upturn in industrial production figures reported in
December had gone into reverse in the first quarter of 1982.
Nevertheless, equities had risen to 564 on the eve of the

budget in mid-March, taking heart from a £2.5 billion package, including another cut in base rates to 13%, designed to cut industry's costs, create jobs and promote new investment, to be paid for in part by increased excise duties and balanced by reductions in public spending and additional asset sales. A fall in the rate of growth of average earnings and of retail prices both to 11%, reported later in the month, was accorded more weight than the appointment of a receiver for **Stone Platt** and the near-collapse of **Turner & Newall**, but a strong advance in equities and gilts was stopped dead in its tracks by the outbreak of the Falklands War.

Who dares wins

There is no question but that the decision to order the naval taskforce to set sail was a huge political gamble. Failure then to achieve an Argentinian withdrawal, either voluntarily or forcibly, almost certainly would have meant the end of three years of Conservative rule and an abrupt reversal of policies. As it turned out, a 20-point fall in the FT 30 and one of nearly three points in gilts was regained within days as US support seemed to guarantee a successful outcome to the conflict. After reaching a new all-time peak of 590.6 in mid-May, 35 points were lost over the next few days as a run of Argentinian successes prompted further consideration of the degree of military and political risk involved.

A rally to 592.6 on the eve of the Argentinian surrender was followed by a near 50-point reaction by the end of June as investors returned to contemplation of the familiar peacetime problems of excessively high US interest rates, still rising public spending, stagnant output and the ever-present threat of industrial disruption. To these worries were now added fears about the impact on the international banking system of the developing countries' debt crises, led by Mexico, and of a spate of bankruptcies among major multinational corporations. All were weighed down by heavy debts accumulated when interest rates were negative and were now cruelly exposed to real rates as recession and disinflation set in. However, there was a silver lining in that these signs that his disinflationary policies were working to the extent that they now threatened a disastrous financial collapse, seemed to persuade Paul Volcker that enough was enough. Accordingly, in late July he announced that the Federal Reserve Board would adopt a more flexible monetary approach by tolerating money supply growth at the upper end of the permitted range, while still maintaining his anti-inflationary goal. The Dow did not respond immediately and after dipping below 800 on a short-lived upturn in interest rates, it rallied strongly, topping 900 on the last day of August in very active trading. At the same time the danger was perceived that a policy of maintaining brutally high interest rates as disinflation takes hold, would create a demand for money in distress borrowing which the banks could not satisfy without putting their own liquidity at risk. On the other hand, not to satisfy it would lead to the collapse of many over-stretched companies and the non-repayment of the bank's existing loans. This was a 'no win' situation as evidenced by the troubles of Continental Illinois and of International Harvester, but to quote former Federal Reserve chairman Dr Arthur Burns, "The banks have been foolish. Let us hope they continue to be so." The popular view was that the shock to confidence of the recent debt crises had gone a very long way towards killing inflationary habits and expectations, and that borrowing and monetary growth would begin to recede naturally. Activity would remain depressed but as debt service costs became bearable for sound borrowers, reconstruction would gradually get underway with any defaults absorbed in banking profits.

In early October, Volcker suspended the money supply growth target while restating his commitment to restraining the growth of money and credit to "appropriate levels" to keep inflation under control, and the next day the Dow broke through the 1000 level on the second highest volume in its history.

Two record breakthroughs

Meanwhile, back in the UK base rates were down to 9% and gilts were seemingly in accord with the US view that the inflationary momentum of the 'sixties and the 'seventies had been broken. Thus on the same day that the Dow topped 1000, the Government Securities index added nearly two points to 82.83, its highest level since 1964. Equities, too, confirmed this measure of world economic interdependence and broke through 600, closing above it for the first time at 606.1. But if the rise in equities was justified by the prospect of falling debt service costs coming straight through to profits, with any rise in sales as icing on the cake, and the rise in gilts by the reduction in inflation, the longer-term future of both depended to a large extent on the Government controlling the growth of the public sector and thereby its tendency to pre-empt available resources. That task still lay ahead, and given that the public sector had been insulated for so long from competitive pressures, it was not going to be accomplished without a struggle.

Earlier governments of both persuasions had tended to avoid confrontation but Mrs Thatcher was determined to get across to public service workers the message that there is a link between pay, productivity and jobs. In any case, the hard-pressed private sector was making heavy calls on available funds, and there seemed to be no good reason for the overmanned, inefficient and often loss-making elements of the public sector to continue to be protected from the pains of disinflation.

By the time of the Chancellor's autumn statement, the FT 30 was up to 630, but despite its cautious tone, the belief by overseas holders of sterling that with the oil price depressed, he might be tempted to allow the currency to depreciate further, forced the rate below $1.60 at the end of November. Equities followed it down to reach 588, but rallied as the pound revived in response to the Chancellor's denial that this was what he had in mind, reinforced by a 1% rise in Base Rate to 10%. With the rise in retail prices and average earnings both below 7% in November and no growth in corporate profits over the year, there was some evidence that the Government's disinflationary goals were being achieved. Accordingly it was thought unlikely to continue to pursue policies which could risk prolonging and deepening the recession. Thus despite the most severe industrial recession since the War, the FT 30 managed to gain 12.5% on the year to 596.7 while the All Share did even better, up 22.5% at 382.2. Gilts, although below the best, plussed a remarkable 30% to 81.19, while FT Gold Mines gained 85% to 556.6 as the bullion price recovered, strongly boosted by the Falklands conflict and a run of sovereign debt defaults seen as threatening to the stability of the international banking system.

Racal pulls Decca around

Racal entered 1982 in fine style with a 45% advance in first half profits to £38.4 million, largely thanks to a £10.5 million turnround by Decca. The momentum carried on into the second half and pre-tax profits for the full year came out at £102.6 million, up 39% on sales up by just 20%. On the announcement in June, the shares added 22p to 450p where the yield was 1.6%, but at year end they had risen to 595p boosted by news that Racal had obtained the cellular radio contract, which before the end of the decade was to add another important division to the group.

BTR consolidates

1982 was a year of consolidation for **BTR** with continuing rationalisation measures in the UK operations serving to prevent profit figures from achieving the most optimistic predictions. As a consequence, the £90.1 million total for 1981, up 28% on sales up 25%, included a £4 million drop in UK profits to £26 million, and first half profits for 1982 showed only a 13% gain to £48.7 million despite a small contribution from Serck. The UK workforce had been reduced from 18,500 to 10,500, and although earlier forecasts of a £110 million total for the year were beginning to look unlikely to be met, the prospect of rationalisation benefits coming through in due course helped the shares to end the year at 378p.

Berec pays off for Hanson

Hanson's first half profits were up by no less than 21% to £22 million and after this demonstration of how good management can weather the worst recession in fifty years, due note was taken of the Chairman's pronouncement that there was evidence of the recession bottoming and signs of recovery. In July a successful £15 million bid was made for **United Gas Industries**, and the following month a move to increase the group's borrowing powers from twice capital and reserves to three times was assumed to be the prelude to further acquisitions. Full year figures also recorded a 21% advance bringing the total to £60.4 million with Berec making a nine-month contribution of £14.2 million. The shares closed the year at 271p, effectively doubling over the period.

Polly Peck expands

The placing of 1.3 million shares in **Polly Peck** out of the Restro holding brought in £4.5 million from a consortium of Middle East investors in January. The placing price was around 350p but at the time of the release of the interim 1981/82 figures in June showing a profit of over £3 million, the shares were still only 342p and selling on a P/E of under 5, a rating considered by the *FT* to be "overdoing the caution" for a company which had proved the sceptics wrong by turning a moribund East End rag trade outfit into a major force in international packaging. At the same time expansion plans were announced for the packaging plant in Northern Cyprus and in mainland Turkey, and the £10 million forecast began to look no longer unrealistic. Sister company **Cornell** had been suspended in August at 165p and came back in September with a £2.76 million rights issue designed to fund its investment in a 64% stake in a mineral water bottling plant at Niksar in Turkey with the aim of tackling the huge market in the Middle East.

This rapid expansion of the Polly Peck empire now began to attract a great deal of speculative as well as investment interest, and the share price rose in a straight line, topping £16 by the end of November when the full year profits were revealed to be £9.04 million. The accompanying statement referred to expanding packaging production and also to plans to exploit the substantial market believed to exist in Turkey and the Middle East for locally manufactured products, particularly in the field of television and video and in pharmaceuticals. A merger of the three companies, i.e. Polly Peck, Cornell and Wearwell, was said also to be under discussion. The degree of official backing from the Turkish government was emphasised in the form of an 8-year tax holiday in acknowledgement of Polly Peck's key role in the economic development of the region. The prospect of profits of around £20 million for 1982/83 was now being aired and the shares advanced further in the final quarter to end the year at £23.

Williams goes to first base

The new managers of **W. Williams** wasted no time in rationalising the business and at the interim stage they had cut the deficit from £599,000 to £199,000 on turnover practically halved to £1.55 million. By this time the share price had risen to 40p as a number of institutions gave their backing to Rudd and McGowan. Then in November, they made their first big move with a £3.1 million agreed cash bid for loss-making **Ley's Foundry**, a Derby-based foundry and engineering company best known for its Ewart chains and Beeston boilers.

Bio-Isolates makes its debut

Bio-Isolates was a start-up flotation on the USM by Chandra Singh's London Venture Capital group. Operating from rented space in a Swansea dairy, the company had devised and patented a process for extracting protein from whey, and although the value of the product was questioned by local food producers the concept managed to catch the imagination of the public. Floated at 33p in an offer for sale of 41% of the company's equity, the shares established a 16p premium on the first day of dealing, and ended the year at 270p with a market capitalisation of just over £20 million. Interestingly, shortly after the flotation, one of the family of the founders disposed of a large holding in contravention of the undertaking given in the prospectus.

Among the year's new issues, the most notable were **Amersham** and **International Signal & Control**. The former was unique in that it was the first flotation of a "high-tech" company involved in radioactive materials used for medical and industrial research purposes. At the offer for sale price of 142p the P/E was a relatively demanding 19 and the yield a modest 3.5%, but the issue was well over-subscribed and the 40p premium established on the first day of dealing prompted a political row about the shares being sold too cheaply. Neither was there anything on the London market quite like **International Signal & Control**. Founded by US entrepreneur Jim Guerin in 1971, the company specialised in defence electronics and had a glittering record. Since 1978 pre-tax profits had risen five-fold to £5.3 million on sales trebled to £75.8 million and the P/E of 18 at the offer price of 155p was not considered overdemanding for a company in its line of business. Jim Guerin had brought ISC to London because the SEC in the US insisted on fuller details of his principal customers, which he was not prepared to supply for security reasons. Investors thus had to take the company on trust. They were happy to do so, bidding the shares up to 226p when dealings started.

1983

FT 30 INDEX 1983

New peaks for the indices

With markets having made modest progress in the last three recession-hit years, hopes were high that a more significant advance would be recorded in a year which looked likely to see the end of recession. Even the Chancellor's uncompromising New Year message, promising no relaxation in the fight against inflation and designed to discourage speculation in the City that the March budget would be expansionary, failed to deter buyers and the end of the first week in January saw both the FT 30 and the All Share at new record levels of 621 and 396. The pound and gilts, however, both fell sharply on oil price weakness and on Labour's pledge to devalue, but steadied after a 1 per cent hike in Base Rates to 11%. As a measure of the change in sentiment, whereas not so long ago weak sterling and a weak oil price might have been interpreted bearishly, the first was now seen as boosting corporate profits and the second as aiding world recovery as well as having a negligible impact on national revenue. Thus ahead of the budget on 15th March, on OPEC's agreement to a $5 cut in the oil price to $29 a barrel, the FT 30 actually rose 2.5 points to 665.8 in recognition of the fact that the fall in the pound, since the autumn, had more than offset the decline of the dollar-denominated oil price.

A Conservative landslide

The budget made some useful personal concessions in terms of raising tax allowances and child benefits as well as increasing duties on petrol, drink and tobacco again, and although it was well received by markets, all eyes were now on the impending election called for 9th June. With Mrs Thatcher's standing boosted by the Falklands victory and CBI surveys reporting a "substantial recovery in business confidence", the Conservatives were odds-on favourites but if there were any doubts, they were dispelled by Labour's election pledges. They included withdrawal from the EEC, renationalisation, reimposition of exchange controls, repeal of industrial legislation and closure of all nuclear bases in the UK, as well as an immediate increase in public expenditure by £7.5 billion and an increase in the PSBR from £8 billion to £14 billion. The FT 30 crossed the 700 mark for the first time in the fortnight ahead of the poll, but reacted sharply after topping 730 following the Conservatives' re-election with a 144-seat majority. Profit-taking was only to be expected after such a well discounted outcome, but the new Chancellor, Nigel Lawson, managed to create some anxiety, not least among his Cabinet colleagues, by demands for massive public spending cuts out of expenditure planned for 1984/85 in the wake of reports that 1983/84 spending was

Nigel Lawson took over as Chancellor of the Exchequer in 1983 and inaugurated dramatic personal and corporate tax reductions

already well above target. Another unsettling factor at this time was the miners' call for a "substantial pay rise" and the threat of a strike if it was not met.

By the end of July, the FT 30 had moved above 700 again, encouraged both by a parallel revival in the US economy to which the Dow had responded by successfully challenging the 1200 level and by President Reagan's continuing commitment to sound money evidenced by Paul Volcker staying on for a second term of office at the Federal Reserve Board.

If markets remained hesitant throughout the summer, there had been a record number of rights issues to absorb as well as the £525 million **BP** tender offer scheduled for late September. It sold effortlessly, and then towards the end of October the market suddenly sprang to life in response to **ICI**'s third quarter profits which were up over 150% at £147 million, showing an acceleration of the trend evident in the first two quarters. Investor enthusiasm was helped by another flurry of takeover activity with **BAT** vying with Allianz for control of **Eagle Star** and on 28th November the FT 30 reached a new peak of 743.9 on growing confidence that a spontaneous economic recovery promoted by market forces with the minimum of government assistance, was now underway. In the run-up to Christmas, the jobless figures fell again, as did the Retail Price index. The November trade figures pointed to a surplus for the year of over £1.5 billion, and further good company results confirmed expectations that corporate profits would show a gain of around 25% on the year with dividend growth restored in real terms.

After several years of disappointed hopes, it appeared that the UK industrial recovery had arrived, and with the OECD confirming that prospects for world recovery were showing "a big improvement", the FT 30 closed the year at 775.7, up 29.5%, with the All Share trailing at 470.5 for a gain of 22.5%. The superior performance of the FT 30 was due to the fact that the painful rationalisation and reorganisation of 1980 and 1981 had begun to show through in dramatic productivity gains and profit rises, particularly among the capital intensive cyclicals, led by ICI, which dominated the index. This was also the year in which US fund managers had discovered the UK, becoming big buyers of stocks like ICI and Glaxo after the decisive election win by the Conservatives in June. Gilts put up a less impressive performance in 1983, held back by anxieties over the US deficit and by the downtrend in sterling over the year, and recorded a modest gain of just 2% at 83.12.

Racal slows down

Racal's interim figures for 1983/84 showed a very creditable 22% jump in profits to £47 million on an 18% sales gain, but warnings of a second half slowdown due to the recession and growing competition in the field of data communications disappointed the market and the shares fell 62p to 485p on the announcement. Full year forecasts were scaled down from £120 million plus and the eventual total of £112 million was not greeted with any enthusiasm. Orders from OPEC countries were well down and data communications remained a problem area, but also affecting investor sentiment was a patent dispute between Racal-Milgo and Motorola-Codex which looked like being settled in the latter's favour.

Tilling falls to BTR

BTR, by contrast, had an excellent year. Profits for 1982 came out at £106.7 million, up 18%, and taking advantage of the fact that it was now a firm favourite of the investment community, in April BTR launched a dawn raid on industrial conglomerate Thomas Tilling. Having picked up only 6%, a week later BTR made a full bid which valued Tilling at £576 million. The target argued that the offer price was "totally unreflective of its underlying worth and assets", but after raising its bid to £660 million, BTR won control. Interim figures of the combined group recorded a 20% gain to £58.3 million but they included a loss in the period for Tilling which contrasted sharply with a £95 million full year profit forecast in its defence document. BTR also announced a 100% scrip issue, and the shares ended the year at 424p, an effective gain of over 100%.

Hanson expands in the UK

Hanson Group began the year with a £264 million agreed counterbid for **United Drapery Stores**, then the subject of an approach by a consortium led by Heron. In the course of the contest, Hanson made a full year profit forecast of £75 million which was already looking conservative at the time of the interim figures in June, which showed a 53% jump to £34 million. Hanson wasted no time in trying to recoup the major part of the UDS purchase price, and by the end of September had agreed to dispose of the Richard Shops, John Collier, Timpson and Orbit for some £152 million. In December full year figures revealed an overall 51% advance to £91 million, a sparkling result that proved to be the prelude to a £170 million bid for **London Brick**. During the year the market capitalisation of the whole group topped the £1 billion mark for the first time.

Polly Peck grows and grows

The announcement of Asil Nadir's plans to double capacity at Uni-Pac and to acquire two cargo planes and two cargo ships to strengthen its monopoly position in the region, together with his confident statement at the AGM in mid-February that **Polly Peck** was "on the verge of becoming a very large international concern with unlimited trading potential", sent the shares soaring to a peak of £35. Before the end of that month, however, they had collapsed to £17, at which level they were suspended pending a statement to answer charges that the company was exploiting sequestered Greek property in Northern Cyprus, thereby prejudicing a political settlement, and that the claimed tax holiday did not have the official blessing of the Turkish government. A brief statement answering the charges in general terms was made, and the suspension lifted, but the shares plunged afresh to £10 before rallying into the £15-£20 range. Even interim profits rocketing to £8 million did not help matters greatly and the accompanying statement was criticised as being woefully inadequate in the light of the rapid expansion of the group. In September £13 million was raised by a placing of 6.3% of the group with a consor-

tium of Middle East investors and brokers to the company,
L. Messel, then began a series of institutional presenta-
tions. By the time of the announcement of the results for the
full year in early December, Polly Peck's share price had
recovered to £24 where the market capitalisation was £175
million. Profits came in at £24.7 million on turnover of £62
million, and much was made of the expansion of activities
serving to make Polly Peck a much more widely based
manufacturing and trading group. Legal & General
disclosed that it held a 5.1% stake, and just before
Christmas Asil Nadir announced a 10 for 1 share split and
another placing with Middle East investors to raise £5
million. The shares had recovered their poise and closed the
year at £26½, or 265p in their new form.

The Turkish Connection

In 1983 the phenomenal success of Polly Peck prompted
investors to look for others that might follow the same path
literally, given Polly Peck's origins, from rags to riches.
Their first target was **Mellins**, an obscure loss-making
manufacturer of lingerie and babywear in which Mr Tukar
Suleyman, a gentleman of Turkish descent, acquired a 29%
stake. Despite his declared intention to return the company
to profitability by remaining in the same area of operations,
the shares rose from 6p in November 1982 to a peak of 246p
in February 1983 on rumours that Mr Suleyman was
related to Mr Nadir and on the confident expectation that
new businesses would be injected into the company. A rights
issue in April at 100p to raise £660,000 seemed to be
nothing other than confirmation of these expectations, but
the subsequent purchase of a stake in loss-making store
Bambers gave rise to doubts when the deal was shelved
following revelations of exceptional losses at Bambers. By
the end of the year, Mellins' share price was back to 62p as
investors changed their allegiance to late runners, **Bellair
Cosmetics** and **Harold Ingram**, both of which became
subject to bids from Wasskon, a Liechtenstein-based
company run by Mr Akcay and Mr Tecimer, both of Turkish
origin. Wasskon had paid 8p for a controlling stake in
Bellair in April and the shares soared on the news to end

the year at £11¾. During the intervening period no announcement was made beyond "the company knows of no reason for the rise in the share price". The case of Harold Ingram followed much the same pattern. Wasskon's controlling stake was acquired at 65p a share in August and the shares promptly rose to 350p by the end of December, again on no news.

A darling of the market

Sinclair Research was riding high in 1983 on founder Sir Clive Sinclair's reputation for imagination, innovation and salesmanship, and in January a £20 million placing of 10% of the company (to exclude the electric car project) was

Electronics genius, Sir Clive Sinclair, at the launch of his revolutionary single-seat, battery-operated car, the C5.

made with institutions. The valuation had been made on the basis of pre-tax profits of £10 million in 1981/82 on turnover of £27 million, and a forecast of practically doubled turnover in 1982/83. Profits for the year rose to £13 million and expectations were boosted by booming home computer sales, news of a new mini-TV to sell for £50, and of course hopes for the revolutionary electric car. A public quotation was said to be scheduled for the following year.

New directions

Many of the new issues during the year were indicative of the new directions the UK economy was taking in the 'eighties. **Pineapple**, the dance studio company, got off to a fine start, and soon followed by Eric and Julia Morley's **Miss World.** Placed at 60p, the shares had the rare distinction of opening at more than twice the issue price, touching 132p on the first day of dealing. Then came Michael Green's **Carlton Communications**, which achieved a quotation on the USM via a reverse bid for Nigel Wray's **Fleet Street Letter**. The declared aim was "to expand in TV work." Later in the year, **Tottenham Hotspur** came to market, but while it received an enthusiastic reception from the small investor with its offer for sale at 100p, it failed to gain significant institutional support.

1984

FTSE 100 INDEX 1984

The last battle

Expectations that the economic recovery would continue
and broaden in 1984 did not go hand in hand with a widespread belief that the stock market would repeat its
sparkling performance of 1983. Rights issues were not
considered likely to match last year's record of £2 billion but
there was no doubt that they would still lay claim to a large
slice of available institutional cash, as would the continuing
stream of privatisations scheduled to include the record
breaking £3.9 billion **British Telecom** offering. However,
January soon demonstrated that institutional buyers had
more than enough resources to cope with anything the
market might throw at them, and equities advanced on a
broad front on record volume. Within a matter of days the
800 level was penetrated decisively with US buyers prominent, and by the end of the month the index had topped 840
in company with other markets around the world also
hitting new highs.

A sharp setback on Wall Street in response to Paul
Volcker's expressions of concern over the inflated US
budget deficit led to a reaction in London but it was short-
lived and a renewed buying wave carried the FT 30 up to
865 ahead of the budget in mid-March. The market was
delighted with the new Chancellor's tax-reforming
measures, especially the phased reduction in Corporation
Tax to bring it down to 35% by 1986/87, the halving of
Stamp Duty to 1%, and the abolition of the investment
income surcharge. The phasing out of first-year capital
allowances and the removal of artificial incentives in the
savings market, including the axing of premium relief on
new life insurance contracts, did not pass without criticism
but there was no question that industry was the gainer in
this budget. The PSBR target for 1984/85 was set at £7.25
billion or 2½% of GDP, the money supply growth range
was to be 6-10%, and the Retail Price index was expected
to be growing at no more than 4.5% per annum at year end
as against 5.1 % in February. A week later the FT 30 had
crossed the 900 level for the first time with the new FT-SE
100 share index, launched in January with a base figure of
1000, touching a peak of 1130.7.

Scargill rocks the boat

The market had risen too far and too fast since the beginning of the year and it was time for a pause. No one needed
to look very far for reasons for caution. At home the miners'
strike, which had started in the first week of March, was
becoming more bitter and protracted, seriously hitting
output and the balance of payments and undermining
foreign confidence in sterling. Continental Illinois,
America's eighth largest bank, had to be rescued by the
Federal Reserve Bank after sustaining huge losses on South
American and energy-related loans, and a soaring dollar
and a weakening oil price aggravated the situation by
ruling out the chances of any decline in interest rates. But
after dipping briefly below 800 at the end of May, the FT 30
recovered in June only to collapse again in July as a run on
the pound prompted a sharp rise in Base Rates to 12%. At
the same time the dockers decided to throw in their lot with

the miners, and in late July and early August, the fortunes of Mrs Thatcher's government were at their lowest ebb. It was now her turn to call off a 14-day tour of the Far East to stay in London to deal with the crisis. However, better money supply growth figures led to a rapid reduction in Base Rates to 10½% in mid-August and, interestingly, the cuts continued despite sterling becoming progressively weaker in line with a still falling oil price. Perhaps the market sensed the implications of the defeat of the miners' challenge to the Government, seeing it as a test case the outcome of which would settle the issue of "who governs the country" once and for all.

By this time the public sympathy which the miners could claim at the outset of the dispute had all but disappeared. The scenes of violence witnessed daily on TV together with the reluctance of other unions to become involved in the strike to the detriment of their own members were factors which tended to isolate the miners and to refute their argument that they deserved "special case" treatment. Scargill's fund-raising efforts in Libya and Russia did not endear him to the general public either, evoking memories of the Betteshanger colliery strike in 1941 during the darkest days of the war, and of the fact that such industrial action did not cease until Russia joined the Allies following the breakdown of the Nazi-Soviet Pact and the German invasion in June of that year.

Mrs Thatcher stands firm

By September things were beginning to look a lot better for the Government. The dock strike had crumbled after more and more dockers decided to cross the picket lines, and the miners' strike seemed more likely to end with a whimper than the bang so desired by Scargill as the drift back to work gained momentum. Markets survived the **Johnson Matthey** collapse, taking heart from the speed with which the Bank of England came to the rescue. There was another nasty moment in late October when the pit deputies' union debated whether or not to strike, but the threat was lifted and by November the FT 30 was over 900 again. Sterling was still drifting down towards $1.20 under the influence of a weakening oil price and the fear that the miners might still be bought off on the lines of the 1974 settlement, but sentiment improved by the end of the year on OPEC's agreement to production cuts and Mrs Thatcher's refusal to negotiate over the issue of pit closures or to introduce a new Plan for Coal. The landslide re-election of President Reagan on his "You ain't seen nuthin' yet" platform and the Dow's surge above 1200 again was another plus for the London market, but the overall firmness throughout the year owed more to two other factors.

One was the sheer magnitude of the recovery in corporate affairs under the Conservative administration. Trading profits had doubled since 1980 and were likely to rise another 20% in the current year. Corporate liquidity was at its highest level for six years, while balance sheet gearing at 20% and a strong cashflow meant that capital spending could be financed without recourse to bank borrowing. Admittedly, the recovery was from a low base, but it was nonetheless real, and the extent of the previous state of endemic overmanning was demonstrated by the fact that unemployment was continuing to rise. What had happened was that the burden of supporting it had moved from the private sector to the public sector with all that it implied for the borrowing requirement.

The other factor was sterling seemingly coming to terms with its place in a floating currency world in which the UK economy was fully exposed to world competition in a capital as well as a goods and services market. In such a context capital would go wherever it found the best return and an exchange rate was no longer an instrument of adjustment but simply a market price. Hence the Chancellor's efforts to cut back on public spending overheads and to combat wage inflation to ensure that excessive costs did not squeeze the profits of UK Limited and in turn lead to capital outflows which would rapidly undermine the pound. The fall in the pound since its heyday as a petrocurrency in 1981 was part of the process of finding a new market price, and judging from the strong recovery in exports and orders, it was close to doing so. The fact of an exceptionally strong dollar pushing sterling to too low a level temporarily then became a matter for internal adjustment, and once again the process would become self-correcting as the level of the dollar made US industry uncompetitive and that country ultimately less attractive to foreign capital. At least, that was the idea.

The Chancellor's autumn statement forecasting growth of 3½% and an inflation rate down to 4½% in 1985, and hinting at tax cuts of up to £1½ billion in the coming budget, helped the market to end the year on a very firm note. Investors also took heart from the enthusiastic reception accorded to the huge **British Telecom** offering, when the partly paid shares practically doubled on the first day of dealing, the last in a line of outstandingly successful privatisations in 1984 including **Enterprise Oil** and **Jaguar**.

The FT 30 ended the year at 952.3, up 23%, much in line with the FT-SE at 1232.2, while the All Share beat them both by gaining 26% to 592.9. Gilts had a quiet year but, down only 2% at 81.7, had stood up remarkably well in the face of the slide in sterling from $1.40 to nearer $1.15, although a further drop in base rates to 9½% helped at the end of November. The Dow was actually down on the year at 1211, but recovering strongly as the new Republican administration, with the cooperation of the Federal Reserve Board, began to shift the emphasis of its policy from fighting inflation to resuscitating the economy, cutting a point off the discount rate to 8 % in December.

Racal buys Chubb

Racal's half year figures for 1984/85 continued to reflect the problems that had caused the slowdown in the second half of the previous year. Up only 2½% to £48.7 million, profits had been hit by a dearth of new tactical radio orders, but reports of a strong recovery at Racal-Milgo and a growing order book for defence and marine radar helped to keep the share price steady at around 210p. Earlier estimates of a total for the year of around £130 million were revised to £120-125 million, but the actual figure of £119 million was accepted with good grace with an eye to the potential of the cellular radio division expected to move into substantial profits in 1988/89. Expectations of additional delayed benefits were aroused in August when Racal bid for **Chubb**. Given the trend towards electronic security systems, the

expertise of Racal allied with the customer base and celebrated brand name of Chubb, promised to prove a winning
combination.

Tilling pays off for BTR

The second half of 1983 began to demonstrate the benefits
of the Tilling acquisition for **BTR** and full year profits came
in at £170 million, up 60%, with a contribution of £44
million from Tilling. At the interim stage, profits doubled to
£115 million and "marked progress" was forecast for 1984, a
phrase which analysts interpreted to mean a total for the
year of something like £270 million. Crewe House, the
magnificent building in Mayfair that had been Tilling's HQ,
was sold during the year for £37 million to Saudi Arabia for
use as its embassy. The shares ended the year at 614p,
having added 130p since the interim announcement in
September.

Hanson wins London Brick

Despite forecasts by **London Brick** of a remarkable
recovery in profits for the coming year, **Hanson** managed to
win the day but only after boosting its offer to £247 million
in cash or convertible stock and by requesting an extension
of the period for acceptances. This success was followed in
April by a $400 million bid for US Industries, a diversified
manufacturing group, typically just completing a major
reorganisation and getting back into profits after a major
loss in 1981/82. Hanson eventually had to pay $530 million,
but then offset part of the increase by selling Seacoast, one
of its first US acquisitions, for $30 million. US Industries
added $1 billion to Hanson's US sales, taking them up to
$2.2 billion. In June, interim profits weighed in at £64.4
million, up 90% on a sales gain of 40% at £900 million.
Analysts pencilled in a full year figure of £150 million, only
to see it handsomely beaten at £169 million. This was
Hanson's 21st year of operations. Sales now totalled £1.7
billion, evenly divided between the UK and the US, and at

278p the shares were selling on a prospective P/E of 11 assuming profits of around £220 million in the current year. Hanson rounded off 1984 with an ultimately unsuccessful £150 million bid in the week before Christmas for **Powell Duffryn**, a diversified engineering group with a lacklustre record, further depressed by the miners' strike.

Williams returns to profits

The new management at **Williams** had spent most of 1983 rationalising and integrating Ley's Foundries with the original business. High-volume, low-margin work was dropped in favour of smaller production runs carrying increased prices, and losses gradually fell to £76,000 for 1983, down from £312,000, on turnover up from £5.6 million to £27 million. Then towards the end of 1983, the first profitable business was acquired. This was **Garford-Lilley**, a specialist engineering, plastics and woodworking group operating in a number of relatively underexploited niche areas. The acquisition neatly supplemented the recovery trend in the rest of the group, and the first half of 1984 saw a dramatic return to profits with a total of £753,000. By this time Rudd and McGowan were winning increasing institutional support and the shares had risen to around 165p to give a market capitalisation of some £16 million.

Polly Peck pauses

1984 was a year of consolidation for **Polly Peck**. The long-awaited merger with Wearwell took place in May when the half year figures were announced. They were in line with expectations at £18.6 million, up from £8 million, on sales 150% higher at £45.3 million. Analysts' forecasts for the full year centred around a figure of £50 million, and the actual total of £50.5 million was regarded as disappointing for a company accustomed to exceeding rather than meeting forecasts. At the AGM in December, Asil Nadir said that he planned to spend £40 million in 1985 and that he was in discussions with Daihatsu about manufacturing their cars

under licence in Turkey, and with Racal over a defence electronics project. The shares ended the year at 220p where
the P/E was still a cautious 4.

The year was not a good one for the Polly Peck look-alikes.
Mellins was suspended at 30p in February while refinancing negotiations were embarked upon and a month
later the receiver was called in. **Bellair** was also
suspended, but at its peak of £13¼, on the failure of the
directors to provide any explanation or substantiation of the
extraordinary rise. At the AGM in August, mention was
made of plans to manufacture cosmetics under licence in
Turkey and of the purchase of a 5.8 acre factory site to this
end, but the developments were judged by the board to be
"not sufficiently mature" to justify application for restoration of the listing at this time. **Harold Ingram** made no
mention at all about moving away from its rag trade origins
and after reaching 450p in January, fell back to close the
year at 120p.

Two not of a kind

Among notable new issues of 1984 were **Body Shop** and
Blue Arrow, both on the USM. Body Shop's novel concept
of natural-based beauty products in simple refillable packs
caught the public imagination and despite the exceptionally
high prospective P/E of 24.4 at the 95p offer price, the
shares practically doubled on the first day of dealing,
boosting the market capitalisation to almost £10 million.
Blue Arrow began public life with a placing of 18.4% of its
capital at 75p a share to give a market capitalisation for the
collection of 34 staff recruitment agencies of just over £3
million. The shares were bid up to 89p on their first day.

Fatal Distraction

Lonrho's seven-year tussle with **House of Fraser**
appeared to have ended in November when Tiny Rowland
agreed to sell his 29.9% stake in the stores group to the Al

Fayed brothers for £138 million. However, within a matter of weeks Rowland had begun buying again, building up a stake of over 5% to enable him to carry on the battle with House of Fraser's prospective new owners.

Tiny Rowland is the most enduring of the controversial characters of post-War years. Starting in 1961, he transformed the obscure London & Rhodesia Mining and Land Company (Lonrho), then making a profit of £160,000, into a pan-African enterprise embracing many of the mining and agricultural activities of the developing countries in that Continent. Businesses acquired in the UK and in Europe included the exclusive importing concession for Volkswagen and Audi cars, as well as a string of hotels and casinos, and by 1979 Lonrho's annual profits had risen to over £90 million. But while Rowland's buccaneering style had won him the admiration of Lonrho's small shareholders, it had upset a large and influential section of the political and financial establishment. The problems began in 1973 when unilateral actions on his part came to light involving overseas payments to directors allegedly designed to avoid tax, and led to accusations that he regarded Lonrho as his own private domain. They even prompted Prime Minister Heath to say that the affair represented "an pleasant and unacceptable face of capitalism". A DTI enquiry was launched, and although the boardroom battle that followed was won by Rowland, thereafter he remained an outsider as far as the City was concerned. His unorthodox courting of Harrods, which began in 1977 did not help, although paradoxically his aim was to achieve international respectability by owning the world's premier department store.

Rowland's initial acquisition in 1977 of a 24% stake in SUITs, which owned 10% of House Fraser, and Sir Hugh Fraser's agreement to step down as chairman in favour of Rowland, who also became Deputy Chairman of House of Fraser, caused consternation both in Parliament and in the City. Within months Rowland had boosted his holding in SUITs to 30% and bought the 20% stake in House of Fraser held by US stores group, Carter Hawley Hale. His decision to bid £40 million for the whole of SUITs prompted a reference to the Monopolies Commission. After a year of argument, it was decided that he could go ahead with his bid, now revised to £60 million, but by that time Sir Hugh Fraser had bowed to family and City pressure and turned against Rowland. A new boardroom struggle ensued, but Rowland managed to win Sir Hugh over yet again to his side. Thereafter, Rowland's tactics were based on extending his control over House of Fraser, but he continued to meet fierce opposition from the bulk of the board and from their adviser, Warburgs, who planned to install a new Chairman, Professor Roland Smith, in place of Sir Hugh, now the subject of widespread criticism for his gambling problems. Faced with losing both his reputation and his position, in 1980 Sir Hugh decided to back Rowland's £230 million bid for House of Fraser. Victory seemed at last to be within Rowland's grasp, but the City establishment still had one decisive card to play. The bid was referred to the Monopolies Commission. His bid earlier that year for *The Observer* had succeeded but it still managed to stir up more controversy and helped to lose him a favourable judgement on the House of Fraser bid. The Commission's grounds for rejection were not convincing, and even the popular press now sided with Rowland. The contest between Rowland and the House of Fraser board continued, and then in 1984 yet another Monopolies Commission was set up to investigate a Lonrho bid for House of Fraser.

This time Rowland was hoping for a decision in his favour but once again was disappointed. It was at this point that the Al Fayed family came on the scene and apparently having given up all hope of ever attaining his goal of winning control of House of Fraser and Harrods, Rowland agreed to sell his 29.9% stake to the Al Fayeds for £138 million. Everyone thought that was the end of the matter, but they were wrong....

Sinclair falls from favour

Things began to go wrong for Sir Clive Sinclair in the second half of 1984. Capacity had been expanded rapidly in 1983/84 and costly marketing strategies put in place to meet booming demand in the home computer market, but there was a flood of new entrants and competition became intense. As sales fell, so did the share prices of the other players, and in February the postponement of the planned flotation was announced on the grounds of "adverse stock market sentiment towards companies in the computer sector".

But there was still the electric car. Barrie Wills, managing director of Sinclair Vehicles, and a former de Lorean executive, said that at under £1000 it would appeal to a wide market, embracing commuters, shoppers and the younger generation, and could be expected to have as big an impact on the vehicle market as the inventor's low-cost products had had on electronics. In the event the C5 Electric Car was not at all what the market had been led to expect and even at the low price of £399, no one except the manufacturers believed that the sales target of 100,000 a year was a realistic one. In June Robert Maxwell decided not to proceed with a £12 million rescue operation for Sinclair Research, and in October a receiver was appointed for Sinclair Vehicles. Only 4500 C5s had been sold, there were another 4500 in stock and the company had debts of £7.75 million. Six months later Amstrad was to buy the computer interests for just £5 million.

FT Stock Exchange 100 Share Index (FT-SE)

To meet the need for a market barometer capable of instant computation in order to support a new futures contract based on the UK equity market, the FT-SE was introduced in February 1984 with a base figure of 1000. It is made up of the country's top 100 shares, i.e. those with the largest market capitalisations. Like the Actuaries indices, the FT-SE constituents are weighted and subject to change from time to time.

1985

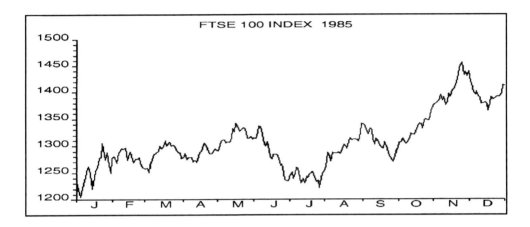

FTSE 100 INDEX 1985

Crossing the 1000 barrier

Hopes were high that the New Year would see a continuation of the favourable trends in growth, inflation and corporate profits established in 1984, but if there were doubts, they centred on the price of oil, sterling, the US economy and the Chancellor's strategy. OPEC was still in some disarray faced with an oil price that looked likely to continue to weaken, sterling showed no sign of arresting its downtrend, the twin deficits appeared to threaten the US recovery, and the record level of unemployment, at over 3 million, meant that the Chancellor would be under intense political pressure to reflate with all the attendant dangers.

In the event, anxiety over a continuing slide in sterling to $1.12 in the first half of January and a 2½% hike in base rates to help stop it, quickly turned into something like euphoria on further consideration of the benefits to UK industry of a lower exchange rate. The FT 30 crossed the 1000 mark for the first time on 18th January, held above it for a week, and then slipped below it again as the pound continued to fall and base rates were raised another 2% to 14%. The index lost over 40 points in the next two days but then steadied in the belief that a brief period of high interest rates was a necessary corrective action and that it would not have much adverse effect on a corporate sector in such a strong financial position. Even a renewed plunge of sterling towards parity with the dollar at the end of February failed to spark any further decline in equities and by mid-March the FT 30 was over 1000 again, helped by some excellent company results, bid activity, strong US buying of the leaders, and the official ending of the miners' year-long strike.

The dollar peaks

Paul Volcker's hints of official intervention at the end of February as the dollar continued to soar and the pound touched $1.0525 (70.9 on the trade-weighted index) marked the end of the dollar's extraordinary rise and simultaneously saw the Dow break into new high ground at 1299. This move heralded the start of the worldwide equity boom fuelled by cheap oil, cheap money and a cheap dollar that culminated in the crash of October 1987. For the moment, however, the event came as a considerable relief, assisting Chancellor Lawson in the task, outlined in his Budget speech in March, of resisting any further fall in the pound by keeping interest rates at whatever level might be necessary to maintain the downward pressure on inflation. In addition he reaffirmed his commitment to the MTFS, tightening the money supply growth targets to 5-9% for M3, the broad measure, and to 3-7% for M0, the narrow measure. Next year's PSBR target was £7 billion now that the figure for the current year had overshot so alarmingly as a result of the miner's strike. In an effort to reassure financial markets only £700 million, less than half what had been expected, was to be given away in tax cuts, leaving room for incentives and job creation measures. Duties were increased on drink and tobacco, but 400,000 people were taken out of the tax net altogether, and National Insurance contributions were restructured to reduce the cost of hiring lower paid workers. Capital gains were to be indexed. The next day base rates were cut by half a point to 13½%, and a week later they came down to 13% as investors switched out of a falling dollar, pushing the rate up to $1.24.

Problems for the Chancellor

A stream of rights issues kept the equity market subdued in April and May but the FT 30 managed to stay close to the 1000 level until June. Then a flurry of heavyweight offerings, totalling almost £2 billion, together with some shockingly bad results from the electronics sector and a pound soaring towards $1.40, started a slide in the index which saw it back almost to 900 in late July. **ICI** blamed a fall in second quarter profits on the strength of the pound and given that some 40% of the profits of the constituents of the Actuaries Industrial Group represented overseas earnings, with another 10% coming from direct exports, the reaction was understandable. At the same time, the market had to bear in mind that the pound's plunge towards $1 had undermined the Government's anti-inflation strategy by sending the rate of growth of the Retail Price index up to 7%, or twice the level achieved in 1983.

This de facto reflationary effect carried all the disadvantages in the form of higher prices with no benefit at all to the unemployment figures, and the Chancellor's room for manoeuvre in this area was limited further by the fact that his £5 billion public spending contingency reserve was already pre-empted thanks to lower oil revenues as the dollar price fell. Furthermore, the degree of overspend was a clear threat to his promised tax cuts, and he needed either more economical methods of funding or to continue disposing of public assets at attractive prices as a substitute for tax revenues. The political dimension of the Chancellor's problems was emphasised in July when the Conservatives lost their seat at the Brecon-Radnor by-election, a result widely taken as a verdict on his economic policies.

New highs all round

In August events began to take a turn for the better. As sterling continued to rise, half a point was taken off base rates in mid-July bringing them back to 12%, and the rate of growth in the Retail Price index slowed and then reversed to 6.8%. There was a further fall to 6.2% in the figure for August and the view was gaining ground that the policy of keeping short-term interest rates relatively high together with a stable exchange rate in order to restrain inflation would enable the Chancellor to relax his fiscal stance in the coming budget. After all, growth was already well established, industry seemed to be able to live with the current level of interest rates, and so did the public, judging from the record rise in retail sales on the back of a record level of consumer debt. And reservations about the fact that the money supply growth targets were being exceeded month by month could be countered by stressing that methods of calculating them were known to be highly unreliable. The dollar, too, was no longer a worry. The Plaza accord of the G5 nations in September had agreed on a policy decision to push it lower and get the locomotive of the US economy rolling again. Whatever remaining doubts there may have been in investors' minds had disappeared by the end of November as the FT 30 swept through 1100, the FT-SE through 1400, while the Dow crossed the 1400 level for the first time.

December was an exciting month, witnessing three of the biggest bids of all time with **Argyll** offering £1.8 billion for **Distillers, Elders IXL** £1.8 billion for **Allied Lyons**, and **Hanson** bidding £1.9 billion for **Imperial Group. GEC** also made an ultimately abortive £1.2 billion offer for **Plessey.** The economic numbers seemed to set their seal of approval on this enthusiasm as the rate of inflation fell to just over 5%, and the trend in the unemployment figures at last began to turn down.

The FT 30 closed the year at 1131.4, slightly below its November peak of 1146.9, but still up 20% influenced by its preponderance of bid targets, while the FT-SE was up 14% at 1412.6. Gilts steadied after dropping below 80 in February during the pound's slide and the raising of base rates to 14%, and recovered to end the year at 82.81, up 2%. The Dow reflected a growing optimism about the outlook for the US economy in the context of the recent G5 accord and a falling oil price, ending the year at its peak level of 1546.7, a gain of 27.6%.

Racal shocks the market

The shares of **Racal** fell 48p to 240p, taking them back to their level in 1982, on the shock announcement in January that profits for the year would be "substantially below expectations" following a £1.55 million fall at the interim stage to £47.2 million. The reason was a "major hiccup" in the US at Racal-Vadic involving a loss of £15 million. Chubb was not pleased with the news and complained to the Takeover Panel about the forecasts made in the offer document, but Racal was cleared on the grounds of genuinely unforeseen circumstances arising. The share price continued to weaken and full year profits eventually came in at a very reasonable £123.6 million, but the announcement was accompanied by yet another warning that interim profits for 1985/86 would be below last year's £47.2 million. The shares did not take kindly to this second disappointment, falling 36p to 156p and taking the whole sector down with them. The reasons given for the expected setback were the increased costs of cellular radio development, higher interest charges, and an exceptionally slow order intake in the US. Further confusion was caused by the prediction of record sales and profits in the year as a whole and the share closed the year at 160p after falling as low as 120p in November on reports of problems at Racal-Milgo.

BTR takes Dunlop

BTR began the year with a £34 million bid for debt-ridden **Dunlop,** quickly opening negotiations with the target's bankers to get them to continue their support if BTR won. Given that Dunlop's debts totalled £500 million, this was no mean achievement, and encouraged BTR to pay up to £101 million in order to secure an agreed deal. Meanwhile BTR's profits for 1984 managed to exceed all expectations at £284 million and the shares plussed 21p to 664p. Interim profits announced in September did not disappoint either, recording a 31% gain to £151 million.

Hanson boosts its war chest

Hanson Group's interim profits for 1984/85 announced in June were a little below best expectations at £106 million, but the market was worried much more by the mammoth £520 million rights issue which came out a week later. It knocked 50p off the share price and depressed the whole market to such a degree that 50% of the issue was left with the underwriters. July saw the sale of Interstate United, originally acquired in 1977, for $92.5 million, and then in August Hanson launched its biggest US bid yet with a $745 million offer for SCM, the group best known for its Smith Corona typewriters but also with important interests in foods and chemicals. The company tried hard to avoid Hanson's clutches, using complex defence systems and appeals to the US courts, but eventually was forced to capitulate after the offer was raised to $926 million. Hanson's full year figures published in December showed profits up 5% to £253 million. The whole group now had an equity market capitalisation of £3 billion.

Williams expands

In March, Rudd and McGowan were able to report profits over £1 million for the first time at £1.17 million, and later in the month they launched their biggest bid yet with a £24 million offer for the forgings and plastics group, **J & HB Jackson**. In order to secure agreement they had to raise the paper and cash alternative bid to £32.4 million. The acquisition was especially important to **Williams** in two respects. It took the group into the US where Jackson was a major distributor, and it also brought in a lot of cash which served to reduce Williams' gearing from 100% to 33%. Interim profits for 1985 duly rose by a remarkable 88% to £2.7 million, and by this time the shares had risen to 340p where they sold on a prospective P/E of 16 assuming a total for the year of close to £6 million.

The last two months of the year saw both a £11.5 million purchase of Rawlplug from **Burmah Oil**, the first big-name acquisition in the important DIY and home care market, and an agreed £7.3 million bid for **Spencer Clark**, manufacturers of structural and special steels. The shares now stood at a little over 400p.

Polly Peck misses a forecast

Polly Peck boosted its cash position in February with a £40 million rights issue, and then in May pleased the market with a 32% increase in interim profits to £28.2 million. The shares were a firm market at 280p following a company visit to Turkey by over fifty London fund managers earlier in the month. Margins continued to hold up at around the 40% level, and it was pointed out that while costs were denominated mainly in Turkish lira, receipts were in harder currencies. The rest of the year did not proceed quite so smoothly. Brokers to the company, L. Messel, reduced their profits forecast for the full year from £85 million to £68 million because of the likely "adverse impact of currency movements". The shares dropped 52p to 173p on the news but managed to maintain that level even though profits eventually turned out to be no more than £61 million.

F.H. Tomkins is transformed

In 1983 Greg Hutchings (35), a former corporate development manager with the Hanson Group, had become a major shareholder and chief executive of **F.H. Tomkins**, an industrial fasteners distribution company. At that time the share price was around the 50p mark. His first purchase was Ferraris, a distributor of motor parts, for £2.2 million, a deal that helped profits in Tomkins' first year under his

Greg Hutchings, Chief Executive of Tomkins, turned his early experience at Hanson Trust to good account by building his own individual empire.

control to rise by 50% to £2.4 million. His second was Hayters, the well-known private manufacturer of lawn-mowers, for £4 million, and in May 1985 an £11.7 million rights issue was made, giving a clear indication that more acquisitions were on the way. The following month Hutchings paid £14 million, half in shares and half in cash, for seven engineering and distribution subsidiaries of GKN. Full year profits for 1984/85 announced in July came to £3.5 million and on the basis of confident predictions of a total of over £7 million in 1985/86, the shares at 200p were selling on a prospective P/E of 18.

What Reebok did for Pentland

In August 1981, Stephen Rubin of tiny Pentland Industries had made what must rank among the most successful investments of all time. He paid $77,500 for a 55% stake in a start-up venture struggling to estab-lish itself as a distributor in the US of athletic and leisure footwear. The name of the company was **Reebok.** After a slow start, Reebok's sales really began to take off in 1983/84 on the back of the fitness boom and its fashion associations. Thanks to Pentland's experi-ence of manufacturing in the Far East, Reebok was able to cope with the meteoric increase in demand for its products, and in that year accounted for 70% of Pentland's turnover and a rise in profits of 65% to £1.65 million. Meanwhile Pentland's shares had risen from 55p at the beginning of 1984, to just over 100p in May. There was talk of a total of £2 million in the current year, but when first half profits came in at no less than £2.5 million, sights were raised to £5 million. The shares were still relatively slow to respond

Stephen Rubin, Chairman of Pentland Industries, in 1981 paid $77,500 for a 55% stake in struggling US sportswear distributor Reebok, thereby making one of the most profitable investments in history.

and by the end of August had risen only to 128p even though in March Stephen Rubin had obtained Reebok's world distribution rights. From that point on, however, the share price began to rise almost as fast as Reebok's sales. From £3 at the end of 1984, the share price had reached £10 in mid-June of 1985 when a six-fold increase in Reebok sales, to £57 million, helped Pentland's profits to £12.9 million against earlier estimates of £5 million. The decision was made to let part of its holding go in a US flotation of Reebok to value the company at over $300 million while Pentland still retained over 40% to keep producing profits as an associate.

WPP is born

May 1985 saw Martin Sorrell move into **Wire & Plastic Industries**, a manufacturer of supermarket trolleys and baskets and animal cages, that was soon to become WPP, the largest marketing services company in the world. In company with stockbroker Preston Rabl, Sorrell took a 27% stake in Wire & Plastic as a result of issuing themselves with 1.36 million shares at 38p. Martin Sorrell had already made a name for himself as finance director of Saatchi & Saatchi and the idea that he wanted to branch out on his own proved an attractive one to investors. The shares doubled to 75p on the news and moved up throughout the year to reach 290p in December when the first acquisition was made. This was graphics company VAP, for £2 million in shares, and at the same time it was announced that Saatchi & Saatchi had taken a 10% stake in WPP.

New issues in 1985

A record £6 billion was raised in the London securities market in 1985, up 72% on the previous year, and among the more notable new issues was **Coloroll**, the fast-growing home furnishings group run by Business Man of the Year, John Ashcroft. Half the capital was offered for sale at 135p a share giving a market capitalisation of £36.8 million. The issue was ten times oversubscribed but still managed to open at small discount.

Laura Ashley's popularity was less in doubt even though the P/E, at the 135p offer price, was a heady 23. Queues up to a hundred yards long formed the day the prospectus was issued and the issue was forty times over-subscribed. The shares touched 200p on the first day of dealing, closing with a premium of 59p.

1986

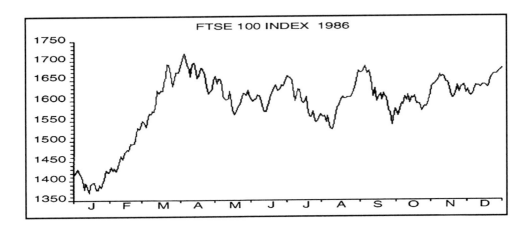

FTSE 100 INDEX 1986

Stoking the furnace

With an election looming in just over a year's time, few
doubted that the Chancellor would manage to keep the
economy on a growth track until then, and at the same time
spread his largesse a little more widely wherever it might
be needed. A further decline in the price of oil could pose a
problem but it was a development where the benefits to the
non-oil sector and to the world at large were still seen as
outweighing the disadvantages on the revenue front. Asset
sales could always fill the gap. Anxiety over sterling also
seemed to be unnecessary. The pound had weathered the
storm that the fall in the oil price had created in 1985, and
there was little reason to doubt that the Chancellor would
be able to maintain a stable exchange rate in order to
achieve his inflation target of under 4% by year-end. As for
the equity market, the prospect of low inflation and a
reasonable rate of growth looked certain to provide the rise
in earnings and dividends required to validate a prospective
yield of around 5% and a P/E of 11.

Not surprisingly the markets opened the New Year with
a broad advance, and after hesitating on the political upset

created by the Westland takeover supposed "fix" and a 1% increase in base rates to steady the pound after a sharp drop in the oil price, they recovered to close the month at record levels. There was no doubt that sentiment was aided by the sight of predators being willing to compete with each other and pay ever higher prices for what had once been thought of as rather dull companies. Thus **Imperial Group** and **Distillers** went for £2.5 billion each, some 25% above the opening bids, in hard-fought and no holds barred contests between determined bidders.

The oil price continues to fall

Despite an oil price now below $20 and still falling, an event that might have been expected to prompt another rise in interest rates, markets continued to surge ahead in February in company with the Dow which crossed the 1700 level on the last day of the month. The fact that buying of gilt-edged was pushing yields below 10% seemed to point to lower, not higher interest rates on the way, a view given substance in early March when the Federal Discount Rate was reduced to 7%.

The budget in mid-March provided markets with yet another boost. A penny was taken off the basic rate of tax bringing it down to 29p, the 25p target was reaffirmed, and thresholds and allowances were raised by just over 5% to provide a £1 billion fiscal boost where it was most likely to be spent. Significantly, the M3 target growth range was raised to 11-15%, Personal Equity Plans (PEPS) were intro-duced, and base rates were lowered to 11½%, moves which prompted Lex in the *FT* to call it a "budget for equities". Within days the FT 30 was over 1400, the Government Securities index over 90 and the Dow into 1800 plus terri-tory.

Meanwhile, the price of oil had collapsed to below $10, a level not seen since 1974. However, worries had not disap-peared completely. The rapidity and extent of the fall in the price of oil was certain to cause problems in the US banking system given the huge amount of energy-related loans, and while the Chancellor had said that he could live with halved oil revenues on the basis of $15 a barrel, $10 might prove to be quite another matter regardless of what the OECD might say about benefits to the world. At that price revenues from the North Sea would be no more than £3 billion in 1986/87 compared with £11.5 billion in 1985/86.

Red lights on the M3

April was a significant month in that it witnessed a further cut in base rates to 11% on the day that the money supply figures were released, showing it rising at an annual rate approaching 20%. The clear implication was that monetary targeting was a thing of the past, and when in May the rate of growth in M3 rose even more sharply, only to be met with a 1% reduction in base rates to 10%, there was no doubt. The fact that the same month had seen no improvement in the unemployment figures and also an unexpected drop in manufacturing output, suggested the reason for this policy change. The industrial world was still in recession. To the surprise of politicians and investors, it had not responded to lower oil prices as quickly as they had expected. Inflation had been conquered – RPI growth was down to 2.8% in May – but the problem facing the politicians in particular, with electoral timetables to keep, was how to combine low inflation with full employment. They had fallen victim to the Butler Miller Paradox (so-called after the two economists who had detected it) which states that since people want to hold more money when inflation is falling because it then represents a better store of value, a greater supply of money is going to be needed to finance activity during this period. The politician is thus faced with two more problems. One is that the store of liquidity built up as inflation was falling is not necessarily going to be held on a lasting basis but is likely to be spent, thereby adding to the excess liquidity already being pumped into the system. The other is that it will then add to the difficulty of imposing an effective monetary squeeze to reduce the ensuing inflation.

Preparing for the election

These warning signs did not go unremarked but since a bull market needs nothing more than its own existence to justify it, the investor in mid-1986 was not overly concerned about the fragility of its foundations. After all, the time for them to be tested was still some way off, and meanwhile there was money to be made in a brave new world of low inflation, low interest rates and rapid growth to be built on the ruins of OPEC.

April and May saw a 100-point fall in the FT 30 after the market had to absorb £1.8 billion in rights issues in a month, but after a strong rebound in June and July on signs of the private investor taking the place of the institutional investor, whose liquidity had shrunk to practically nil, buying petered out and the index spent the rest of the year mainly in the 1200-1300 range. The price of oil falling below $9 and a sharp deterioration in the balance of payments did not help, and with output still falling and unemployment still rising, for a time markets seemed to be anticipating even laxer financial controls with all their attendant dangers.

Nerves steadied in August after OPEC managed to agree on a plan for production cuts and the oil price rose by almost 40% to $13.95. Then in mid-October, base rates were raised by 1% to 11%, a move which the Chancellor said should be "enough to keep the anti-inflation strategy on track". His autumn statement the following month seemed to confirm the worst fears of those who thought he might be tempted to spark a pre-election mini-boom. By announcing plans to increase public spending by £10 billion over the next two years, and asset sales of £5 billion a year for the next three at the same time leaving the PSBR for 1986/87 unchanged at £7 billion, Nigel Lawson was suspected of following much the same pre-election path as his predecessor who had set tight spending targets and then allowed them to be overrun. To be fair to both Chancellors, however, they had to cope with exceptional events in the form of the Falklands War, the miners' strike and the collapse of the oil price, making overruns inevitable, and at least the money was going to a public sector that had undergone a measure of reform. It was no longer money down the drain in the form of a subsidy from taxpayers to protect nationalised industries and public services from the consequences of the huge losses incurred as a result of grossly inefficient operations. Nevertheless, the low PSBR was largely an illusion created by the Government's asset sales. Public spending had risen steadily in real terms over the past seven years and, as a percentage of Gross Domestic Product, was higher than in the last year of the Labour government.

There was a cynical view current in the closing weeks of the year that the Chancellor had abandoned monetary and fiscal restraints, accepted devaluation and let loose a consumer boom as a gamble to secure an election victory. Once this had been achieved, it was argued, the screws could be put on again in order to repair the damage done in the shape of higher inflation, higher interest rates and the first balance of payments deficit since 1979. If getting unemployment down was more important than adding a point or two to inflation in an election year, it was perhaps a gamble worth taking, especially since figures released in mid-November showed the first real decline in the numbers of jobless as well as a pre-election poll giving the Conservatives a one-point lead over Labour.

School for scandals

Markets were under something of a cloud in November and December as one scandal after another came to light. First of all Geoffrey Collier, a senior executive at Morgan Grenfell, resigned after insider dealing allegations. Then US arbitrageur, Ivan Boesky, who had been an active participant in many of the year's big bids in the UK, was fined $100 million by the SEC. After weeks of rumours, December saw a DTI investigation ordered into the Guinness takeover of Distillers, closely followed by the revelation that Guinness had "invested" $100 million in Boesky's arbitrage pool of funds. On the last day of the year, Roger Seelig, the Morgan Grenfell executive who had looked after the Guinness bid, resigned from his post at the bank. Although these events were truly exceptional in the light of the high standing of the persons and the companies involved, they did not prevent a good Christmas rally developing in a market which also had to absorb the £5.6 billion offering from **British Gas**. The advent of dual capacity and automated quotations with Big Bang in October seemed to have no particular influence on the course of markets at the time. The FT 30 closed the year at 1313.9, well below its peak, but still a gain of 15.5%, while the broader-based All-Share and FT-SE were up 20% and 23.5% at 835 and 1679 respectively. Government Securities were up a modest 1.25% at 83.62. The Dow recorded a gain of 22.5% closing at 1896.

Hanson wins Imperial Group

Imperial Group and **United Biscuit** both thought that Lord Hanson was being kept too busy in the US courts over his takeover of SCM, to concern himself with their proposed merger. His £1.9 billion bid therefore came as a surprise, although he had had his eye on Imperial for a long time. It was one of the few remaining asset situations in the UK market and an obvious target for the Hanson treatment. The referral of the Imperial-United merger to the Monopolies Commission, but not **Hanson**'s bid, was a major victory for the Hanson camp, but Sir Hector Laing of United Biscuits countered by proposing a reverse £2.5 billion bid for Imperial and getting over the Monopolies hurdle by agreeing to dispose of Imperial's Golden Wonder subsidiary. A rise in the price of Hanson's shares in the ensuing weeks put the value of both bids on a par, and a combination of a balance of institutions favouring the Hanson option and buying in the market, eventually delivered the prize.

Within the next six months, Hanson managed to dispose of enough parts of SCM to recoup the whole $926 million outlay and still retain half the original group. Boise Cascade bought the paper interests for $160 million, ICI the titanium dioxide division for $580 million and Reckitt & Colman paid $120 million for Durkee Famous Foods. The Park Avenue head office was sold for $36 million. Meanwhile Hanson Group's interim profits for 1985/86 had come in at £157 million, up 50%. The second half of the year saw the beginning of disposals from Imperial Group. In July the hotel and restaurant division was sold to Forte for £190 million, and two months later Elders IXL paid £1.4 billion for Courage. Golden Wonder went next for £87 million to Dalgety. There were also some relatively minor disposals in the US but they went a long way towards funding the $200 million purchase price of Kaiser Cement, that country's fifth ranking cement producer. Full year profits totalled £464 million, a gain of 83%, leaving the shares at 190p on an historic P/E of 11.

Racal recuperates

In line with the warning given the previous June, **Racal**'s interim profits more than halved to £23.2 million, but to sweeten the pill "very satisfactory" results were forecast for 1986/87. Profits for the full year were £90.2 million, representing the first reduction in profits since 1955, but once again Racal followers demonstrated their loyalty and the shares not only held their ground but edged ahead, reacting to analysts' forecasts that profits for 1986/87 would be back to around the £130 million mark. In December the announcement that Racal was buying out its minority partners in Vodafone for $161 million cash, indicated that Racal was in control, and the shares ended the year on a firm note at 192p.

BTR goes for Pilkington

BTR opened 1986 with the sale of Tilling's insurance subsidiary, Cornhill, for the very good price of £305 million. Rationalisation and integration of recent major acquisitions helped provide a 47% gain in final figures for 1985 to £362 million and then the half year figures saw a further strong advance to £203 million. BTR was very long on cash and in a climate where the megabid had now become almost the order of the day, everyone was waiting for BTR to pounce. The selected target turned out to be **Pilkington**, manufacturers of an everyday product but with an unimpressive record, and an ideal subject for the BTR treatment. The £1.16 billion bid was rejected immediately.

Williams and Tomkins extend their Empires

In January **Williams Holdings** laid the foundations for its biggest bid yet, by taking a 6% stake in **McKechnie**, an engineering group twice its size, already involved in a bid of its own for **Newman Tonks**. The following month Williams made a £140 million offer for McKechnie conditional on the Tonks bid being dropped. In the event, McKechnie shareholders voted for the bid to go ahead, and Williams' consolation for its first failed bid was a £2 million profit on the sale of its share stake. Its own shares were riding high, adding 26p to 548p on the news in March that 1985 profits had topped best expectations at £6.4 million. Its next move was the purchase of Fairey Engineering from **Pearson** for £22 million and then in April an agreed £79 million bid was made for **Duport**. It was hardly surprising that first half 1986 results were up by almost 200% at £8.5 million, or on recent experience, that the announcement was simultaneous with a £58 million offer for **London & Midland Industries** (LMI). Before the end of the year, 21 of LMI's subsidiaries had been sold for £20 million, a move that effectively reduced Williams' gearing from 20% to zero. The next major bid could not be far away.

F.H. Tomkins also had a busy year. Profits for the first half of 1985/86 doubled to £2.4 million and the shares at 237p were selling on a prospective P/E of 21. With £12 million in cash another bid was expected before long, but few expected anything quite so ambitious as a £175 million all paper bid for **Pegler-Hattersley**. After upping the price to £200 million, Tomkins managed to secure its prize. Full year figures comfortably exceeded expectations at £7.4 million, and by then the shares had risen to 310p where the prospective P/E was down to 14.

Polly Peck goes shopping

Shares of Polly Peck were a nervous market in 1986. They began the year with an unexplained 20p drop to 138p, but confident statements about trading saw them back to 200p at the end of May in time for the interim report. Profits were slightly below expectations at £31.2 million but an accompanying announcement about expanding produce sales into Western and Eastern Europe and improving currency management, served to reassure the market. Full year profits revealed in December were up by 15% to £70.4 million and were closely followed by news of the purchase of TI's small appliance division comprising Russell Hobbs and Tower Housewares for £12 million cash. The acquisition was welcomed for providing some top brand names to boost Polly Peck's consumer sales in the Near East as well as a UK

earnings base. The shares closed the year at 180p, still on a
P/E of no more than 3.5.

The Guinness Affair

Ernest Saunders was
appointed Chief Executive of
Guinness in 1981 with the
task of reversing the group's
ramshackle and unsuc-
cessful diversification policy
which had left it with over
250 operations ranging from
film finance to babywear.
Within five years more than
half of these had been
disposed of and Guinness
was firmly established in
just three key areas –
namely brewing, retailing
and publishing. In the
process, profits recovered
dramatically and market

Ernest Saunders, Chief Executive of
Guinness, won and lost his reputation
by turning the company into an international giant.

capitalisation rose from £90 million to £500 million.

The merger with Distillers in 1986 was to be Saunders'
crowning achievement and he was to stop at nothing to push
rival bidder, Argyll Foods, off the scene. This he succeeded in
doing but the methods he employed soon came under
scrutiny, and in January 1987 he was forced to step down
along with his Finance Director, Olivier Roux. Apart from
upsetting the Scottish lobby by failing to honour an undertaking to appoint Sir Thomas Risk as Chairman, his big
mistake was to ensure success for his bid by covert means.
There was nothing new about trying to persuade institutions
to support the share price of one bidder rather than that of a
rival in the case of a paper bid, but it was usually done by a
nod and a wink over lunch or at informal meetings. The
subsequent court proceedings revealed that Saunders'
support had been won not only by using Guinness's own
money but also by offering 'no loss' guarantees and performance fees – which were readily accepted – to helpful
financiers, including the already discredited Ivan Boesky.

1987

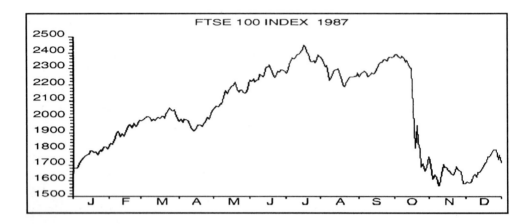

FTSE 100 INDEX 1987

Jeux sans frontières

Prospects for the New Year looked promising, not only in the UK but in all the major industrial nations. There were high hopes of what the Plaza Accord might achieve in terms of getting the surplus countries, principally Germany and Japan, to stimulate their economies in order to help reduce the trade imbalance between themselves and the US. Markets were prepared to take a great deal on trust and by the end of January practically all of them were at new peaks. The Dow had cracked the 2000 level for the first time, the Nikkei Dow, 20000, and in London the FT 30 and the FT-SE had broken through the 1400 and 1800 levels respectively. Leading UK industrials, like Glaxo and ICI, were becoming firm favourites with international fund managers impressed by the remarkable transformation of the country's economic status. Export-led growth was accelerating, productivity was continuing to improve, government revenues were above estimate, the trade account was in balance and unemployment was falling. In addition, political continuity and stability were virtually assured by the prospect of a renewed term for the Conservatives.

The picture looked almost too good to be true, but for every commentator who thought it was just that, there were two or more ready to justify a continuing rise. Thus the potential problem posed by the high rate of growth in average earnings was explained away on the grounds that it was merited by improved productivity and overtime working in certain industries, while the level of output was said to be understated since the figures gave too much weight to declining industries. As for the renewed decline in the dollar and the possibility that it could force the Federal Reserve Board to impose another squeeze at the risk of causing another world recession, clearly it was the duty of Germany and Japan to take on the locomotive role by stimulating their own economies more. In any case London was cheap by international standards as the wave of foreign buying demonstrated. There was also a distinct air of excitement in markets as the public climbed on the privatisation and new issue bandwagons. Long queues formed outside the issuing houses for prospectuses and multiple applications became the order of the day. Since an allocation invariably resulted in an instant profit, the new private investor soon came to see the stock market as a moneymaking machine. Even the scandals became a bull point by making the whole business of "investment" risqué and alluring.

Betting on a Conservative win

By early March, markets had surged to new record levels ahead of a budget likely to predate the election only by a matter of weeks. Helped by a ½% cut in Base Rates to 10½%, the FT-SE crossed the 2000 level for the first time in the week before the budget, then paused and regrouped ready for another run in anticipation of a Conservative victory in June. The budget did nothing to harm this prospect. The basic rate of tax was reduced by 2p to 27p, and thresholds and allowances were raised. Both moves were widely regarded as "fiscally responsible" in that the Chancellor was using half his buoyant revenues for tax cuts and the other half to reduce borrowing. The PSBR target for 1987/88 was now down to £4 billion, 3½% growth was forecast for the non-oil economy, inflation was expected to fall to 4% by year-end, growth in M0 (bank deposits with the Bank of England and notes and coins in circulation) was to be targeted in a 2-6% range, and the current account deficit was considered unlikely to exceed an acceptable £2.5 billion. Gilts liked the package too and the Government Securities index stood at 90.9 on budget day, having risen steadily since the beginning of the year. Within a week of the budget, base rates came down another half point to 10%. Some anxiety was expressed about the rapid growth of private credit and the consumer spending boom, but that too was rationalised by the consideration that, unlike corporate or government borrowing, consumer borrowing is eventually repaid.

New worries about the dollar

It was a sudden fall in the dollar at the end of March that began to spoil this apparently rosy picture. A further meeting of the Group of Five in Paris in February had produced the so-called "Louvre Accord", whereby in return for a US commitment to stabilise the dollar, the Germans and the Japanese had promised once again to undertake their own expansionary measures. However, this renewed fall in the dollar gave rise to the suspicion that the US authorities were reverting to the policy of "benign neglect" of the early years of the Carter administration, in an attempt to force the issue. That suspicion became a certainty when it became known that Paul Volcker was not to be invited to carry on for a third term as head of the Federal Reserve Board but was to be replaced by a supposedly more pliant Alan Greenspan. The worry now was that the US would overplay its hand in this game of international financial poker, and fail to win an improvement in its trade deficit since a whole series of devaluations meant that the adverse impact of the latest rise in import prices would always serve to mask the benefit of a turnround in exports.

By contrast, the UK had managed a very successful devaluation against the DMark over the past two years without courting inflationary dangers because it took place at a time of falling oil and commodity prices and when the labour market was particularly slack. Not surprisingly, the pound now became a firm favourite with overseas investors, giving great importance to the Chancellor's supposed exchange rate targeting policy. It seemed clear that a link with a non-inflationary currency like the DMark provided the ultimate backstop against inflation, for as long as the exchange rate target was maintained, a lid would be put on all costs and prices subject to international competition. Furthermore, on the domestic front selective monetary easing could be carried out without too much risk of inflationary side effects.

A landslide victory for Mrs Thatcher

The ramifications of an exchange rate targeting policy took very much second place in the minds of investors, institutional and private, in the weeks ahead of the election on 11th June. Two half-point reductions in base rates had brought them down to 9% by early May, **Sock Shop**, oversubscribed 53 times, opened at more than double the 125p offer price, and **Tie Rack** did even better, attracting subscriptions of over £1 billion for the £12½ million of stock on offer. **Rolls-Royce** was hugely oversubscribed and opened at 147p partly paid against an offer price of 85p, while **Polly Peck** at last moved into new high ground thanks to a wave of buying of its new ADRs by US investors who did not share in London's "residual scepticism". Against the trend and with masterly timing in May, co-founder of **WPP**, Preston Rabl, placed his 5.6% stake in the company with institutions, and two months later Saatchi & Saatchi followed suit.

The Conservative win with a majority of 100 seats was up to the best expectations of the market and the FT 30 added another 27.1 to a record 1767.9, the FT-SE 40.2 to 2289.5, and the Dow provided moral support by advancing 17.6 to 2377.7. But with the yield on equities at just over 3%, or one third of that obtainable on long-term government stocks, the ratio was now at a record level. In addition, money supply growth of M3 was rising at well over 20% a year, oil prices were firming, commodity prices had stopped falling, and growth in earnings was edging over 8%. Not surprisingly consumer spending was at record levels and house prices were soaring along with those of other non-financial assets.

Twin peaks

There was still a month to go before London hit its peak for the year, and yet another six weeks before New York did the same, but although the warning signs multiplied there was no broad consensus that markets were riding for a fall. Oddly enough Tokyo had taken a 10% tumble between June and July, and given its status as the most expensive of all markets, its rapid recovery to a new record was seen as a vote of confidence in world share prices. Also the downward drift of the dollar had halted and a degree of stability had returned to currency markets, giving rise to hopes that with its trade imbalance no longer widening, the US would be able to survive the strain of its double deficit pending further progress in the field of international monetary co-operation. Even fears of a Third World debt crisis began to recede as commodity prices firmed, thus relieving the pressure on the hard-pressed debtor countries while the Western banks began to make multi-billion dollar provisions against potential loan losses. But as far as London was concerned, these global factors were less important than a deluge of new issues and rights which the market was simply unwilling and then unable to digest, as well as a run of disappointing, even alarming, economic numbers.

Nearing the summit

The indices peaked on 16th July with the FT 30 at 1926.2 and the FT-SE at 2443.4, but significantly with the Government Securities index at just under 91, some 2½ points short of its high. On the same day the Dow reached a new record of 2496.97 but from then on London was more concerned with its own problems.

A week later markets were shocked by a dramatic increase in the trade deficit for May to £1.16 billion after a steep rise in imports. At the end of the month, top stockbrokers Barclays de Zoete Wedd called an end to the long bull market, the Government Securities index had fallen another three points to 87.66, and the yield ratio had risen to a multiple of 3.3, higher than the peak in 1972. There was also an enormous and growing settlement backlog aggravated by the active trading of small investors in penny stocks with an insatiable appetite for rights issues.

Then in the first week of August, just three years after joining the USM with a market capitalisation of £3 million, **Blue Arrow**, still with net assets of only £21 million, announced the biggest rights issue ever of £837 million to finance the takeover of Manpower in the US, the world's leading recruitment agency. The *FT* described the move as one of "stunning audacity" and warned that the surplus liquidity in the system that made such deals possible carried the danger that increased leverage in the securities and property markets would make any setbacks very painful. **WPP**'s £177 million rights issue to help finance Martin Sorrell's bid for J. Walter Thompson, of which only 35% was taken up, did not bode well for the Blue Arrow issue, and the uncertainty was compounded two days later when a surprise 1% rise in base rates to 10% in response to "domestic monetary conditions" knocked the FT-SE back to 2261, 56 points down on the day. Along with a rights issue of £700 million from **Midland Bank**, and the **British Airport Authorities** (BAA) £500 million issue, underwriters were calculated to be coping with some £3 billion, two thirds of which they now seemed likely to be left holding.

Over the top

Still ready to look on the bright side, investors took the view that with the mammoth sale of £7.2 billion of **BP** stock scheduled for the third week of October, the Chancellor was following the Grand Old Duke of York strategy by knocking markets down in August ready for a run-up ahead of this much-publicised offering. In any case the Dow was still marching onward and upward, reaching a peak of 2722.42 on 25th August.

London began to rally in early September, survived another horrendous set of trade figures both in the US and at home, and entered October approaching the 2400 level with sentiment aided by **TSB**'s £777 million bid for **Hill Samuel**, **AB Food**'s £767 million offer for **S & W Berisford**, and **Benlox**'s £2 billion break-up bid for **Storehouse**. Meanwhile **Saatchi & Saatchi** had made an abortive approach to **Midland Bank** as well as to **Hill**

Samuel, and **Blue Arrow**'s rights issue was reported as only 48.9% taken up with the balance placed by Phillips & Drew with "outside investors". In a climate of such frenetic activity, the feeling was that a rising share should not be sold in case there was something about to happen and that a falling share should not be sold either in case it attracted a bid.

With manufacturing output now rising strongly, unemployment still falling and confident CBI surveys, markets were looking forward post-BP to a period of calm and consolidation with no privatisations for at least six months. This reasoned appraisal of the investment situation changed abruptly at the end of the first week in October when a sudden rise in US prime rates from 8¾% to 9¼% coincided with an all-embracing "sell" recommendation by respected Elliott Wave analyst, Robert Prechter. The Dow responded with a record points drop of 91.55 to 2548.63, and a hesitant recovery at the beginning of the second week was snuffed out abruptly by another disappointing set of trade figures followed by a renewed slide in the dollar. On Wednesday 14th October, the Dow lost 95 points, the following day another 57, and no relief was in prospect for Friday after a hike in prime rates to 9¾%.

At one with the elements

The London market had not been upset very much by the news from New York, and the FT-SE closed at 2322 on Thursday 15th October. There was a widespread conviction that "they" would ensure a firm market for the BP sale later in the month at 330p but any investor who might have been tempted to cut and run on Friday morning after learning of the prime rate rises would have found it practically impossible to deal. The previous night had witnessed one of the worst storms in living memory with London and the South East especially hard hit. Falling trees had disrupted road and rail services as well as telephone lines, and most stockbrokers and marketmakers were unable either to get to their offices or even to communicate with them. As a result Friday in London was a non-event for all practical purposes and the news next morning that the Dow had fallen a record 108.36 ensured that there would be pent-up panic selling on

Monday. Systems failures meant that there were no figures available for Friday, and Monday's record 249.6 drop in the FT-SE was measured against Thursday's close.

There was worse to come on Tuesday following Wall Street's Black Monday when the Dow dropped 508.32 points to 1738.42, its worst ever fall, inviting parallels with the Great Crash of October 1929. The FT-SE lost another 250.7 bringing it back to 1801.6 and Tokyo fell by a record 3836 to 21910. With BP back to around 280p against almost 350p a week earlier, the outlook for the offer at 330p was not promising, but appeals by the US underwriters to have the issue abandoned were rejected by the Chancellor. Instead a buy-back floor price was conceded which meant that the Government actually benefited from the Crash by buying back at 70p shares it had sold three weeks before at 120p in partly-paid form.

Rescuing the dollar

To the extent that it was the continuing weakness of the dollar as a result of the failure of the US authorities to live up to their part of the Louvre Accord that had set the scene for the October Crash, the event inevitably made the problem more acute and the dollar promptly fell to new record lows against the currencies of its major trading partners. The latter, already fretting that the huge amounts expended on trying to support the dollar earlier in the year had done nothing but boost their own money supply and undermine their own low inflation policies, now had no alternative but to continue to play the game according to the American rules. Accordingly, they embarked upon a round of interest rate cuts on the post-Crash assumption that everything possible had to be done to halt the dollar's slide and restore confidence in the international financial system. The US authorities had won their poker game but the danger remained that it would prove to be a Pyrrhic victory unless a programme of fundamental corrections was embarked upon in the US as a quid pro quo for the supportive actions of its trading partners.

The aftershock of the 'quake that hit world stock markets on 19th October continued to reverberate for the rest of the year and beyond. However, fears of a rapid initial impact on consumer confidence and on investment as a result of the sharp reduction in financial wealth and the increased difficulty of obtaining equity finance appeared to have been exaggerated when evidence of any adverse effect on real activity proved hard to find. Indeed, the concerted efforts to avoid recession served to prolong artificially a boom that had already outlived its natural life. The day of reckoning had been postponed, not averted, but many took comfort from the thought that the Crash had occurred as a result of the temporary breakdown of a relatively untried, oversophisticated computerised trading system faced with a sudden and dramatic increase in cross-border activity. Also blamed was the huge amount of trading in futures and "derivatives" with their unquantifiable effect on "real" shares in the here and now. It was even suggested – with considerable justification – that the collapse had been a blessing in disguise in that it had pricked the bubble of asset speculation arising from five years of irrational concentration on capital gains rather than income, and heralded a return to more orthodox values.

Chancellor Lawson's contribution to this international rescue operation for the dollar was three ½% reductions in base rates, one at the end of October, one at the beginning of November and one at the beginning of December, bringing them back to 8½%. With the exchange rate at $1.86 at year-end against $1.68 at the time of the Crash, the reductions did not do much to help the dollar, but they may have eased the after-effects of Black Monday by helping to restore a degree of confidence in some investors, private and institutional, burdened by underwriting commitments and nursing massive losses on shares bought only weeks earlier. County Natwest, for example, reported losses of £69 million, £49 million of which was accounted for by Blue Arrow. Certainly an upbeat Autumn statement provided no case for base rate reductions, and the market remained nervous on fears that the Chancellor was following the example of the US and putting other policy objectives above the fight against inflation. Still, such anxieties did not prevent a useful rally developing in December, taking the FT-SE out of its 1550-1650 trading range up to nearly 1800 before closing at 1712.7 for a gain of just 2% on the year but down 30% on the mid-July peak of 2443.4. Over the same period the average dividend yield had risen from 3.3% to 4% while the

P/E had fallen from 15.1 to 12. **Eurotunnel**, however, was substantially undersubscribed and opened at 100p discount to the 350p offer price. Gilts ended the year at 88.99, well below their peak on inflation fears, but still up 5% overall, demonstrating the appeal of quality bonds for investors who had witnessed the devastating vulnerability of even the most blue chip of equity investments. Wall Street's performance was much in line with that of London, losing practically all the year's gains and ending not much better than at the start of the year, up just 2% at 1938.8.

Hanson buys Kidde

Hanson had another successful year. A run of relatively minor disposals preceded the interim figures which exceeded best expectations with a 97% advance to £312 million, including a six-month contribution from Imperial. Then in August came the biggest US bid yet with an agreed $1.7 billion offer for Kidde, a conglomerate with over a hundred subsidiaries all operating in basic industries and ripe for rationalisation. Hanson's earnings growth in 1988 was now assured. Results for the first nine months of 1986/87 announced in late August saw the shares up to a peak for the year of 195p on a prospective P/E of 14 given a likely full year total of around £725 million. This remarkable performance did not prevent the savaging of the shares in the wake of the October Crash, and even though the annual profits came out at £741 million, they ended the year at 127p, down 35%. Hanson also took two "investment" stakes during the year, one of 3% in **Morgan Grenfell** and one of 5% in **Midland Bank**, typically both "name" companies fallen on hard times.

Vodafone underpins Racal

Racal's 8.4% gain at the interim level to £25.2 million was notable for the first move into the black by the telecommunications division based on Vodafone. The figure was a modest £97,000 against a loss of over £7 million, but forecasts of a £10 million profit were made for 1987 ranging up to £100 million in 1990. Even the failure of group profits to match estimates of £110 million for the full year by 10% failed to dent investor enthusiasm, and the shares surged ahead to a peak of 348p in September on confidence that Vodafone would ensure a total of at least £150 million in 1987/88. The shares suffered more than most leaders in the post-Crash shakeout and ended the year at 222p, down 36%.

Pilkington gets away

BTR's year began with a disappointment for new Chief Executive John Cahill, who had taken over from Sir Owen Green in November, when they were forced to drop the Pilkington bid. The proposed takeover had raised a major political storm as a result of the Government's failure to refer the bid to the Monopolies Commission, even though there were no obvious grounds for doing so. The Pilkington family had a lot of political clout and made good use of it in a climate where sentiment had turned against the megabid in the wake of the Guinness affair. The full year figures for 1986 provided some compensation in that they were considerably above best market expectations at £505 million, a 40% advance marking the company's twentieth successive year of growth. Interim profits for the current year announced in September showed a continuation of this trend with a 38% gain to £280 million and most commentators agreed that at this stage, BTR had the edge over Hanson in the "organic growth" stakes. The shares peaked at 374p in September and managed to lose 100p, or 27%, in the final quarter.

Williams and Tomkins keep buying

Williams achieved the peak of its popularity in 1987, overcoming any disappointment that might have been caused by the narrow failure of its £540 million bid for veteran engineering conglomerate, Norcros. Profits for 1986 more than tripled to £22.9 million on turnover doubled to £206 million, and the shares rose another 10p on the news to 738p where the market capitalisation was £347 million. Then in June the shares were suspended at 835p ahead of the purchase for £250 million, to be funded by a share placing, of Reed International's DIY division, comprising some of the best brand names in the business in the shape of Crown Paints and Polycell as well as the paint interests in North America. This deal was widely regarded as a major coup for Rudd and McGowan and the shares continued to gain ground ahead of the interim results due in September. They did not disappoint either and the figure of £18 million was taken as an indication of full year profits of over £50 million, leaving the shares at 927p on a prospective P/E of 15. After a 2 for 1 scrip, the shares topped out at 347p and ended the year at 219p, down 37% as the high-flying conglomerates tended to fall out of favour with investors.

The year was also a brilliant one for Greg Hutchings and **F.H. Tomkins**. January saw interim profits for 1986/87 practically quadrupled to £9.3 million, and in May he announced the purchase of US gun makers Smith & Wesson for $112 million in cash and shares. This 135-year-old company, with one of the best known brand names in the world, had a 30% share of the US market but had recently run into problems, losing an important US Army contract to Beretta. The deal had been masterminded by Hutchings' alter ego in America, Roger Carr, in a partnership clearly based on the Hanson-White model. Full year profits once again exceeded best expectations at £30 million, also quadrupling, and estimates for the following year were pencilled in at £42 million plus, as rationalisation benefits continued to flow. After peaking at 320p, the shares ended the year at 220p, down 31%.

Polly Peck finds new friends

Continuing with his plans to diversify geographically and to reduce **Polly Peck**'s dependence on the Near East, in March Asil Nadir contrived a £20 million placing of stock at 203p with institutions, the proceeds to be spent on expanding the produce distribution network in Western Europe. The shares moved ahead steadily in the first half of the year, passing the old £36 peak in May thanks to vigorous buying of the new ADRs by US investors whose shareholdings now topped 20%. The interim results, with profits up 18% at £36.9 million, did not disappoint and at 296p the shares were selling on a prospective P/E of around 6 assuming a full year total of £83 million. The shares continued to advance throughout the summer, eventually reaching a high of 422p just before the Crash on the announcement that the electronics business was being expanded four-fold by the acquisition of Capetronic in the US for $35 million. Full year profits revealed in December were above target at £86 million, and the shares, now back to 260p, were on a prospective P/E of 5. They rallied strongly during the rest of the month to close at 288p.

Picking up the pieces

Among the principal casualties of the Crash were the "shells", tiny quoted companies with a vestigial business, control of which had been bought by one or more entrepreneurs. Suspended pending reorganisation and refinancing, they would then return to the market after tranches of the increased capital had been placed with friends of the new management and favoured institutions. The first day of dealing would see a mad scramble for stock by small private investors, alerted to the situation by the City pages and by the specialist 'penny share' publications, resulting in a meteoric rise in the share price.

There was nothing new about the idea. Slater had done it in 1964 with H. Lotery, and more recently so had Asil Nadir with Polly Peck. But now with a bull market roaring away and mass public participation, everyone was trying to get in on the act. Entrepreneurs of whom no one had ever heard had to do no more than announce that they had gained control, raise some money on the strength of as yet unspecified acquisitions, and the share price would soar away. They were then in a position to use their paper to take over established companies and to come out with rights issues to raise even more cash.

The South Africans, always keen to sense a favourable business climate, were early on the scene following in the footsteps of Michael Meyer who had made such a success in building up **Emess Lighting**. Kenneth Maud took control of tiny **Peek Holdings** in August 1986 with the aim of turning it into a leader in applied electronics and industrial technology, and after a rights issue at 2½p saw the shares soar to 160p at their peak in the summer of 1987. Over this period he managed to make some useful acquisitions, but too late to do so were Daryll Phillips who tried to build a media services empire with **Acsis**, and Bruce McInnes who planned to turn **Charles Baynes** into a specialist engineering group. They did not make their move until late in June 1987 and although the impact on their respective share prices was instantaneous and dramatic, it did not last long enough to enable any really advantageous acquisitions to be made. More successful was Hugo Biermann with **Thomson T-Line** which, thanks to a well-structured acquisition policy taking in bookmakers J. Coral, he managed to sell to Ladbrokes.

Other darlings of the small private investor – and of more than a few large institutions – were **Blacks Leisure**, **Platignum**, **Eagle Trust** and **James Ferguson** of Barlow Clowes fame, along with a number of fast-growing property developers like **Dares Estates**, **Randsworth**, **Speyhawk** and **Marina Developments**. The October Crash was a watershed for these speculative favourites as investors clamoured to sell in an unwilling market where the size had contracted and the spread had widened alarmingly.

1988

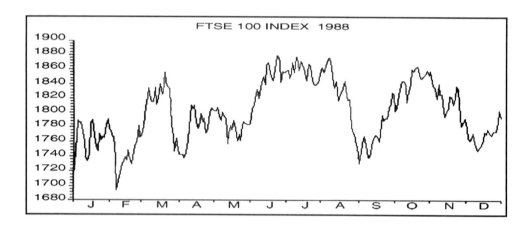

FTSE 100 INDEX 1988

Fuelling the spending boom

As far as the real economy was concerned, Black Monday witnessed the "crash that never was". The vision of world recession and financial collapse that had seemed so frightening then had quickly faded as consumers continued to spend and profits kept on growing. The rate of growth in 1987 looked like exceeding the estimate in the budget, actually accelerating in the second half, but for many commentators this remarkable performance evoked memories of the last days of earlier "dashes for growth" in 1964 and 1974 and their aftermath. The key question was over the nature of the motive power behind the boom, and in particular whether it owed more to rapid money growth and credit expansion than to increased productivity and competitiveness. The consensus seemed to be that it was a mixture of both, in which case the Chancellor would have to be ready to apply a touch of the brakes by raising interest rates and at the same time going easy on his promised tax cuts.

The situation was made even more delicate by the fact that the dollar was continuing to fall, still with no visible effect on the trade imbalances and thus the background remained as unstable now as it had been in the run-up to the October Crash. The consolation for investors, however, was the thought that a dollar that had halved against the yen and the DMark since 1985 was bound to have a dramatic effect on the competitive position of US exports before long, and that with stock markets in London and New York both down by some 30% from their 1987 peaks, the downward adjustment was in line with the post-War bear market average and the scope for a further decline had to be limited.

The Chancellor's dilemma

A sharp rise in the dollar in mid-January after a 25% fall in the US trade deficit was taken as some indication that policies were beginning to work and both markets rose, but London quickly relapsed when the Chancellor reacted to record bank lending figures and a higher than expected trade deficit in December, by raising base rates by half a point to 9%. The move was described by Shadow Trade and Industry Secretary, Bryan Gould, as "a body blow to British industry", an interesting comment in the light of Labour's criticisms during the 1992 election campaign of the immediate post-Crash rate reductions. Thereafter the London market became increasingly dominated by concern over the deteriorating trade deficit, the excessive growth in money supply, and the unrelenting pressure for higher pay in key public and private sectors. The Bank of England was already issuing warnings that interest rates might have to go up again in order to bear down on inflation but during the second quarter of the year the Chancellor chose to let an appreciating exchange rate do the job, at the same time giving himself room to compensate industry by cutting interest rates.

This phase began with the "radical, reforming" budget in mid-March which took 2p off the basic rate of tax bringing it down to the promised 25p, and slashed the top rate to 40%, as well as indexing allowances at twice the rate of inflation, all adding up to a £4 billion giveaway package. The equity market responded to the reduction in interest rates to 7½% by mid-May, rising above the 1800 level on the FT-SE, but was unable to maintain it for long after the Chancellor abruptly changed tack. The problem facing him was two-fold. One aspect was that lower interest rates were much less important to low-geared UK industry than a high exchange rate, and the balance of payments deficit continued to rise alarmingly. The other was that lower interest rates helped to inflate domestic demand by fuelling a private sector borrowing binge, thus adding to inflationary pressures. The situation was aggravated further by the absence of a PSBR which had the reverse effect of "crowding out", leaving the field clear for the private sector, and by the fact that foreign investors saw sterling as a one-way bet.

Double jeopardy

Thus faced with the choice between letting the pound appreciate and further hurt the competitive position of industry, or cutting interest rates and abandoning his anti-inflation policy, the Chancellor decided to hang on to the anti-inflation policy at all costs and opt for a high exchange rate and high interest rates. Base rates rose in four half-point steps in June from 7½% to 9½%, and were increased progressively to reach 13% by the end of November, their upward march accompanied by an ever-widening trade deficit and rising inflation figures, as August's "temporary blip" at 5.7% began to take on a permanent air. The risk was that in due course an unsustainable "go" phase in the economy would be brought to an all too sustainable "stop" as a rising exchange rate reversed much of industry's competitive gains since 1986, and rising interest rates hit a personal sector that was historically grossly overextended, particularly in an obviously vulnerable property market.

The Autumn Statement, however, was looking for a controlled slowdown with a "soft landing" for the economy in 1989 as GDP growth slowed to 3% from 4½% in 1988, and the inflation rate topped out at 7% the following summer, falling back to 6¼% in the fourth quarter before returning to 5% in 1990. The dramatic expansion of the trade deficit was not explained away altogether satisfactorily by the official view that the balance of payments provided a safety valve for excess demand at home, and that the deficit would ultimately be self-correcting as inflationary pressures were tackled at their source. Indeed, a rise from £1 billion in 1986 to £2.7 billion in 1987 rising to a likely £15 billion in 1988, seemed to indicate that the "teenage scribblers" in the stockbrokers' offices had been much more prescient than Mr Lawson in June when they predicted a £10 billion trade deficit and base rates rising to 12%.

The year ended on a relatively cheerful note, helped by a buoyant Wall Street in the wake of the re-election of the Republicans, and by a sharp reduction in the November trade deficit, but there was no runaway enthusiasm. The massive intervention in support of the dollar since the October 1987 Crash had had an expansionary effect on the world economy in 1988, but while US trade performance had improved, the familiar pattern of current account deficits in the US matched by surpluses in Japan and Germany persisted. The problem had been managed, not solved, and it was clear that hopes for future macro-economic coordination rested very much on the working out of the international political progress.

All in all, it had been a year of low activity in London with the institutions tending to sit on the fence and top up their holdings by way of rights issues, while the majority of private investors had gone to ground completely, switching their allegiance from shares to property. Even so, the £2½ billion public offering from **British Steel** was more than three times oversubscribed and the shares opened at a small premium in December. The FT-SE closed the year at 1782.8, up just 2%, while the FT 30 was barely changed at 1447.8. Gilts continued to reflect inflation fears and Government Securities lost 1.5 points to 86.85. Gold shares remained depressed with FT Gold Mines down from 296 to 161 on the continuing failure of the bullion price to derive any benefit from the Crash. The Dow at 2144 gained over 10% on the year on growing expectations that the dollar was bottoming out and that the US economy was on course for a soft landing. Tokyo managed the best performance of all, crossing the 30000 level on the Nikkei Dow into new high ground by year-end.

Hanson prefers to be a seller

Hanson opened 1988 with an agreed £69 million cash bid

for UK brickmaker, George Armitage, but it proved to be the sole purchase in a year which Lord Hanson later referred to as one for selling rather than buying. The following month another part of Kaiser Cement was sold for $195 million, a deal which meant that the whole of the acquisition price had now been recouped leaving Hanson with a rump making $20 million a year. First quarter profits were well up to expectations, recording a 12% gain to £169 million, but conglomerates were still out of favour, and at 137p the shares were selling at a 15% discount to the average market rating. A total of £800 million was pencilled in by analysts at this point, but this estimate was raised to £840 million after first half profits came in at £356 million, up 14%. August saw the sale of Kidde Fire Protection to UK's **Pilgrim House** for $254 million, and a nine-month profits total of £605 million which promptly raised full year hopes into the £845-850 million range. Before the end of the year another division of SCM, Durkee Industrial Foods, was sold to Unilever for $185 million bringing the total proceeds from the $926 million acquisition in 1986 to $1.3 billion, and Kidde Credit brought in another $70 million. A proposal almost to double the group's borrowing powers to £11 billion raised speculation about the next bid target, and the year ended with the encouraging news that profits for 1987/88 had exceeded all estimates at £880 million. The shares were now 157p and the P/E was in single figures.

Racal floats Vodafone

Racal's figures continued to be dominated by the extraordinary growth of its telecom division, and first half profits recorded a gain of 73% to £43.4 million, confirming hopes of a likely total for the year of around £150 million. In April the decision was made to float 20% of **Vodafone**, now to be called **Racal Telecom**, in order to generate cash for the parent company to pursue its ambitions to expand its security and datacom operations in Europe. The shares rose 72p on the news to 319p on the expectations of the effect on Racal of a growth valuation being accorded to its remarkable offshoot. Full year profits of £159 million did not disappoint, but everyone was waiting for the terms of the Racal Telecom flotation in October. At the 170p offer price the new shares were being sold on a prospective P/E of 30.5 on a forecast of profits practically doubling to £71.7 million. This put a valuation of £1.7 billion on the new company, which meant that with Racal still retaining an 80% stake, the whole of the rest of Racal was being valued at no more than £300 million, an anomalously low figure even bearing in mind a static profits performance. Interim profits announced in December were up 44% at £62.4 million, a gain due entirely to a further dramatic advance by Racal Telecom. Given their high rating at the flotation price, Racal Telecom shares received a cautious welcome from investors but quickly attracted buyers and closed the year at 184p.

BTR's results for 1987 proved something of a disappointment when the 17% gain in profits to £590 million fell short of forecasts ranging up to £700 million. The discrepancy was blamed on exchange rate effects, and did not prevent the shares from out-performing the averages later in the year as investors acknowledged the attractions of BTR's diversity of businesses and locations at a time when domestic concerns were dominated by rising interest rates and a consumer squeeze. The last quarter of the year saw two significant overseas purchases in Rockwell's measurement and flow control division for $437 million cash, and New Zealand carpet and soft furnishings company, Feltrax, for $572 million. The shares recorded a modest gain on the year at 294p.

Williams collects more "names"

The year opened for **Williams** with the completion of the purchase for £138 million of Berger Paints from Hoechst, a deal which left them as the country's second largest paint business. By the time the 1987 results were due, the shares had advanced to 274p and profits of £57.2 million did not disappoint. Estimates for the full year fell into the £115-120 million range, and interim profits of £50.5 million in September indicated that they were well on course. Meanwhile, in pursuit of market-leading brand names, Williams had taken a 3.9% stake in **Yale & Valor**, and added upmarket kitchen supplier **Smallbone** to its collection. The final deal of the year was the acquisition of electrical and electronic group **Pilgrim House** for £330 million in cash and convertible stock. The move was seen as providing Williams with a better balance of interests, effectively doubling the size of its industrial and military products divisions and increasing overseas exposure. The shares ended the year practically unchanged at 225p.

Tomkins looks to the US again

First half profits up 81% to £16.8 million pleased followers of Greg Hutchings and prompted forecasts of a total of around £44 million for the full year. This figure was comfortably exceeded at £47 million with the help of a $16 million contribution from Smith & Wesson, and the acquisition of Murray Ohio Manufacturing for $224 million was seen as providing scope for further substantial earnings growth in 1989. However, the shares did not do well over the year while investors chose to stay on the sidelines to see how the newer conglomerates fared in less favourable trading conditions.

Polly Peck expands its network

1988 was the year in which Asil Nadir began to expand his fresh produce distribution network. In February a Spanish packer was bought to complement recent acquisitions in Marseilles and Rotterdam, in May a base was established in the Far East by buying the Rainbow Orient Company in Hong Kong for £36 million, and in June an American and another Dutch distributor were added.

Interim profits were well up to best expectations with a 30% advance to £48 million and the shares rose 29p to 318p on the announcement. In October a £133 million rights issue was launched with the declared object of reducing borrowings in preparation for a series of acquisitions designed to increase the company's geographical diversity and to raise the quality of earnings. The move was welcomed both for cutting gearing from 135% to 60% and for reducing the dependence on the Near and Middle East from 36% to 10%. The make-up of the whole group now looked much better balanced with Agriculture falling to 39%,

Electronics rising to 48% and Textiles static at 13%, with Leisure and Pharmaceuticals expected to grow to 10%. In addition, next year's profits were forecast to top £142.5 million on over £1 billion of turnover. Profits for 1987/88 were £107.3 million and the shares ended the year not much changed at 268p ex-rights.

1989

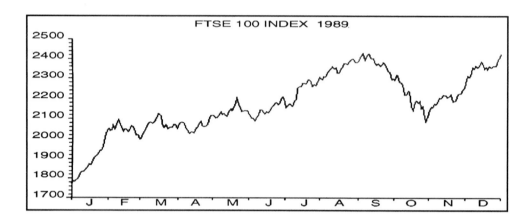

FTSE 100 INDEX 1989

You can't buck the market

Equity markets greeted the New Year with considerable enthusiasm, casting aside the caution of the last days of 1988, and the FT-SE surged through the 2000 level at the end of January on record volume. The confident expectation seemed to be that high interest rates were working and that growth would slow to a more sustainable level of around 3% while inflation would fall back below 5% again. In any case, an average P/E of a little under 10 and a yield of over 5% was not taking too much on trust. Sentiment was boosted further by takeover fever when GEC and Siemens launched a £1.7 billion bid for Plessey which was promptly followed by a £7 billion consortium bid for GEC as part of Plessey's defensive tactics.

After reaching 2072 at the end of the first week in February, the market began to have second thoughts when inflation registered yet another upward "blip" as the Retail Price index rose 0.7% to 7.5%. Worse was to come later in the month, when the Richmond by-election saw the Conservatives' majority slashed from nearly 20,000 to just over 2,500. The index dipped below 2000 again and fears were expressed that a credit-based boom as well entrenched as this one would not succumb quickly or easily and that the persistence of inflationary pressures could lead to a new round of rate rises with the attendant risk of overkill. However, the setback proved very short-lived and the FT-SE rebounded to 2125 in mid-March in response to a budget designed to be tough on inflation as well as providing help for the lower paid and for savings. There were no changes in the basic rate of tax but thresholds and allowances were raised at a cost of £2 billion. The trade deficit was forecast to remain broadly unchanged at £14½ billion, inflation to fall to 5½% by year end and growth of money supply (M0) was to be held in the 1-5% target range. Growth in GDP over the year was scaled down from 3% to 2½%.

Too much, too late

The budget estimates were viewed with a degree of cynicism by many commentators who suspected that to date the Chancellor had chosen to give short-term growth priority over the longer-term battle against inflation, and that his choice had left the economy of the UK as the odd man out in an industrialised world whose policy-makers remained determined to keep up the fight in spite of rising unemployment and painfully high interest rates. The further implication was that he would soon be forced to change tack as the UK fell increasingly out of line with its trading partners and sterling came under pressure. This is precisely what happened towards the end of May when the pound fell sharply against both the dollar and the DMark, and base rates were raised to 14%.

The dilemma facing the Chancellor was given even more point the day after when the April trade deficit was seen to have widened dramatically, indicating a total for the year approaching £18 billion against the budget estimate made barely a month earlier. A deficit at this level looked much more than a symptom of excess domestic demand. There was a much publicised clash of opinion between the Chancellor and the Prime Minister backed by her personal adviser, Sir Alan Walters, over the management of the exchange rate, with the former wishing to peg the pound at close to DM3 while the latter wanted to let it find its own level, and if this had a lot to do with the deterioration of the trade deficit as Mrs Thatcher prevailed and the pound soared to over DM3.20, Mr Lawson also came in for criticism for underestimating the strength of demand in the wake of the abolition of credit controls and his failure to reduce wage inflation. Now he found himself unable to bring down interest rates without precipitating another sterling crisis, and if he kept them where they were or even raised them again, then he would run the risk of tipping the economy into recession.

Weight of money rules

Throughout the summer months the problems facing the Chancellor and the economy made no impact at all on the equity market. By the end of July the FT-SE had crossed the 2300 mark to record a new high for the year, totally ignoring gloomy surveys from the CBI, falling retail sales figures, and a further deterioration in the trade deficit. A much greater influence was the strength of institutional cash flow, relatively few rights issues and a number of major bids including the £13.5 billion consortium bid for **BAT**s, **Boots** paying £900 million for **Ward White, Bass** buying **Holiday Inns** for £2.6 billion, and the sight of the Dow actually surpassing its August 1987 high point.

On 1st September the FT-SE moved above the 2400 mark, but a month later worse than expected August trade figures, followed by a 1% rise in German interest rates, prompted an increase in base rates to 15%. The index lost over 100 points in three days as the pound failed to benefit but instead fell sharply to below the DM3 level. Simultaneously, Wall Street took its worst knock since Black Monday with a 190-point fall on news of the collapse of the United Airlines buy-out following the failure to syndicate the required $7.2 billion financing. The Bank of England added to the general air of despondency with a warning that base rates at 15% "challenged the assumption" upon which much of the record £30 billion of bank lending for property development had been based. Then Nigel Lawson rocked the market at the end of October by announcing his resignation as Chancellor. The news sparked an 80-point fall in the FT-SE to 2082, not least because it served to emphasise the deep divisions within the Cabinet, but within three days the index had made up all the ground lost as the new Chancellor, John Major, declared his commitment to the defeat of inflation and the maintenance of a "firm exchange rate".

John Major becomes Chancellor

The ex-Chancellor made no secret of the reason for his resignation, which essentially was over exchange rate policy and the Chancellor's "right to manage", and all eyes were now on John Major to see how he would manage both the economy and Mrs Thatcher. The autumn statement in mid-November made it clear that it was not going to be a simple task. A sharp slowdown was forecast for 1990 with domestic demand stagnant and inflation rising to over 7%. The balance of payments deficit, now likely to total £20 billion in the current year, was expected to fall to £15 billion in 1990 while growth, which had already been downgraded to 2% in 1989, was predicted to fall further to 1¼% in 1990 or ¾% ex-oil.

This depressing picture was given substance a week later when **Coloroll** reported halved interim profits, **Tarmac** issued a profits warning, and a whole string of companies announced lower earnings or losses and dividend cuts. Equity buyers, however, looked at Ford's £1.6 billion bid for loss-making **Jaguar**, sterling being allowed to slip below DM2.80, questioned the strength of Mr Major's dedication to a firm exchange rate, and pushed the FT-SE to over 2400 again by year end, oversubscribing £5.24 billion of water privatisation issues in the process.

John Major succeeded Nigel Lawson as Chancellor on the latter's resignation in October 1989.

The Christmas rally was given further impetus by the failure of a Thatcher leadership challenge in the first week of December and by the Dow moving back into new high ground to 2753.2 on the back of prime rate reductions and the lowest trade deficit in five years. Given that the forecasts at the beginning of the year for inflation and the trade gap had both turned out to be gross underestimates and that the growth prediction also had to be scaled down drastically, equities did well to record a gain of about a third in 1989, taking the FT-SE to 2422.7. Expectations still favoured a slowdown in growth rather than outright recession, and gilts similarly looked upon inflation as a greater threat than deflation, their index losing 3% over the year to 84.29. Tokyo rounded off an exciting year by hitting a new all-time high point in December of 38915.

Measure for Measure

One of the great problems arising from the pursuit of monetarist policies was the difficulty of establishing a yardstick upon which to base those policies. A growing realisation of this fact as the 'eighties progressed led the Bank of England, after a survey of the relative merits of the various methods of calculating broad money, to conclude that "any choice of dividing line between those financial assets included in, and those excluded from, broad money is to a large degree arbitrary, and is likely to be invalidated by developments in the financial system." By the end of the decade, M3, M4 and M5 had come to be regarded as simply a useful source of information, and not indicators whose behaviour should prompt an automatic policy response. M0, the narrow measure, comprising mostly notes and coins in circulation and bank deposits at the Bank of England, was now the only monetary aggregage targeted by the Government to judge if high interest rates were working.

Hanson buys Goldfields

The year began quietly enough for **Hanson** with a string of US disposals from Kidde, SCM and Kaiser totalling some $33 million, and then Hygrade Foods was sold for $140 million. First quarter profits were well up at £195 million, a rise of 15%, and net cash holdings of over £1 billion were reported. The next few weeks saw this figure augmented by £224 million from an MBO of Allder's plus £25 million from Elizabeth Shaw Chocolates, with another £26 million coming from the sale of Barbour Campbell in Northern Ireland. Before the end of June $400 million came in from the sale of Smith Corona and the stake in Midland Bank was disposed of for a "substantial premium". Then came the biggest bid ever with a £3.1 billion offer for **Consolidated Goldfields**, already strenuously resisting a £3.2 billion offer from rival South African mining house, Minorco. That bid had been deadlocked first by a reference to the Monopolies Commission and then by complex challenges in the courts, and typically Hanson timed its intervention to maximum advantage. Goldfields finally agreed to accept an offer of £3.5 billion and Hanson walked away with a considerable prize. Disposals were not long in coming and simultaneous with the release of the nine-month figures showing a 23% advance to £742 million, the sale of the South African Goldfields assets for £368 million was announced. By November the London head office had been closed down and all the staff dismissed, and four of the US subsidiaries went for $650 million. Hanson rounded off a bumper year with profits topping £1 billion for the first time against £880 million. The shares were now 228p, well up on the year but still selling on a modest enough P/E of 11.

Racal Telecom takes over

Despite some relatively minor acquisitions in the US and an ADR listing for **Racal**, 1989 was still very much **Racal Telecom**'s year. Thus the latter's profits surge from £37 million to £85 million helped the parent to a 29% advance for 1988/89 to £178 million. Accelerating demand resulting in a 72% rise in RT's turnover to £194 million had much the same effect in the first half of 1989/90, when its profits rose 146% to £75 million and Racal's, 32% to £82.5 million. During the year RT's share price reached a high of 557p, more than three times the original issue price, while Racal's also benefited from its popularity, topping 575p.

BTR back in the fast lane

If **BTR**'s 1987 results had caused some disappointment, the company redeemed itself with those for 1988. A 39% advance to £819 million on turnover up by 32% was in the best BTR tradition, fully justifying the 75p rise in the share price during the first three months of the year to 370p. Organic and acquisition growth figured roughly equally in this result and with £1.5 billion to spend in the current year, there was no hint of a slowdown. Two European acquisitions were announced in March, one for $28 million in Italy and one for $10 million in France, both makers of roll covers for paper-making machinery. August saw a sharp rise in the share price to over 450p on a statement from US financiers and deal-makers, Kohlberg Kravis & Roberts, that they intended to buy 15% of BTR with the aim of creating a partnership of their financial clout with BTR's industrial management skills. Given BTR's superb track record it was difficult to see what KKR could do for the company, and some commentators saw it as an attempt by a speculative and opportunistic operator in a nearly played out market to hitch its wagon to a more solid and reliable star. BTR's interim figures were well up to the mark at £513 million, a gain of 40%, and the shares closed the year at 465p.

Williams takes it easy

Williams' profits for 1988 announced in March fell neatly into the target range at £116 million to record a 101% advance on turnover up by 78%. It was announced that no major acquisitions were planned for 1989, and the emphasis in the following months was much more on disposals. In April, four engineering businesses were sold to B. Elliott for £22.5 million, and in May, American Electrical Components went in an MBO for $40 million. Then at the time of the interim figures in September, up almost 50% to £75 million, it was announced that the motor distribution business, **Pendragon**, would be given to shareholders. The shares did not live up to best expectations, and after a brief flurry in November on a false takeover rumour which sent them up to over 300p, they closed the year at 267p with a P/E of under 10 on fears that the DIY slump would affect profits in the current year and beyond.

Tomkins consolidates

Interim profits of £19.1 million, up from £16.8 million, were not as spectacular as followers of Greg Hutchings had come to expect but nonetheless they demonstrated solid growth. This low profile but creditable performance continued in the second half and full year figures came out at £65 million for a gain of 38%. The shares rose 11p to 266p on the announcement with buyers reassured by the fact that the group had done well over a difficult period, was ungeared and had £300 million to spend.

Polly Peck buys Del Monte

Asil Nadir continued his buying spree aimed at expanding Polly Peck's geographical network. In January a West German fruit importer was bought for £15 million, 90% in shares, together with one on the West Coast of the US, and March saw the acquisition of a 21% stake in a Hong Kong supplier of household appliances. Results for a 16-month period to end December 1988 announced in April saw the forecast total of £142.5 million comfortably exceeded at £144 million, and Lex commented that as Polly Peck "continued to raise the quality of its earnings and reduce its geographical dependency on the Near East, it was shifting from an erratic and opportunistic trading group into a truly international electronics and agricultural business". The writer added prophetically that the group had "not entirely put its reputation for nasty surprises behind it", and expressed concern that borrowings continued to rise to pay for capital expenditure yet to be reflected in earnings. He added that the group had generated less cash in the last 16 months than in the previous 12, partly because of inexplicably large cash adjustments of £99 million to compensate for the weakness of the Turkish lira, but that a P/E of 7 with the shares at 320p took "that sort of thing" into account. June saw a listing obtained on the Swiss exchanges, and also the unexplained resignation of managing director, Tony

Reading. Then in September a £283 million rights issue was announced to help fund the purchase for $875 million from Nabisco of Del Monte fruits. The shares surged to 369p on the news given the obvious strategic logic of buying on 12 times earnings probably the world's leading fruit brand name which could be used to cover all Polly Peck's produce. Since Del Monte was No. 1 in pineapples and No.3 in bananas, the deal made Polly Peck into the world's third largest fruit company. There was an added bonus in that Polly Peck would continue to benefit from the huge advertising budget of Del Monte's canned fruit operations retained by Nabisco. At the same time interim profits of £64.4 million were announced, representing a gain of 34% on turnover up 65% to just over £500 million.

Nadir reaches his zenith

Asil Nadir was now achieving for his company the aura of respectability that had eluded it for so long, and during the remainder of the year he continued to make all the right moves. A 30% stake was taken in Sansui, the troubled Japanese electronics company, rescuing it and at the same time providing Polly Peck with tied manufacturing capacity to feed into its distribution network. Then the textile division was sold for £38 million and a sale and leaseback of Del Monte's cargo ships was planned to bring in another $200 million plus, all with the aim of reducing gearing, which had crept up again thanks to recent purchases, to 105% this year and to below 75% by the end of 1990. The shares closed the year at around 400p, near to their best ever level. Polly Peck now had an equity market capitalisation of some £1.5 billion and had joined the FT-SE 100 index of the country's leading companies.

Ferranti bites the bullet

In September 1987, defence electronics and missile manufacturer **International Signal & Control** (ISC) had merged with **Ferranti**, a move widely acclaimed as one of mutual benefit with the marketing abilities of James Guerin and his team being enhanced by Ferranti's technical skills. All seemed to be going well until May 1989 when Mr. Guerin and associate Claude Ivy announced that they were quitting the group to "pursue their private interests in the preferred environment of a small, privately owned company". The shares fell 3½p to 104½p on the news and on County Natwest's modest downgrading of their profits estimate, but Ferranti was still regarded as a "good two-way bet" on a bid and on its order prospects. A month later the shares fell 15p to 82p on a statement from the company that profits could fall by as much as 20%, and in mid-September they were suspended at 73½p given the likelihood of "a substantial loss on overseas contracts managed by ISC subsidiaries", unofficially estimated to be around £150 million. Later in the month Ferranti quantified the figure by writing off £185 million, and legal proceedings were launched against Mr Guerin who, it now transpired, had sold all his 31.8 million shares in July and August.

The giant killers

1989 was the year the fee-driven superbids came to Britain. Devised by merchant bankers, they targeted well-known conservative companies with the avowed aim of "maximising shareholder value", and the necessary cash was provided by a consortium of banks, institutions and companies specially created for the purpose. The first bid was unveiled in January as a tactic in Lazard's defence against **GEC**'s unwelcome approach to **Plessey**, but the £7 billion counterbid failed to get off the ground. The plan to break up a cash-rich and admittedly rather staid GEC with a view to giving the company "a new strategy and direction and maximise shareholder value" was not convincing in the light of Lord Weinstock's obvious achievements, and one by one the consortium's prospective members dropped out or joined the GEC camp. Within ten days it was all over, to the considerable embarrassment of Lazards and of Barclays which was to lead the consortium.

Then in July came a £13.5 billion bid for **British American Tobacco,** making it the biggest ever launched in the UK. It had been thought up by Jimmy Goldsmith, Jacob Rothschild and Kerry Packer, who planned to unbundle what they saw as an untidy mix of Third World tobacco interests and First World financial services, once again with the ostensible aim of benefiting shareholders. BATs put up a vigorous defence and shareholder loyalty won the day for Sir Patrick Sheehy and his board. Shareholders of both companies clearly viewed their conservative managements as to be supported rather than prodded into more adventurous paths. Before long, the banks and institutions that had created **Isosceles** to pay over £2 billion for supermarket chain **Gateway**, with only a 10% equity base, must have wished that their bid too had failed.

The collapse of the $7.2 billion financing plan for the buyout of United Airlines marked the end of these attempts to channel all the loose money in the system into frankly speculative deals, but did not prevent the BIS from commenting ruefully on the "apparent propensity of the banking system to make repeated mistakes on a rather grand scale".

1990

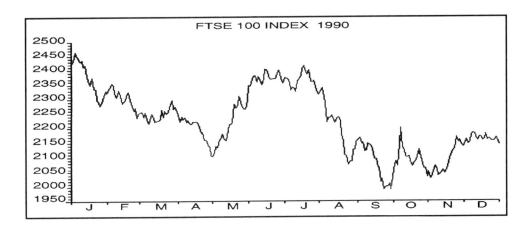

FTSE 100 INDEX 1990

'If it isn't hurting, it isn't working'

An FT survey of analysts' forecasts at the beginning of January revealed that most believed the UK economy would still manage to avoid a recession in 1990 and return to steady growth in 1991. Base rates were predicted to fall to 13% by the end of the year and to 11% in 1991, while inflation was expected to fall from the present rate of 7.7% to 5.5% in 1990 and to 4.8% in 1991. A similar downward path was forecast for the trade deficit from £20 billion to £15 billion to £12.5 billion. However, little change was looked for in the number of unemployed at 1.7 million. Chancellor Major's New Year message included the celebrated phrase "if it isn't hurting, it isn't working" but the clear implication that the earlier excesses which had resulted in a huge balance of payments deficit and an inflation rate well above the OECD average would have to be paid for by a corresponding period of below average growth, failed to upset the market, at least initially.

The first week of the New Year saw the FT-SE at last breaking through its July 1987 peak to reach 2463.7 accompanied by the Dow moving above 2800 for the first time. Frankfurt, too, was hitting new highs as investors took the view that a united Germany would create a new powerhouse in the European bloc. This burst of enthusiasm proved to be short-lived as bond markets worldwide suddenly weakened dramatically on fears that inflation was more likely than recession as governments found it difficult to maintain their resolve in the face of an economic downturn. By the end of the month the Dow had lost some 250 points and Tokyo over 2000, while London's FT-SE was back to 2322 on growing signs of corporate distress in the retail sector as a result of the virtual collapse of consumer demand. **Lowndes Queensway** and **Magnet** were finding out all too soon the double disadvantage for leveraged buyouts in industries where demand is also interest rate-sensitive.

Given a continuing run of adverse company news and economic numbers pointing to a far more serious slowdown than had been expected, the London market held up surprisingly well throughout the spring. Institutional investors still seemed to be taking the view that the means of achieving lower inflation had to be painful and thus apparently bad news was regarded as indicative of good news further down the line. This resilience was tested just as severely by the Government's political problems as the storm over the poll tax raged and Labour opened up a nineteen-point lead ahead of the Mid-Staffordshire by-election and then won it, overturning a 14,654-seat Conservative majority in the process.

The budget was seen as neutral with a touch of laxity, evidencing John Major's preference for gradualism in contrast to overkill, but anxiety began to grow in mid-April when both the earnings and inflation figures rose sharply to 9.5% and 8.1% respectively, putting paid to hopes of an early cut in interest rates. Another big rise in the trade gap for March plus news that a receiver had been appointed to major construction company **Rush & Tomkins**, knocked the FT-SE back almost to 2100 at the end of April. It then staged a rapid recovery into the 2300-2400 band on growing speculation about the benefits to the economy that would flow from joining the European Exchange Rate Mechanism

(ERM). This was what Nigel Lawson had wanted to do in 1989, but now that Mrs Thatcher had dropped her opposition to the idea, the way was clear for John Major to do so.

To join or not to join ...

The pros and cons of joining the ERM were debated vigorously throughout the summer months. Those in favour saw it as the surest way to introduce a degree of monetary discipline into an inflation-prone economy with a long tradition of "muddling through". They had no illusions that it would be an easy process since industry and unions would have to learn to take decisions on no-devaluation assumptions instead of looking for a lower exchange rate to validate their failure to control costs. In fact, they saw ERM membership as presenting the only possible remedy for the long-standing defects of the UK economy in that a combination of rising costs with a fixed exchange rate would soon solve the problem of excessive wage rises, and do so the hard way. After all, Chancellor Lawson had done his bit by sharply reducing direct taxation and it was now up to the private sector to fulfil its part of the bargain by accepting the discipline of a firm exchange rate in the absence of any credible policy based upon voluntary restraint.

Those who opposed entry did so largely on the grounds that the country's financial and industrial systems were incapable of producing sustainable non-inflationary growth and that the greatest economic successes had taken place during periods of devaluation. Furthermore, they argued, giving up the freedom to juggle with the exchange rate would be the last in a long line of abdications ranging from import controls, exchange controls, incomes policies, low-cost food imports and credit controls, leaving the UK economy rudderless.

Iraq invades Kuwait

Given that informed opinion believed ERM entry would take place some time in the autumn and that the equity indices remained close to the tops of their trading ranges, it was clear that markets saw membership as a bull point. Certainly it was enough to offset a run of corporate disasters as **Coloroll** and **Lowndes Queensway** went to the wall and rumours swirled around **Parkfield**, but the Iraqi invasion of Kuwait at the beginning of August added a quite different dimension of uncertainty and markets fell sharply. A rocketing oil price seemed to assure both higher inflation and a global economic slowdown and the consequences if a shooting war developed were almost too awful to contemplate.

By the end of August, the FT-SE had dropped to 2100 while the oil price had risen to over $30 a barrel, reviving sterling's petrocurrency status and evoking memories of what high interest rates, together with an overvalued currency, had done to UK industry in the early 'eighties. The Dow was a little more resilient on ultimate safe haven considerations outweighing normal economic calculations, but Tokyo, which had been falling throughout the year, crashed through the 25000 level. Worries about the course of the oil price were relieved to some degree by OPEC's agreement to raise production to counter the shortfall from Iraq and Kuwait, but fears remained about what would happen to oil production if a full-scale war broke out in the Gulf.

Meanwhile in the UK, evidence of acute corporate distress was mounting almost daily. **Parkfield**, once the best performing share in the All-Share index, collapsed under the weight of its bank debt, **Polly Peck** was obviously in serious trouble, and the share price of prominent property development companies nose-dived as asset values sank and debt servicing costs rose. The FT-SE responded by dipping below 2000 at the end of September. Interestingly, this gloomy background failed to deter **Ratners** from continuing to demonstrate its "insatiable appetite for deals" and paying $400 million for Kays, the loss-making US jewellery store chain.

The good news on the anti-inflation front, if it could be called good in such a context, was that money supply growth in terms of M0, the narrow measure, was back into the 1-5% target range. It was now clear that the monetary squeeze, begun in mid-1988, was working by curbing output and demand with distressing consequences for companies and individuals but as yet with no discernible effect on prices and wages, both now rising at rates in excess of 10% per annum. This left the Chancellor with the unenviable problem of how to head off a wage/price spiral developing later in the year without precipitating a recession, which could prove disastrous for the Conservatives' electoral prospects, all at a time when a degree of relaxation looked essential after base rates had stayed for a whole twelve months at 15%.

Sterling joins the ERM

John Major chose to try to solve the problem on 8th October by joining the ERM, and at the same time lowering base rates to 14%. The joining rate was DM2.95 in the wider band with a permitted 6% fluctuation either side. Despite the immediate obviously adverse impact on the open market sectors of the UK economy, markets welcomed the move and the FT-SE recorded a gain of 130 points over the next two days to 2200. All of this and more was lost by the end of the month, partly on fears of full-scale war breaking out in the Gulf but also on John Major's admission that the slowdown had turned into recession after a fall in output for two consecutive quarters. ICI's 48% profits fall in the third quarter plus the announcement that it planned to cut capital spending by 10% in the coming year, did not help and neither did the loss of a Conservative "safe seat" to the Liberal Democrats at the Eastbourne by-election. Sir Geoffrey Howe's resignation speech in early November, which precipitated another leadership crisis, was the last straw and the FT-SE reacted almost to the 2000 level.

John Major becomes PM

The rapid resolution of the leadership issue by the election of John Major in place of Margaret Thatcher was greeted with great relief by markets and the FT-SE rebounded to around the 2150 mark. The recovery was maintained until the end of the year, buoyed by UN backing for the use of force to expel the Iraqis from Kuwait and by the first decline of the year in the rate of inflation as the Retail Price index fell from 10.9% to 9.7%. Nevertheless the background was not encouraging enough to spark the sort of Christmas rally needed to prevent 1990 from becoming the first year in the last twelve in which the equity indices had not recorded an advance.

Hopes that interest rates had peaked were being balanced against a CBI survey revealing that industrial confidence was at its lowest level for ten years and that the recession was spreading with retailers reporting their biggest sales slump since 1980. It could still be argued that the recession was in the price, but the argument lacked conviction given the uncertainty surrounding the probable length and depth of the downturn together with the huge question mark that

Norman Lamont took over as Chancellor when John Major became Prime Minister.

hung over the situation in the Gulf. This last factor threatened to dash all the hopes of the "peace dividends" that had been expected to flow from the break-up of the Communist bloc and the reunification of Germany. In the event the FT-SE closed the year down 11.5% at 2143.5. Gilts, by contrast, although still down 2.5% on the year, had staged a significant recovery from their low point in the summer as bonds worldwide strengthened on "safety first" attractions and UK gilts specifically attracted buyers on post-ERM considerations that they now represented a clearly definable and lower currency risk.

Wall Street fared much better than other world markets, declining only 4.3% to 2633.6, buoyed by its growing "safe haven" characteristics, patriotic fervour and lower interest rates. Tokyo, on the other hand, went from bad to worse on fears over the stability of its banking system and the impact on the Japanese economy of the sharp increase in the price of oil. The Nikkei Dow closed at 23848, down 39% on the year.

Hanson proposes and disposes

For **Hanson**, 1990 was a year for sorting out some of the more complex aspects of its recent acquisitions, especially those arising from the takeover of Consolidated Goldfields. The release of first quarter results, up 15% to £225 million, was accompanied by the news that $504 million was to be paid for a large stake in Peabody Coal, the company which held the balance of the shares in Newmont Gold acquired by Hanson via Consgold. Later the rest of Peabody was bought for $715 million, giving Hanson full control of Newmont, the biggest gold producer in the US. A plan to make a public offering of Newmont failed to get off the ground, and then in a surprise move in October, a swap was arranged with Jimmy Goldsmith for his US timber and oil interests. Further disposals were made during the course of the year, notably of the housewares group Tucker (ex-Kidde) for $185 million. Serious discussions also were entered into with the Government over the possibility of Hanson buying Powergen ahead of the planned public offering.

Full year figures recorded a useful 21% advance to £1.29 billion and with cash balances of almost £7 billion plus an enlarged borrowing capacity, it was clear that nothing was out of Hanson's range. Nevertheless the shares ended well down on the year at 185p, overshadowed in the final weeks by talk of vastly enlarged provisions at Peabody Coal to cover possible health claims.

Racal talks of demerger

Racal Telecom's full year profits for 1989/90 recorded a 95% gain to £165 million, while those of **Racal** were up only 13% at £201 million. It was clear that the offshoot would soon overtake its parent, and demerger talk became rife when interim profits for 1990/91 showed those of Racal Telecom at £122 million surpassing Racal's figure of £97.5 million and also making it clear that but for its share of the former's profits, Racal would have made a loss. In a dull market, the shares of both companies closed the year well down from their highs at 172p and 257p respectively.

BTR gets a new Chief

BTR's 1989 results, showing a 22% advance to £1.06 billion, were accompanied by the launch of its biggest bid since the abortive one for Pilkington. The target was **Norton Inc.**, a US abrasives, plastics and ceramics business with 113 plants in 26 countries and operating on margins of less than half those of BTR. The $1.6 billion offer was rejected but while acceptances continued to mount, the French glass giant St. Gobain entered the contest and managed to get Norton's agreement to a much higher offer. This was another major setback for BTR's ambitions and a $10 million profit on the sale of its stake in Norton was no consolation. BTR's urgent need to get its teeth into an important new acquisition was demonstrated by the half-time figures in September showing only a 6% gain to £530 million with earnings growth down to just 4%. The shares fell 40p to 318p on the news, which also led to a down-grading of full year forecasts and was taken as having adverse implications for the whole market.

In December John Cahill stepped down from the post of Chief Executive in favour of Alan Jackson (54), who came in from BTR Nylex, the Australian associate which he had built from almost nothing in 1984 into Australia's largest industrial manufacturer providing 40% of BTR's overall pre-tax earnings. The appointment was widely welcomed but the shares still ended the year well down from their high point at 320p.

A testing time for Williams

Williams' profits advance to £153.5 million in 1989 was viewed as strictly historic for a group with a 40% exposure to the UK consumer market, and in order to justify its reputation as another Hanson or BTR it would have to do more than simply consolidate in a recession. Some fast footwork by Messrs Rudd and McGowan in May saw the sale of the UK and Irish paint interests for £240 million cash, a deal which at a stroke cut their dependence on the UK consumer to 25% and also reduced gearing from 60% to zero. The move, however, did nothing for Williams' popularity and when the interim profits in September showed an £11 million fall to £61 million, the shares dropped 13p to 217p for a prospective P/E of 9 on a downgraded total for the year of £120 million.

Tomkins survives a difficult year

With 35% of operating profits arising in the UK, **Tomkins** was reckoned to have done well to record a 22% gain to £23.3 million for the first half of 1989/90. The US side was also doing well with Smith & Wesson winning an important FBI order which served to compensate for its earlier pre-Tomkins loss of a US Army contract to Beretta. Then in June a major US acquisition was made in the form of Philips Industries, a diversified Ohio-based industrial company, for $550 million. At the same time a full year forecast was made of "not less than" £76 million, a figure that turned out in due course to be £77.1 million. The shares held up well for the first part of the year but suffered along with the other conglomerates, large and small, to end the year at 225p.

The bid that never was

Polly Peck began the year promisingly enough with the purchase of a Dallas-based fruit distributor, and the establishment of a joint venture with a French company to manufacture colour TVs in Turkey. The results for 1989 announced at the end of March showed profits well ahead at £161 million and Lex commented that this was a "familiar picture of startling but slightly impenetrable success with as usual no detail to speak of on the group's operations".

The shares were now 393p for a P/E of 7.6 and reservations about the still 100% plus gearing began to fade as, first, the sale and leaseback of the Del Monte ships brought in £142 million, and then the flotation of Vestel on the Istanbul market, together with the injection of all the electronic interests into Sansui, raised another £100 million. The shares reached a peak of 462p shortly afterwards but were back to just below 400p on Gulf influences in mid-August when Asil Nadir made an unscheduled announcement about his plan to stage a buy-out for the balance of the group he did not own. His declared reason was that Polly Peck was undervalued by the market, and the shares duly responded by rising 24p to 417p. Less than a week later he said he had dropped the idea after approaches from "significant institutional and private shareholders". The shares reacted instantly, losing 78p on the day to 324p.

An inspector calls

Things now began to go badly wrong for Asil Nadir. For one thing, the Stock Exchange was concerned that he did not appear to have discussed his buy-out plan with Polly Peck's board or its advisers and for another, the fact that funding for the buy-out was not in place, meant his announcement on 13th August could constitute an offence under Section 47 of the Financial Services Act by giving a false impression of the value of the shares. The company's fall from grace had been so rapid that considerable confusion and uncertainty existed. Even Polly Peck's Head of Public Relations, Dominick Henry, was quoted as saying "None of us here has any idea why the hell this is happening", as the share price fell another 15p to 265p at the end of August. All eyes were now on the half-time results due on 3rd September. They were better than expected with a 72% gain to £110.5 million after a £29 million first contribution from Del Monte, but the fact that net borrowings were still high at £864 million pointed out the problems of financing a buy-out. The following week saw exceptionally heavy trading in the shares on reports that Asil Nadir was buying at around the 285p level, and 21 million shares changed hands on a single day.

Then towards the end of the third week the shares began to slip and after falling 135p to 108p on 20th September, they were suspended on the Polly Peck board's request for a DTI investigation into recent events. Simultaneously Asil Nadir was interviewed at the Serious Fraud Office. There was a statement from the board in early October that a liquidity problem existed but hopes of a bail-out by the Turkish government were soon dashed and loan payments were halted. The shares were still being traded on the Zurich exchange but they had collapsed to 1 cent by 24th October when administrators were appointed, offering little hope for UK investors. Subsequently Asil Nadir was arrested to face a number of charges relating to theft and false accounting, although he claimed that the downfall of his empire was the result of a Greek-inspired political conspiracy.

The rise and fall of Polly Peck ranks as the most spectacular of all booms and busts in stock exchange history, going from practically zero to £1.5 billion in nine years and then back to zero in five weeks. The full story has yet to unfold, but large and constant capital spending funded by debt seems to have stayed persistently ahead of returns from normal trading operations, with the true picture concealed in a fog of figures involving exchange rate juggling which regularly understated the former and overstated the latter. Once again quite where the auditors fitted into the picture is uncertain.

Parkfield overwhelmed by debt

The other principal corporate disaster of the year was as much a shock to the company's devoted fans as the downfall of Polly Peck was to its followers. It involved **Parkfield**, transformed by the American, Roger Felber, since 1983 from a loss-making foundry company by a series of acquisitions into a specialist engineering and distribution group making profits of £23 million in 1989. In the process it had become the best performing share in the All Share index, turning a stake of £1000 into one worth £120,000 by early 1990. The group's most recent move was into video distribution where it had become the market leader with a third share of the 60 million videos sold or rented in the UK. 1990 began encouragingly enough with the report of interim profits up 79% to £13.9 million, but the *FT* commented on the company's "irritating habit of taking profits from asset sales above the line", and then added that the prospective P/E of 12½ reflected a balance between growth prospects and the "long overdue corporate mistake". A few days later the shares touched their all-time high of 518p at which level the equity market capitalisation was just over £260 million. In fact it was not such a fair balance in that the "corporate mistake" when it came was of such magnitude that it destroyed the company.

By mid-February the shares had lost nearly 60p to 465p, but the first hint of real trouble came – as it so often does – with the sudden and unexplained resignation of a director. The shares fell another 30p on the news to 430p, but nothing more was heard from the company until late June, by which time the shares had slipped back to around 360p on persistent rumours of problems in the entertainment and video division, originally headed by the resigned director. This first official statement warned that following a sharp fall in second half profits for 1989/90, profits for the current year were unlikely to exceed last year's total of £23 million against widespread expectations of around £35 million. Attributing the prospective shortfall to management problems in the entertainment and video subsidiaries, Roger Felber added, "we are not talking about a disaster". The shares responded to the news by plunging to around 150p but persistent selling on what the company called "unfounded rumours" eventually led to their suspension at 48p in mid-July "pending clarification of the company's financial position". A few days later administrators were appointed, to discover that liabilities, mainly in the form of bank borrowings and leasing commitments, were far higher than expected at over £300 million. They certainly were talking about a disaster, and over the ensuing months the company was sold off division by division while Mr Felber departed for South America.

Sunk without trace

After making his name as boss of highly successful money-broker, **Exco**, in the early 'eighties, John Gunn was invited to join the board of the long-established and conservatively run **British & Commonwealth** shipping and insurance empire founded by the Cayzer family. Before long he was appointed Chief Executive and the share price rose dramatically in anticipation of what new blood could do for this asset-rich but relatively undynamic group. Unfortunately a string of diverse acquisitions included **Atlantic Computer**, a leasing company, for the hefty sum of £417 million. Questionable accounting practices at Atlantic subsequently suggested that it was probably worthless at the time of purchase and its collapse in April 1990 brought a critical spotlight to bear on all the businesses bought by John Gunn. A vigorous disposal programme was already underway but it was too late to save the group and a year later administrators had to be appointed.

1991

FTSE 100 INDEX 1991

The shooting war begins

The New Year opened on a cautious note with investors apprehensive ahead of the 15th January deadline for Iraq to begin withdrawing from Kuwait. The feeling was growing that force would have to be used and the first air strikes came as a positive relief to markets with the FT-SE adding fifty points to 2105 and the Dow 115 to 2623 while Tokyo plussed over 1000 to 23450. After an immediate upsurge in the oil price to $35, within a couple of days it settled at around $20 after the US announced that it would release its reserve stocks. Gold, too, after a quick flurry to $411, fell back into the $360-370 range, which was below the level at the time of the original invasion last August.

The start of the land war two weeks later saw another sharp rise in London and New York which was extended as the war rapidly progressed to a satisfactory conclusion. In fact the war had gone better than anyone had dared to hope, and with oil price worries out of the way the prospect was for a further reduction in inflation which in turn would permit an easing of monetary policy worldwide and the removal of some of the pressures on the banking system. Thus the first week in March saw the FT-SE into new high ground at over 2450, the Dow flirting with the 3000 level and Tokyo topping 26500.

Back to the economy

Unfortunately the victory celebrations could not sweep away entirely the idea that the recession in the UK was unique in the sense that the traditional means of stimulating a recovery, namely devaluation and cutting interest rates, were strictly limited by reason of having joined the ERM. This was all the more worrying given that the recession was showing signs of being more widespread and more severe than earlier predictions had suggested. The last six months had not helped, with UK exporters squeezed between a weak dollar and a strong DMark while facing slumping demand and high interest rates at home, and the reversal of the dollar's decline at the end of the Gulf War together with the first of a series of base rate cuts seemed to have little ameliorating effect. The budget with its 2-year phased reduction in Corporation Tax to 33% was welcomed but the forecast recovery in GDP growth to 2% from mid-1991 to mid-1992 was viewed with considerable scepticism as the numbers out of work rose to over 2 million in March and bank lending collapsed to its lowest level in fifteen years. In this context, the extra 2½% on VAT was not regarded as helpful either.

But perhaps the most worrying point of all was that the supposed constraints on stimulative action since joining the ERM had not prevented a cut in base rates from 15% to 11½% and an 8% depreciation against the dollar by the end of June, quite apart from the stimulus implied by the return to substantial deficit financing announced in the budget. A surplus of £800 million was to turn into a deficit of £7.9 billion in 1991/92, rising to £12 billion the following year before falling back to zero again in 1994/95. Taken in conjunction with CBI surveys revealing that the recession was bad and getting worse, that retail sales figures were casting doubt on the prospect of any consumer-led recovery and that money supply (M0) growth had practically stopped, this meant that the FT-SE at close to 2500 on a prospective P/E of 17.5 looked as out of line with the real economy on the upside as it had been for months after the 1987 October Crash on the downside. Further substance to this view was given by ICI's 52% drop in first quarter profits and the fact that half of the £3 billion contingency reserve had gone in the first three weeks of 1991/92 to help fund rising unemployment and public sector pay deals. The implications of this second point for the budget's PSBR forecast were clear.

Wall Street shows the way

The obvious conclusion was that the London equity market was taking a lot on trust, following Wall Street's lead as the Dow moved above 3000 on indications that the recent cuts in the Federal Discount rate to 5½% were beginning to stimulate the flagging US economy. It may also have been giving some credence to Chancellor Lamont's predictions of an early recovery on the assumption that he still retained some power to assist it, all in the context of an election likely to be postponed until the late autumn or even the spring of 1992 as a result of Labour's recently established lead in the opinion polls.

Time was now on the Chancellor's side and it seemed a reasonable bet that some degree of recovery would manifest itself by then. The corporate sector had been quick to take advantage of the strength of the equity market – as indeed had the Government with its hugely successful power company privatisation – and rights issues of over £5 billion in the first six months of the year had already exceeded the annual totals for 1990 and 1989. But July still saw new peaks for the FT-SE and the All Share index with confidence boosted by another half-point cut in base rates to 11%, a surprise swing from deficit to surplus in the June trade figures, a 1.3% pick-up in retail sales in June, and the Chancellor's forecast of inflation down to 4% by the end of the year. The headline-making collapse of BCCI seemed to have little effect on the broad market despite its devastating impact on the Asian business community.

August and September saw the FT-SE staying comfortably above the 2600 level – apart from a one-day rout on the Russian coup – assisted by another half-point reduction in base rates to 10½% and the Federal Discount Rate coming down to 5%. There were also numerous pronouncements from the Chancellor and the Prime Minister to the effect that the economy was "on course", that inflation was "licked", and that the "clouds of recession" were beginning to lift, views with which the Bank of England, the CBI and the FT poll of 23 economists all now concurred. Even the IMF predicted that the UK economy would grow by 2.3% in 1992.

Recovery? What recovery?

It was in the final quarter of the year, coincidentally around the anniversary of the UK joining the ERM, that faith in an economic recovery began to wane. Inevitably the level of the market then came into question since it had risen in anticipation of a recovery and of the increased chances of a third term for the Conservative administration that such a recovery implied. By mid-November the FT-SE was bumping along the bottom of the 2550-2650 range and then a shock 120-point fall in the Dow on recession fears there, pushed it straight through the 2500 level. Three by-election defeats earlier in the month, a further fall in manufacturing output in the third quarter and a drop in October's retail sales did not help sentiment, and with deflationary worries now coming to the fore, neither did the October Retail Price Index showing the rate of price inflation slowing to 3.7%.

Those who had opposed ERM membership tended to blame the lack of recovery on the Chancellor's inability to apply the traditional stimuli of devaluation and interest rate cuts, contrasting his position with that of his US counterparts who were able to use both measures. The supporters of ERM membership continued to maintain that there should never have been any illusions about it being an easy option or one likely to show quick results. On the contrary, it involved a long and difficult process of adjustment, but it was already showing signs of working as UK interest rates and inflation levels converged towards the German levels. As for the US model, there was just as much anxiety there over a "no show" recovery, despite a weak dollar and the lowest interest rates for 25 years. This last point raised a question that was to concern markets well into 1992. What if the recovery was not just delayed but postponed indefinitely while consumers took the "cold turkey" treatment for structural inflation, giving debt reduction and the rebuilding of savings priority over present consumption? If this was indeed the case then the sharp increase in public spending announced in the budget and again in the Autumn statement – the PSBR was heading for £10.5 billion in the current year with double that in prospect for 1992/93 – did not threaten to "crowd out" private and corporate claims on funds, but rather filled what would otherwise have been a void.

Weighed down by evidence of a general industrial malaise aggravated by incidents like the death of Robert Maxwell, the failure of the **British Aerospace** rights issue and the problems of **Brent Walker**, the FT-SE fell below 2400 at the beginning of December and against such a depressing background there was little expectation of a pre-Christmas rally developing. The signing of the Maastricht Treaty, with its initial favourable impact on the standing of the Prime Minister, sparked a 2-day advance to over 2450, but fears of a German interest rate rise which were soon fulfilled prompted a reaction of 100 points in the week leading up to Christmas.

What eventually turned the tide in the closing days of the year was a surprise cut in the US Federal Discount Rate of one whole point to 3½%. The effect was to send the Dow soaring back up through the 3000 level to end the year at 3168 for an overall gain of 20%. Fired by this example and inspired by the idea that Wall Street was signalling a recovery in the US economy that would give a jump start to the rest of the world, the FT-SE recovered to 2493 by year end to record an advance of 16.3%. Gilts seemed to have put inflationary fears behind them and after peaking at 87.94 in September, closed the year at 86.26 for a gain of 5%, reflecting a growing interest in bonds on the view that a prospective permanent low inflation environment would mean a fundamental change in the relationship between bonds and equities to the advantage of the former. Golds once again disappointed with the FT Gold Mines index down 6% at 140 after bullion had lost nearly $40 over the year to $353. Tokyo continued to reflect anxieties about the health of the Japanese banking system in the wake of the further asset deflation that had taken place during the year, particularly in property and stocks. The Nikkei Dow at the end of December stood at 22,437, practically unchanged on the year, and unlike New York and London, demonstrating no signs of recovery.

Now Hanson slows down

Confirmation of the severity of the recession for those who still needed it, came with the release of **Hanson**'s first quarter profits for 1990/91. At £241 million, they were up by only 7%, and by the end of the first half the figure of £586 million showed that the rate of advance had slowed to 3%. Estimates for the full year suggested that the group would be doing well to exceed last year's £1.29 billion by even the narrowest of margins. Still, Lords Hanson and White, who earlier in the year had announced their intention to stay in control for another five years, retained their capacity for surprise by taking a 2½% stake in ICI at a cost of £240 million, ostensibly "for investment purposes only". Despite this statement, a bid was widely expected and ICI immediately went on the defensive. An undeclared battle was fought by the companies' respective PR agencies, generally considered to have ended in a victory on points for ICI. The tussle did not prevent Hanson from carrying on business as usual and in September a £350 million bid was agreed for **Beazer**, the UK's fourth largest housebuilder, now struggling with debt incurred in its recent takeover of Koppers, the second largest aggregate producer in the US. The deal was financed by part of a $4 billion loan from a consortium of banks over a 7-year period clearly raised with a further US acquisition in mind. Hanson's full year profits managed to maintain its 28-year growth record intact with a 3% gain to £1.31 billion but the shares ended the year only marginally ahead at 200p, with their standing not helped by the criticism levelled at the company by ICI.

The crack-up

The mysterious death of Robert Maxwell served to dispel a great deal of the mystery surrounding his media empire and simultaneously destroyed his reputation. Although never a popular figure, Maxwell was still admired for the ability and energy that had brought him fame and fortune. His early success in building up scientific publisher Pergamon Press, was not without controversy when he clashed with would-be bidder Saul Steinberg of Leasco, but he went on to rescue British Printing Corporation and to defeat the powerful print unions in the process. In 1984 he won control of the ailing *Daily Mirror* and restored its circulation and its profitability. America was his next target and in rapid succession he bought the official Airlines Guide for $750 million and Macmillan's US publishing operations for $2.6 billion, both on borrowed money. As the recession took hold, debt servicing costs soon overtook cashflow and the share price of his flagship company, Maxwell Communication Corporation, began to fall. When a string of strategic disposals failed to stem the slide in the share price, Maxwell, it was subsequently revealed, resorted to a share support operation using money looted from the *Daily Mirror*'s own pension fund.

Racal fights off a bid

Racal, with its shares already well down on the threat to its markets posed by the Gulf War, took another tumble in January on its withdrawal from a potentially very profitable contract to install an internal telephone network linking government departments. However, by the time full year profits for 1990/91 were due in June, the share price had recovered to 230p thanks entirely to a much greater pick-up in the shares of Racal Telecom to 390p. The disparity in performance was explained by RT's 48% profits advance to £245 million beating Racal's £223 million total and confirming indications at half time that the rest of the latter's businesses were making losses approaching £25 million. The demerger terms announced in July were 57 shares in RT, now to be called **Vodafone,** for every 100 Racal. Almost immediately the Racal rump attracted bid speculation on the grounds that it represented an interesting mix of defence and marine electronics, the original core strategic radio business, data communications and security, all with great recovery potential and all undervalued as a result of being overshadowed for so long by Vodafone.

Then in September **Williams Holdings** made a surprise £703 million all paper bid. Racal's Sir Ernest Harrison immediately rejected the bid as "inadequate and opportunistic" and refused to meet or to provide Williams with any additional information. In early December he backed up his case by revealing first half profits recovering to £11.6 million and forecasting a total for the year of "not less than" £50 million, adding that ahead of a proposed demerger of Chubb, an offer of £450 million had been received. Williams promptly raised its bid to £739 million and a war of words began. Sir Ernest Harrison criticised

SirErnest Harrison, Chairman of Racal, transformed a small Berkshire-based company into a major international electronics and communications group (picture by Rex Coleman).

the Williams management on the grounds that they were buyers not builders of businesses, and also for their accounting practices. Williams countered by relating the number of forecasts Racal had missed in recent years, but despite Williams' proven ability to extract higher margins from all its acquisitions, institutional loyalty to Sir Ernest was too strong and only 25.8% acceptances were received.

Third time lucky for BTR

In January a run of aggressive downgradings by analysts of earlier estimates of **BTR**'s full year figures due in March knocked the share price below 300p, but it recovered rapidly to 375p ahead of the event. While still recording an 8% fall to £966 million, the first drop in full year earnings since 1960, the figure showed that the analysts had been overcautious and the shares rose to 402p on the news. There was some speculation that perhaps BTR, in company with Hanson, had reached a size which placed a limit on its capacity to grow, but new chief executive Alan Jackson's declared policy change towards a more aggressive acquisition and disposal programme seemed to carry more weight with investors. August duly saw both the disposal of Pretty

Polly (ex-Tilling) for £117.5 million, and an agreed £197 million offer for Rockware, the UK's leading manufacturer of glass containers. BTR's interim profits recorded a 1.2% advance thanks only to the inclusion of a £90 million profit on the Pretty Polly sale being taken above the line, a move widely criticised for "jumping the gun" on a policy change currently under discussion by the Accounting Standards Board, but all was forgotten the following month when the long awaited "big bid" came along with a £1.5 billion cash and share offer for Hawker Siddeley. The Hawker board had got off to a bad start by forecasting a fall in profits just ahead of the bid announcement and rapidly had to try to redeem the position. BTR spoke of Hawker's "decade of disappointment", and Hawker countered with criticism of BTR's record, implying that it owed more to accountants than to managers, and then came up with a vigorous acquisitions and disposals programme of its own together with a forecast of only a modest decline in profits. The outcome seemed to remain in considerable doubt even though it should have been obvious to the objective observer that Hawker had an uphill struggle on its hands, and a marginally increased bid won the day for BTR with 70% acceptances. BTR now had its major acquisition for the new chief executive to cut his teeth on.

Williams goes for Yale and Valor

Messrs Rudd and McGowan confirmed their reputation for rapidly changing the size and shape of **Williams** to fit in with new business conditions, by opening the year with an agreed all paper £330 million bid for **Yale & Valor** on a modest exit P/E of 12. This gave Williams market leadership in two more established products and boosted group turnover to £1.2 billion divided 44/44 between the UK and the US with 12% in Europe. Net assets of £450 million could be set against borrowings of £50 million, and profits for 1990 came out at £125 million, comfortably ahead of analysts' downgraded forecasts of £120 million. Interim profits announced at the end of August showed that Williams' management was back in form with a 26% advance to £76.5 million despite static sales. The failed bid for Racal had left them with a £77 million stake and a loss of £14 million on cost price, but in the context of Williams' size and Racal's recovery potential, it seemed fair to regard it as a valuable strategic interest not only in Racal but also in the soon to be demerged Chubb.

Tomkins pulls ahead

First half profits for **Tomkins** exceeded best expectations in a difficult market with a 34% advance to £31.2 million, showing that it did not deserve to lag behind its fellow conglomerates at 220p on a prospective P/E of 7½ given full year profits of around £108 million. In the event, the total came out at £112 million thanks to a strong performance from the US interests, especially from the recently rationalised Philips Industries. Greg Hutchings began to attract more fans for his quietly effective acquisition and management style which had not seen one false move since he began the expansion of Tomkins in 1983. The shares ended the year at 414p to record the biggest gain of any of the conglomerates and also the highest rating.

1992

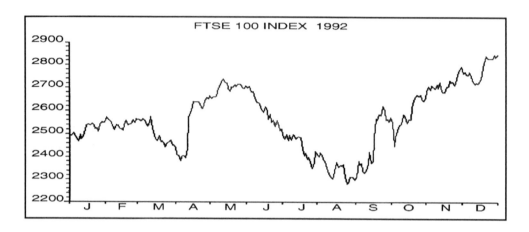

FTSE 100 INDEX 1992

Dragons' teeth

The New Year opened with the Prime Minister admitting that the recession was proving to be "deeper and longer" than expected but adding that a "jagged and irregular" recovery was underway. Given the uncertainty surrounding the election outcome, with both parties running neck and neck in the opinion polls, there appeared to be little upside in equities on a P/E of 17.25 and yielding just 4.5% at a time when dividend cuts were beginning to be presented as prudent policy in line with earnings trends. Thus the push through the 2550 level by the FT-SE in the second half of January perhaps owed more to the extraordinary strength of Wall Street, where the Dow was consolidating its move above 3000 and reaching new highs by the day.

By the end of January the FT-SE had picked up by 10%, recovering all the ground lost since early December when hopes of an imminent recovery had all but disappeared. Expectations of investors now seemed to be pinned on an election-winning budget, albeit one in which any vote-winning concessions could not be represented by the Opposition as political bribes. The weeks leading up to the budget, now set for 10th March, did nothing to ease the problems facing the Chancellor. The unemployment figures announced in mid-February saw a rise to a new peak of 2.6 million, indicating that employers were finding it easier to fit into the straitjacket imposed by the ERM by cutting jobs than by reducing pay awards, which were still running at over 7%. Then towards the end of the month the trade figures showed a practically doubled deficit in January thanks to a sharp fall in exports. Against such a background there was probably nothing the Chancellor could have done to keep everyone happy, but his reduction of tax to 20p in the pound on the first £2000 of taxable income was a benefit bestowed on the lower paid without tampering with the 25p basic tax rate. Of greater significance was the announcement of an increase in the PSBR for 1992/93 of £4 billion to £28 billion, or 4.5% of GDP as corporate tax receipts halved and unemployment continued to rise, an increase which Labour, while saying that it was a figure they would accept, still represented as a bribe to the electorate.

The election looms

The election date was now set for 9th April and the campaign began to hot up. The market did not see the budget as an election-winning one and after losing over 50 points to 2522 on the day, the FT-SE quickly slipped below 2500 as Labour pulled ahead in the polls. But if Norman Lamont's budget did not win the election, there is a case for believing that John Smith's "shadow budget" lost it. Although Neil Kinnock had pledged to repeal any cut in the basic rate of tax that the Conservatives might have introduced in the pre-election budget, and the Labour Party's plans for increasing the higher rate to 50% had been well aired, the publication of the budget Labour would introduce if elected was a "first", leaving no one in any doubt at all about their intentions. It was a move of extraordinary naivety and a gift to the Conservatives who, without fear of contradiction, could portray Labour as the party of high taxation. The idea that the electorate would be prepared to pay higher taxes in return for improved public services might have carried some conviction if people had believed that Labour's plan to "invest" more money in public services would produce any improvement. Rather they suspected that it would result in nothing other than fatter pay packets for public service workers in line with Labour's parallel promise of comparability in pay with the private sector.

Given the depth of the recession, the Conservatives were simply not able to present a very convincing case for re-election, but marginally better news on the recovery front in the form of rising business confidence and suggestions from the CBI of an improvement in manufacturing order books, retail sales up for the second month running and a slightly smaller February trade deficit, helped to narrow Labour's lead during the final countdown.

A fourth term for the Conservatives

The Conservative victory, with a 21-seat overall majority, still came as a complete surprise to markets, and shares, gilts and sterling all soared. The consensus view was that the decisive removal of a serious degree of political uncertainty had created a much more favourable climate for an economic recovery. The FT-SE rose 136 points to 2572, gilts were up to four points better as overseas investors snapped up the latest offering, and the pound pushed up towards the DM 2.90 level again. New York and Tokyo also seemed to be celebrating the event as the Dow added 30 points to 3255 helped by another cut in the Federal Funds rate, and the Nikkei plussed 1252 to 17850, shaking off concern about the banks' exposure to the property and share collapse.

This post-election honeymoon continued well into May with the FT-SE peaking at 2737.8 around the middle of the month just after another half a point off Base Rates had been greeted as an indication that everything was going according to plan. CBI reports that home and export order books were at their best levels since August 1990 and that the economy was "on the turn", helped to keep the index above 2700 for most of the rest of the month, but by mid-June it had lost nearly 150 points on growing fears about the timing and strength of the recovery. The sight of the Dow crossing the 3400 level for the first time was not enough to offset an unrelenting flow of dreary economic news, which included the Danish rejection of Maastricht and the collapse of Olympia & York, and was even counter-productive to a degree in that the rise looked out of touch with reality in the US economy where huge cuts in interest rates and a rapidly depreciating dollar had still failed to produce a recovery.

Disinflation or deflation?

Despite the American example, critics of ERM membership were calling for precisely these "remedies" to bring the UK out of recession, reluctant to recognise that the situation could be one in which such traditional measures simply would not work here any more than they appeared to in America. The ERM continued to take much of the blame but by July there were signs that the real problem was coming to be seen as far more intractable and one less likely to be responsive to any short-term stimulative actions. Quite simply the UK consumer had stopped consuming. Overloaded with personal debt, afraid for his job, and seeing the value of his principal asset, his house, continuing to fall, spending was strictly confined to the essentials of life.

With inflation down to 3.9% in June and base rates still at 10%, real interest rates were actually rising, widening the gap between income and debt servicing costs and causing asset values to shrink further. With much the same process going on at the corporate level, manifesting itself in disappointing results and dividend reductions, it was not surprising that investors should shy away from new issues like the consumer oriented **MFI** and **Anglian** as well as causing the withdrawal of the once eagerly-awaited **GPA** offer, and that by the end of July the FT-SE should be below 2400 albeit still on a P/E of 17 and a yield of 5%. Gilts showed the other side of the coin by hitting a new peak for the year of 89.75 in early July, and although the yield ratio, at 1.73, was now at its lowest level since the depths of the bear market in 1974, few commentators were prepared to regard it as a buy signal. At last the realisation was dawning that the name of the game had changed for the first time in sixty years from "disinflation" to "deflation", and any doubts that this was the case should have been expunged by the sight of the Dow falling on 3rd July when the Federal Discount Rate was cut to 3% in a near-panic response to the worst June unemployment figures in eight years.

Something's gotta give!

Given that the problems of the individual and the corporation in the shape of rising costs and falling income were mirrored at a national level, the divergence of performance between the stock markets of Tokyo, New York and London presented an obvious puzzle, sharing, as they did, the same problems of slow growth, trade disputes and political disillusionment, all within the confines of the Global Village. Indeed, Tokyo, down 60% from its late 1989 peak, was considered by some observers to have come to terms with the new situation rather better than either London or New York, especially a New York which had acquired P/Es more reminiscent of Tokyo in its heyday than of a grid-locked US economy. While the P/E on the Standard & Poor 500 was a forward-looking 29, that on the Dow Jones Industrial index (supposedly more representative of America's industrial heartland) was an incredible 61, assuming a potential for recovery that looked increasingly far-fetched as the likes of General Motors and IBM caused analysts to downgrade already cautious forecasts.

By contrast London looked reasonable value but with a history of downward revisions of growth estimates over the past year with their implications for unemployment and the PSBR, together with the reporting of "financial accidents" by such blue-chip companies as BP and Barclays Bank, few were prepared to take the plunge. To the extent that the case for the bulls rested upon the chances of an enforced policy change, they could point to the fact that the Government Securities index had come back almost two full points from its July peak while sterling at DM2.82 was over eleven pfennigs below its immediate post-election figure, but by now the US example looked much less convincing as dreadful corporate news began to undermine the Dow and the dollar continued to slide.

Into the unknown

Thus the London market entered August with the feeling that the course through uncharted waters had been set back in October 1990 when the UK had joined the ERM, but increasingly voices were heard suggesting that the dangers of holding to that course now far outweighed those of abandoning it. The chief argument of the dissidents was that the background had changed dramatically since October 1990. Germany now had to keep its interest rates high in order to counter reunification-induced inflationary pressures while the US administration in the run-up to an election felt compelled to reduce rates in an attempt to end a recession which was proving much more persistent than originally expected. The pound was caught in the middle, pegged at a hopelessly uncompetitive exchange rate while the Government was forced to maintain interest rates at a level which threatened to turn recession into slump. The result was a ballooning balance of payments deficit, a PSBR out of control, and unemployment heading towards 3 million, all serving to create a situation which was economically and politically unsustainable.

The storm clouds gather

The last week in August saw an intensification of world currency turmoil with the dollar plunging another 7 pfennigs to a record low of DM1.40 while the pound rose to almost $2.00, simultaneously dropping through DM2.80 towards its ERM floor. Speculation grew about the prospects of a UK interest rate rise and the FT-SE responded by falling almost to the 2300 level, seemingly convinced by unequivocal statements from the Prime Minister and the Chancellor alike that ERM membership was sacrosanct and that leaving it was unthinkable, as indeed was even the prospect of realignment within the system. However, though the market was considered to have discounted at least a one-point hike in base rates, no rise came and the pound kept on falling. This anomalous situation was seen as casting doubt on the strength of the Government's commitment to the ERM and speculative pressure continued unabated.

In the first week of September, news that the Government was borrowing £7.3 billion in DMarks to be used in support of the pound, sparked a rally back to DM2.80 (and a low-volume reflex 68.9 point rise to 2381.9 in the FT-SE) but it was shortlived. The foreign exchange market was simply too big for any sort of intervention to have any lasting effect, save for an adverse one on the credibility of the authorities. The situation remained fragile throughout the second week of September although the 7% devaluation of the Italian lira, followed by its departure from the ERM, together with a quarter point reduction in Germany's key Lombard rate to 9.5%, prompted some hopes of lower interest rates all round and further realignments serving to let sterling off the hook. But despite further heavy intervention, the pound continued to fall to within a fraction of its ERM floor of DM2.778, pulling equities and gilts down with it on renewed fears of a rise in interest rates. Sterling had now become a one-way bet on devaluation and the speculators moved in for the kill, convinced that no interest rate rise could avoid it. The 2% hike on the morning of 16th September proved their point, and when the announcement of a further rise to 15% later in the day failed to lift sterling off the floor, the Government bowed to the inevitable, cancelled the second rate rise and dropped out of the ERM. The pound fell immediately to DM 2.64.

Dancing amid the ruins

The confusion surrounding events leading up to sterling's departure from the ERM had left investors uncertain which way to jump but the return of base rates to 10% the following day cleared the air and the FT-SE leapt 105 points to 2483.9 while gilts added nearly a point to 89.22. It might have been a 'Black Wednesday' for the reputations of the Prime Minister and his Chancellor and for the credibility of the Government's whole economic policy, but there was little doubt that the markets saw the move as opening the way to the adoption of policies more in tune with the state of the economy of the UK rather than that of Germany.

Over the next few days talk of an early return to the ERM faded and when the Chancellor reduced base rates to 9%, declaring that "operating a floating regime is not an easy and not a soft option", or in much the same terms as he had spoken previously about ERM membership, it became clear that he was intent on making a virtue of necessity. The U-turn was complete. However, the political fallout augmented by the storm over the pit closures, restrained investor enthusiasm throughout the first half of October, but then another one-point cut in base rates to 8% and hints of more to come, prompted a wave of buying taking the FT-SE almost to 2700 and the Government Securities index to over 94. All eyes were now on the Autumn Statement scheduled for 12th November, in which Chancellor Lamont was confidently expected to re-establish a framework for the Government's economic policy and fill the 'policy vacuum.'

Plotting a new course

This he broadly succeeded in doing by setting forth measures seemingly consistent with going for growth at the same time as keeping up the pressure on inflation. A political as much as an economic package, the mix of monetary and fiscal policies was welcomed by Conservative back-benchers and industry alike, who saw it as restoring the Government's credibility as well as paving the way for recovery. The 1% reduction in base rates to 7% was seen as easing the burden of the debt overhang while the specific measures targeted at the motor industry, industry generally and housing were regarded as bringing relief to where it was most needed. The 1.5% ceiling in public sector pay settlements also won broad approval.

The one aspect of the Statement that caused most anxiety and criticism concerned public sector finances, for given no change in the level of public spending for this year and next with the PSBR forecast to rise to £37 billion and then to £44 billion, and in the absence of new revenue-raising measures, everything appeared to depend upon the early development of a strong and lasting economic recovery. In this context, the revised Treasury forecast of 1% growth in GDP in 1993 was not particularly encouraging and the less so given the implications for export-led growth at a time when the current account deficit was already expected to rise from £12 billion in 1992 to £15.5 billion in 1993. Still the market was prepared to give the Chancellor the benefit of the doubt and the FT-SE moved up 29.6 points to 2726.4, its highest level since the record of 2737.8 achieved in May.

The next few days witnessed some hesitancy, but later in

the month optimism was rekindled by more encouraging economic data on retail sales and wage settlements and by speculation on the prospects for corporate earnings growth in a recovery phase as inflation continued to fall. Some satisfaction was also derived from the sight of sterling apparently enjoying life outside the ERM, while inside chaos still reigned with one currency after another coming under pressure.

Into new high ground

On 25th November the FT-SE surged to a new peak of 2741.8 on high volume, and encouraged by good news from the US in the form of a revision of third quarter growth from 2.7% to 3.9%, it kept going to reach 2792 on 1st December. The pattern beginning to emerge was one of accelerating recovery in the US and the first signs of an upturn in the UK, while Germany and the rest of Continental Europe remained mired in recession. Against such a background, the UK equity market was regarded as having it both ways in that any signs of hesitancy in that upturn would almost certainly prompt a further reduction in interest rates by a Government now firmly committed to a growth strategy.

In the third week of December the FT-SE crossed the 2800 level for the first time boosted by yet another fall in headline inflation in November to 3%, its lowest level in six years. There was a new surge of buying in the final week of the year, sparked by reports of a dramatic 30% increase in new car sales in December and of a hectic start to the post-Christmas sales, and the FT-SE closed 1992 at 2846.5, up 14.2% on the year and just 1.3 points short of its all-time high reached two days before. Gilts too ended on a firm note with the Government Securities index at 94.34, although below its high point of 95.54. Sterling ended the year at DM2.44, 17.2% down on its ERM joining rate, while against the dollar it was practically unchanged at $1.51. With the gold price down $20 on the year to $333, gold shares remained out of favour and FT Gold Mines closed 54% off at 63.9. Wall Street provided some background encouragement, ending the year at just over 3300, still below its June peak but on a rising trend on expectations of continuing recovery and a favourable start for the Clinton administration.

When the going gets tough...

There are some recessions that even the best-managed conglomerates cannot withstand, and **Hanson**'s first quarter fall of 6% in pre-tax profits to £226 million came as no surprise. Neither did the decision not to launch a bid for **ICI** and to sell its stake in the company. The disposal proceeds of some £280 million helped to reduce net debt which had risen to £1.5 billion as a result of the acquisition of Beazer, and the move fitted in well with the new declared policy of disposing of peripheral interests in order to concentrate on building core businesses, including natural resources, through organic growth and acquisition. Thus Jacuzzi (ex-Kidde) was to be floated off and Beazer's US housebuilding side sold to bring in almost $1 billion, and the temptation to bail out Canary Wharf was resisted. By the third quarter the decline in profits had accelerated to 21.2%, aggravated by the sharp fall in the dollar, a performance which appeared to give point to the new strategy. However, the surprise £780 million cash bid for RHM in October prompted many commentators to wonder whether Hanson had broken away completely from its predatory past despite the much-publicised change in policy and the appointment of heirs-apparent to Lords Hanson and White. The counter offer by Tomkins and Hanson's subsequent withdrawal came as something of a relief to Hanson fans, offsetting any disappointment with the small drop in full year profits to £1.29 billion, the first year-on-year decline in the company's history. The shares ended 1993 at 234p selling on a P/E of 11.9 and with a dividend yield of 6.3%. The equity market capitalisation was now £11.25 billion compared with just under £500,000 when James Hanson joined the board in 1964.

BTR, with a rather greater concentration of similar core businesses under its belt and a recent major acquisition to work on, proved more recession-resistant than Hanson in 1992. Pre-tax profits for 1991 had come in 3% down at £917 million, but following vigorous rationalisation measures worldwide, interim profits for 1992 announced in September were up 7% to £548 million on sales 33% ahead at £4.3 billion as benefits from the shakedown of Hawker Siddeley began to flow. The company reported little sign of recovery in the UK, but the downward revision in November by one leading stockbroker of 1992 estimates from £1.03 billion to £984 million carried little weight with BTR followers, and after dipping briefly to below 500p on the news, the shares ended the year at 550p where the P/E was a forward-looking 19.3 and the yield a modest 4%. Estimates now began to be revised upwards again, and buyers were attracted further by speculation that BTR was limbering up for another important acquisition, with Lucas the most likely target. Equity market capitalisation was now close to £11 billion as against under £10 million in 1969 when Owen Green arranged the merger between the original BTR and Leyland and Birmingham Rubber.

Despite rumours to the contrary, in June **Racal** made good its bid-inspired profits forecast of "not less than" £50 million for 1991/92 with a total of £55.6 million, and then kept the excitement going with plans for the imminent demerger of Chubb. The scheme involved consolidating five old Racal shares into one new Racal share plus one Chubb, leaving original Racal shareholders with one share of each company. Debt was to be divided equally between the two companies, a fair split given that Racal had nurtured Chubb with its cashflow since the acquisition in 1984. Both shares advanced strongly following the demerger in early October, and then the first interim results in December seemed to prove the point that the sum of the parts was greater than the whole. Racal turned in pre-tax profits of £23.1 million against a loss of £2.4 million while Chubb's figure almost doubled to £26.9 million, and both declared the same dividend. Meanwhile, in the earlier part of the year Vodafone had come in for some brokers' downgradings as the recession took the shine off the more optimistic estimates of cellular phone demand, but in the event first half profits were well up to best expectations at £160 million, a gain of 23%, and the shares ended the year at a new high of 427p. The combined equity market capitalisation of all three companies now totalled some £5.4 billion by contrast with Racal's value alone of £1.3 million when Raymond Brown and Ernest Harrison took it public in November 1961.

Williams Holdings had a relatively quiet year as the management busied itself consolidating recent acquisitions, many of which were to a greater or lesser degree affected by recession. Profits for 1991 were up 42% at £168 million, but first half figures for 1992 announced in September showed a 6% fall to £72 million despite a further improvement in margins. At the same time a policy change was indicated as a result of the diminishing chances of success of future paper bids given the then modest rating of the company's shares at 247p with a P/E of just 12.3. Accordingly, long-term borrowing facilities were put in place with the aim of helping to fund future acquisitions, but the rapid recovery of the share price in the final quarter of the year to 335p to provide a P/E of 17 suggested that both options remained open for Williams. Equity market capitalisation now stood at £1.57 billion compared with £850,000 when Nigel Rudd and Brian McGowan took control of an obscure Welsh iron-founder in 1981.

Tomkins opened 1992 in fine style, reporting a 40% advance in pre-tax profits for the first half of 1991/92 to £43.7 million on sales up 52% thanks to a continuing strong performance from the US interests. Full year figures announced in July confirmed Tomkins' position as the most recession-resistant of all the conglomerates with an 18% rise to £132 million. Analysts were now estimating a total of £144 million for 1992/93 and the shares rose towards 500p ahead of a 100% scrip issue. Given net cash of £112 million another acquisition was thought to be on the cards before long, but the £935 million agreed counter offer for RHM dismayed many of Greg Hutchings' most devoted followers. The cash and share offer involved a 1 for 2 rights at 200p to raise £653 million net, and Tomkins' shares lost 50p to 212p on the announcement. Despite the fact that he had not put a foot wrong since taking control of Tomkins in 1983, many observers were convinced that with RHM, Greg Hutchings had gone one bid too far. On the contrary, he argued that basic products are basic products and that the same principles of efficient production and distribution apply as much to bread and cakes as they do to nuts and bolts. As the acceptances rolled in with the pattern indicating that Tomkins would end up with little or no net debt, this latter view began to gain ground and the share price had recovered to 256p by year end. Tomkins' equity market capitalisation was now some £2 billion, or just over £3 billion with RHM, as against under £10 million back in 1983.

1993

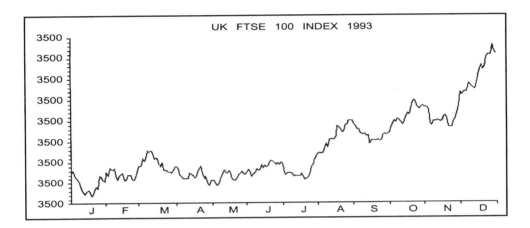

UK FTSE 100 INDEX 1993

The recovery begins

The Prime Minister's New Year message spoke of clear signs of recovery that could mark the start of a "virtuous cycle" of sustainable growth and prosperity thanks to the success in reducing inflation and to the opportunities created by the coming into being of the Single European Market. But while the equity market seemed to agree with him by reaching new highs in the first days of 1993, there were plenty of sceptics who believed that given the existence of the country's huge trade and budget deficits, even a modest recovery would quickly run into serious problems. Their argument was that given the sharp diminution in the UK's manufacturing base in recent years, rising consumer demand would feed straight through to imports instead of benefiting domestic industry. For the same reason, any post-devaluation surge in export demand would run into supply constraints. The net result would therefore be very little if any expansion in activity to the continuing detriment of both deficits, a situation likely to be aggravated and perpetuated by the urgent need to fund a still growing PSBR at the risk of starving the private sector of funds for expansion. Companies would also be keen to rebuild their balance sheets and any advance in the equity market was likely to be subdued by a flood of rights issues.

Those of a more optimistic frame of mind countered the apparent inevitability of this doom-laden scenario by saying that consumer confidence was likely to remain at a low level thanks to a combination of a still high debt burden, a depressed housing market and fear of unemployment, and that the real beneficiary of lower interest rates and low inflation would be a corporate sector already leaner and fitter from the economy measures undertaken during the recession. Thus they argued that perhaps for the first time, a UK Government was in a position to take the action necessary, if devaluation is going to work, of curbing domestic demand and public spending in order to shift resources into productive investment and exports. Indeed the Government no longer had any choice in the matter and to pursue this course was a simple policy imperative.

Fortunately, the Government had a lot going for it. For one thing it was still in the first year of the electoral cycle and growing signs of industrial recovery were already benefiting sterling which, now that it had "escaped" from the ERM, was being spoken of as a "safe haven" currency. Furthermore, the two budgets in 1993 gave the Chancellor the opportunity to use the first one to boost recovery and the second to start to repair public sector finances. Also there was little prospect of widespread industrial unrest forcing the Government to alter its plans as it had in previous devaluations. Add in the prospects of a continuing decline in inflation and there was a real chance that overseas capital could flow in and tide the country over until real growth led to a significant reduction in both deficits.

At first the bulls seemed to have the better of the argument and on 4th January the FT-SE reached a new high of 2861.5. But their triumph was shortlived. Two weeks later the index had shed almost 100 points as investors worried about the prospect of "paper heading towards the market from all directions". The Retail Price Index for December also caused some consternation. The

2.6% rise was the lowest in 6½ years but the underlying rate (excluding mortgage payments) rose 3.7% over the year as a whole. This figure was uncomfortably close to the top end of the Chancellor's target range of 1–4 per cent, largely thanks to the effect of devaluation on prices of raw materials and fuels as well as seasonal food price increases.

A new Governor for the Bank of England

But after falling below 2750 on fading recovery hopes sparked by disappointing December retail sales figures and a shock rise in unemployment to just short of 3 million, equities rebounded sharply at the end of January in response to a surprise 1% cut in Bank Rate to 6%. Despite its welcome by the market, the cut drew some criticism for being a panic reaction to the jobless figure, and Governor-elect of the Bank of England, Eddie George, was quick to caution against expectations of further rate cuts. This view appeared to be well supported by the news that the Retail Price Index rose only 1.7% in January, the lowest figure in 25 years, that private sector pay was rising at a rate of only 3.6%, and that the public sector pay limit of 1.5% looked like being accepted, albeit reluctantly. Chancellor Lamont expressed his agreement with the Governor, but it was a falling pound that effectively ruled out the

Eddie George was the popular choice to succeed Robin Leigh-Pemberton as Governor of the Bank of England on his retirement in June. © Bank of England

prospect of further rate cuts at this stage. Clearly, the foreign exchange markets were not convinced that the UK was entering a new era of non-inflationary growth and in mid-February the pound fell to $1.42 and to DM2.35, establishing a new trade-weighted low of 75.7 against the basket of currencies. The Chancellor's priority in the forthcoming budget was to present a convincing enough fiscal package that would serve to put a floor under the pound by attracting global capital flows, thus leaving scope for more rate cuts in due course. This still left him with the problem of how to strike a balance between measures that would help to establish the Government's anti-inflation credentials and those that might hinder the fragile recovery process. A steady rise in the Government Securities Index from 93 at the beginning to around 98 ten weeks later, suggested that inflation was the lesser fear, but the debate continued.

Six out of the "seven wise men" – economists appointed as special advisers to the Chancellor in the interests of open government – were not in favour of tax rises on the grounds that they would inhibit recovery but all thought that interest rate reductions were needed. Mr. Lamont's dilemma was partially solved by a German rate cut, an unexpected fall in unemployment, and a rise in January's figure for manufacturing output, and by the end of the first week of March, optimism was back in fashion. The FT-SE surged to 2922 and buyers clamoured to buy gilts yielding 8.5%. Additional data showing increased consumer lending, growing business confidence and subdued wage pressures, prompted a further rise to 2957.3 and to 98.04 with sterling recovering too in the week leading up to Budget Day.

A courageous Budget

The Government's defeat in the Maastricht debate put an extra political onus on the Chancellor, and he rose to the occasion by staking all on the recovery taking hold before the financial situation could get any worse. His "wedge" of rising tax revenues, led by the extension of VAT in two stages to domestic fuel and power, to raise £6.5 billion in 1994/95 and £10.5 billion the following year, clearly relied upon the adventurous assumption that gradually improving labour and housing markets would enable the population to take these deferred tax increases in their stride. The rise in employees' National Insurance contributions from 9% to 10% was the measure proposed in John Smith's "shadow budget" a year earlier, and the fact that Mr. Lamont had adopted it, as well as provoking the wrath of his own back-benchers by extending VAT to domestic fuel, did him credit by demonstrating that he saw the nation's finances as a problem to be solved rather than just as a political balancing act.

The budget was broadly welcomed by the markets but over the ensuing weeks both gilts and equities retreated under the influence of conflicting economic numbers. An FT editorial made the point that unfamiliarity with the sight of a recovery led by manufacturing output and exports instead of being consumer-driven, had served to confuse forecasters. Nevertheless, investors still paid more attention to the third successive monthly rise in retail sales figures and to the inflation fears it aroused, than to still rising industrial output. At the end of April the FT-SE fell below 2800 again and Government Securities slipped below 95.

Going for gold

However, the early summer was not lacking in excitement. In mid-March, the gold price had fallen to a 7-year low point of $325, prompting many analysts to predict another drop to $300 and even lower. Thanks to the explosive growth of the derivatives market, gold was no longer regarded as the hedge it had once been. Furthermore, the supply/demand fundamentals appeared to leave no scope for upside potential, and in the words of one dealer quoted by Reuters, "gold is awful, whichever way you look at it." As is so often the case in the markets, such a damning indictment marked the precise bottom of the downswing. Six weeks later, the price was nudging $360 thanks to the buying impetus provided by the well-publicised action of fund manager George Soros in paying $400 million to Sir James Goldsmith for a sizeable stake in Newmont Mines, the largest gold producer in the US. Sir James then added fuel to the flames of speculation by revealing that he had used $300 million of that sum to purchase bullion options. Despite what Lex called "these somewhat dubious origins" behind the rise and analysts reiterating that the physical supply/demand situation did not justify any upward movement, the gold price continued to advance as fund managers climbed aboard the Soros/Goldsmith bandwagon. The peak of $405 was reached on the last day of July, and then reports that China's central bank was selling gave the signal for a general sell-off. By any standards, this engineered rise in the gold price was a textbook example of how a speculative operation should be carried out. A neglected commodity, but one with latent appeal, was selected, the price target was modest, and the timescale was brief enough to leave minimum scope for upsets to occur. If the Hunt Brothers had employed the same tactics with silver in 1980, they would have made money instead of losing the lot. It should also be noted that money was made out of gold shares. The FT Gold Mines index had already risen 50% to 97.6 by the time bullion hit its low point, a move indicative of accumulation, and touched 250 as the price topped $400.

Nightmare on Elm Street

The other principal diversion for investors in May and June was the news that former Polly Peck chief, Asil Nadir, had skipped bail and flown to his base in Northern Cyprus. Mr. Nadir's avowed reason for putting himself outside the reach of British justice was that he could not be sure of getting a fair trial. Remarkably, despite evidence of extensive insider dealing in Polly Peck shares through the medium of a Swiss company, and of illegal transfers of many millions of pounds from company funds in the UK to Turkey and Cyprus, Mr. Nadir and friends still contrived to portray the Serious Fraud Office (SFO) as the villain of the piece.

A new Chancellor takes over

Meanwhile back in the real economy, in May the FT-SE

Kenneth Clarke took over as Chancellor of the Exchequer from Norman Lamont in May and presented the first unified budget on 30 November.

had managed to re-establish itself above 2800 again despite the prospect of more and more rights issues to add to the total of £7 billion so far in 1993. Mr. Lamont greeted the announcement of a 1.3% rise in the Retail Price Index for April as "an outstanding achievement", and it was somewhat ironic that when Kenneth Clarke replaced him as Chancellor a few days later the event should have been followed by a flow of economic data, including a surprise narrowing of the trade gap, confirming the prospect of modest growth without a revival of inflation. These reports saw the FT-SE respond by advancing towards 2900 as gilt yields shrank to 8%. In fact, a half-year round-up showed gilts outperforming equities, rising 10% against the latter's 7%, as the forces of disinflation were seen to have developed more strongly than originally expected against a background of relatively disappointing economic growth.

Up, up and away

July was the month investors decided to put aside their worries and embrace the belief that the industrial recovery was now well established and was going to continue without a resurgence of inflation. That belief was not confined to the UK. In the US investors had experienced the same doubts and fears about recovery and inflation, with the Dow Jones index ebbing and flowing in response to every new set of economic numbers. Now the thirst for yield that had driven both bond and equity markets to their present levels, intensified as the conviction grew that low inflation and low interest rates were here to stay and that corporate earnings were set to rise. Two more factors added impetus to the rise. One was the Group of Seven breakthrough during the Uruguay round of the GATT talks, widely expected to usher in a new era of world prosperity on the back of trade liberalisation. The other was the near collapse of the ERM, untying Europe's depressed economies from the restrictions of German domestic monetary policy, and opening the way for interest rate cuts just like those embarked upon by the UK in September 1992. A forty-vote victory for the Conservatives in a confidence motion called over the Maastricht ratification may also have helped to resolve many of the political doubts raised by earlier disastrous losses in by-elections and at local council elections.

New highs across the board

The advances by gilts and equities were swift and dramatic. Both the Dow and the FT-SE consolidated their moves into new high ground and by the last day of July they stood at 3537 and 2926 respectively. The Government Securities Index also touched a new high of 99.17 on that day. Two weeks later, despite a sharp fall in manufacturing output in June and a rise in unemployment, the FT-SE crossed the 3000 mark, buoyed by the belief that such news made an interest rate cut more likely. Gilts powered ahead to 102 and by then the Bank of England had sold enough stock in the first 4½ months of the financial year 1993/94 to cover 60% of its £50 billion requirement. Also there was no problem for the market in digesting the £5.3 billion total of the third British Telecom offering. Much of it, like gilts, went to overseas buyers.

Money talks

The liquidity-driven nature of the boom prompted some commentators to warn that liquidity flows have a habit of reversing themselves rather abruptly. Thus any sign of an upturn in US rates could cause the managers of mutual and pension funds to take their profits and repatriate their funds. The argument, sound though it was, did not find much support from investors at this time. Apart from a sharp but brief setback at the end of October, markets here continued to move ahead on hopes of further rate cuts if the economic data was disappointing, and of a strengthening economic recovery if it was not. A half point cut to 5½% duly arrived in the last week of November, and against this background the new Chancellor's budget, scheduled for the last day of the month, held no terrors. On the contrary, it caused the year to end in fine style with both gilts and equities embarking upon an almost unbroken run. The keynote was big spending cuts, allied with more slow-burn tax rises designed to take effect as the recovery gained pace. Mr. Clarke's avowed intent to tackle the PSBR "once and for all" caused some surprise but markets were not displeased with the prospect of borrowing being cut by £5.5 billion in 1994/95, £7 billion in 1995/96 and by £10.5 billion the following year, and aiming at zero by the end of the decade. These targets were well below those of his predecessor, just as the tax rises were a significant addition. Gilts added 1½ points on the day taking the index to 104.18, and the FT-SE plussed 31.1 to 3166.9. Sterling firmed to $1.485 and to DM 2.5475.

At the end of December, the FT-SE stood at 3418.4, down from the high point of 3462.6 touched two days earlier, but still up 20% on the year. Much better performances were recorded by individual interest rate-sensitive sectors, and Building Materials and Contracting and Construction rose by 59% and 65% respectively. Financials also showed exceptional strength and while the Financial Group as a whole was up 56%, Properties plussed 85% (aided by the revelation that George Soros regarded commercial property as a good bet), and Merchant Banks gained 80%. There was a great deal of speculative activity among the smaller companies which included many of the year's new issues, and the Smaller Companies index added 32%. The Government Securities index achieved a high of 107.6, up 14%, and the yield fell from 8.42% to 6.37%. With equities yielding around 3.4%, the yield ratio was comfortably under 2, a figure which helped to relieve any anxieties that might have been aroused by a P/E of 24. The Dow Jones index appeared equally cheerful, achieving a new high of 3794.33 in December before shading to show a gain of 14.7% on the year. Gold managed to hold on to much of its advance since mid-March, and at $390.75 was up 17.5% over the year as a whole. Gold shares fared even better and the FT Gold Mines index quadrupled to 257.7.

The last round-up

There was relatively little excitement among the select band of top growth stocks, the fortunes of which we have followed from the day they embarked upon the acquisition trail. With the megabid no longer practical nor fashionable thanks to a dearth of suitable targets and a degree of political unacceptability, minor bolt-on acquisitions accompanied by selective disposals became much more the order of the day. **Racal** had set the pattern back in 1988 with the flotation of **Vodafone**, followed by that of **Chubb** in 1992. Since then the value of **Vodafone** has trebled and that of Chubb more than doubled, demonstrating what Lex termed "constructive divorce in action".

Into 1994

End-year enthusiasm was rife and forecasts by the usual panel of experts of where the FT-SE might stand at the end of 1994 ranged up to 4000 with an average of 3700. Even

WHAT THEY FORECAST				
Name	FTSE100	GDP	Interest Rate	Inflation
Barclays de Zoete Wedd	3,600	2.75%	5%	3.6%
NatWest Securities	3,600	2.6%	4.5%	3%
Nomura	4,000	3.1%	7%	4.2%
Smith New Court	3,618	3%	5%	2.5%
UBS	3,400	3.25%	6%	3.4%
SG Warburg	3,500	2.6%	5%	2.4%
Average	3,620	2.9%	5.4%	3.2%

those who looked for a rise in both inflation and interest rates still expected the market to go higher on the grounds that such developments would arise as a consequence of faster economic growth. Doubts, such as they were, centred upon the fragility of consumer confidence given the insecurity induced by the high level of unemployment and the impact of the deferred tax burden imposed by the last two budgets. A few of the more cautious commentators foresaw a fall in the market later in the year as the cycle of low interest rates turned in response to pre-emptive counter-inflationary action by the Federal Reserve Board...

APPENDIX A

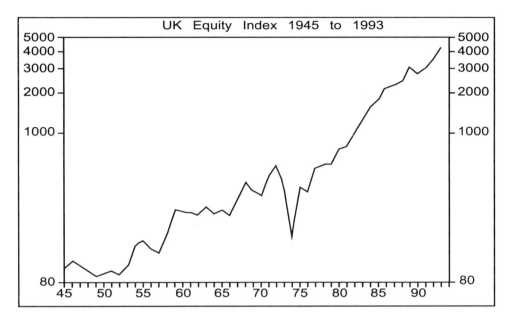

Value of £100 invested in the UK stock market on 31/12/45 (based on FT All Share after 1962 – before then on BZW Special Index)

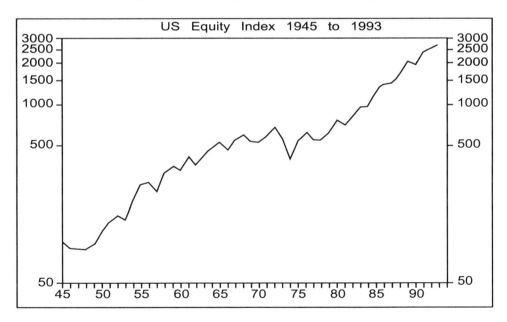

Value of $100 invested in the US stock market on 31/12/45 (based on Standard & Poor 500 Index)

363

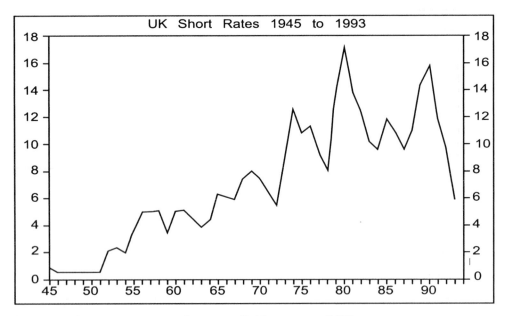

Average interest rates of 3-month Treasury Bills

Gross Redemption Yield of long-dated Gilts. Before 1963 – undated.
1963-1989 – 20 years. 1990- – 15 years.

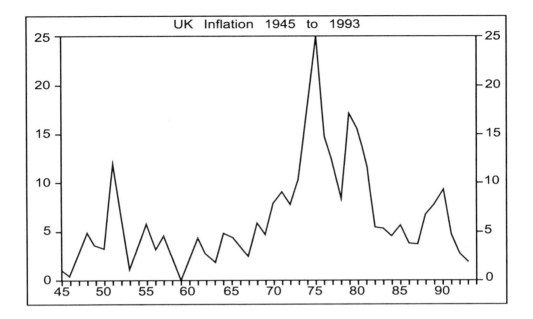

Headline inflation rate (annual % change in Retail Price Index)

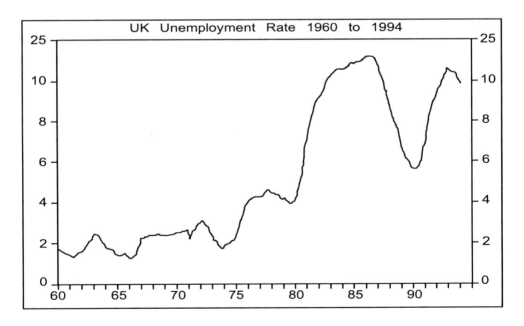

UK unemployment as percentage of working population

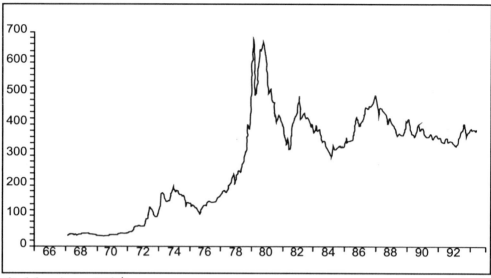

Gold prices (US$)

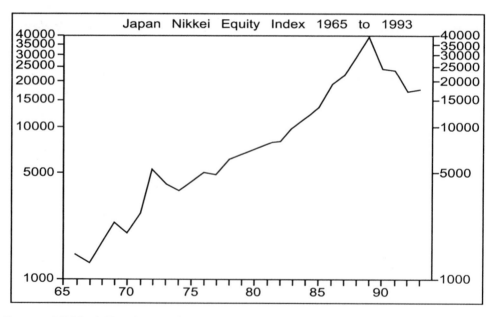

Japan Nikkei Equity Index 1965 to 1993

APPENDIX B

Top 30 UK companies by market valuation at end 1993

	Stock	Price (p)	Yield	P/E	Mkt cap (£m)
1	BT	472.5	4.3	18.2	29,328
2	HSBC	974	2.6	23.3	24,912
3	Shell Transport	727	3.9	22.4	24,100
4	Glaxo	725	3.8	19.0	22,061
5	BP	360.5	2.9	28.3	19,650
6	BAT Industries	553.5	4.3	16.6	17,036
7	British Gas	341.5	5.2	16.5	14,776
8	Hanson	268.5	5.3	19.9	13,540
9	BTR	373	3.7	20.9	12,976
10	Marks & Spencer	453.5	2.3	23.2	12,566
11	Cable & Wireless	522	1.8	27.3	11,390
12	SmithKline Beecham	404	3.0	14.6	10,316
13	Barclays	636	2.5	. . .	10,315
14	NatWest Bank	620	3.6	37.7	10,304
15	GrandMet	475.5	3.5	18.2	9,852
16	Unilever	1,203	2.3	16.4	9,756
17	Guinness	477.5	3.2	17.8	9,588
18	GEC	341.5	3.8	17.1	9,340
19	RTZ	812	3.0	22.9	8,639
20	Lloyds Bank	659	3.6	18.8	8,461
21	Zeneca	840.5	4.1	49.6	7,942
22	J Sainsbury	444	2.9	15.6	7,925
23	Reuters	1,787	1.5	29.5	7,433
24	Prudential	361	4.3	24.0	6,826
25	Abbey National	512	2.9	19.7	6,712
26	GUS	649	2.2	19.9	6,528
27	Boots	598	2.9	23.6	6,213
28	National Power	484	2.9	12.0	6,185
29	Allied-Lyons	680	3.9	18.9	6,018
30	Vodafone	594	1.6	25.8	5,975

INDEX

Where and How to Raise Finance for Your Business

A J Mckeon

(PB, £9.99, 192pp, 229 x 145mm, 1-85252-112-0)

Published with the co-operation of 3i plc

Includes free demo version of Business Architect's acclaimed business plan software.

There has never been a time when small companies found it easy to raise money, but the 1990s have presented them with very special problems.

Here at at last is a comprehensive guide in accessible and inexpensive format to help overcome these problems.

This book lists all the possible sources available to British firms, both within the UK and from EC institutions, and gives practical advice on how best to exploit them. It also contains sections on preparing business plans and the proper presentation to create the best response.

Adrian Mckeon spent a number of years as a financial analyst with Ford of Europe Finance in the City. He now operates as an independent financial and computer consultant.

'Not just a book...More like a complete start-up package - for under a tenner!' *Your Business Magazine*

'Companies that follow its advice will stand a chance of beating the funding challenge.' *Accountancy Age*

The Good Stockbroker Guide

Robert Miller

(PB, £19.95, 176pp, 229 x 145mm, 1-85252-057-4)

A Guide to Private Client Stockbrokers in the UK and Ireland

The Good Stockbroker Guide is a comprehensive guide to stockbrokers and the services they provide. It is designed to help the new investor to choose a stockbroker for the first time or aid the experienced investor in finding a new broker after the ructions following the 'Big Bang' and the rise and fall and rise again of the equity market.

This guide covers the complete gamut of private client investors, from the richest to the poorest, from those investing actively in futures and options to the person who has little interest in investment and wishes to invest passively, leaving to the stockbroker the important decisions about which shares to buy or sell.

Robert Miller, a former stockbroker himself with Kitcat and Aitken, is now with the Institute of Economic Affairs and edits their journal, *Economic Affairs*. He is a regular contributor to the *Observer* on financial and investment topics.

Endorsed by the Association of Investment Trust Companies
